W9-BWO-447

BEAUMONSTER

JESSE ★ DAYTON

BEAUMONSTER

★★★★★ **A MEMOIR** ★★★★★★★★★★

New York

Hachette Books
Hachette Book Group
1290 Avenue of the Americas
New York, NY 10104
HachetteBooks.com
Twitter.com/HachetteBooks
Instagram.com/HachetteBooks

First Edition: November 2021

Published by Hachette Books, an imprint of Perseus Books, LLC, a subsidiary of Hachette Book Group, Inc. The Hachette Books name and logo is a trademark of the Hachette Book Group.

The Hachette Speakers Bureau provides a wide range of authors for speaking events. To find out more, go to www.hachettespeakersbureau.com or call (866) 376-6591.
The publisher is not responsible for websites (or their content) that are not owned by the publisher.

Print book interior design by Amy Quinn.

Library of Congress Cataloging-in-Publication Data

Names: Dayton, Jesse, author.
Title: Beaumonster: a memoir / Jesse Dayton.
Description: First edition. | New York: Hachette Books, 2021.
Identifiers: LCCN 2021021668 | ISBN 9780306846748 (hardcover) | ISBN 9780306846762 (ebook)
Subjects: LCSH: Dayton, Jesse. | Singers—Texas—Biography. | Guitarists—Texas—Biography. | Musicians—Anecdotes. | Concert tours—Anecdotes.
Classification: LCC ML420.D375 A3 2021 | DDC 782.42164092 [B]—dc23
LC record available at https://lccn.loc.gov/2021021668

ISBNs: 9780306846748 (hardcover), 9780306846762 (ebook)

Printed in Canada

MRQ-T

10 9 8 7 6 5 4 3 2 1

I'd like to dedicate this book to my mother, who always inspired her children to read and write and be curious.

★ CONTENTS ★

BEAUMONSTER

INTRO

Unless you're a tried-and-true, longtime cult follower of my solo records, my guitar session work, the hundred-plus annual shows I've been playing globally nonstop for thirty years, my film and TV work, or lastly, a fan of my online rants and writings, then you're probably screaming to your wife or husband, or significant other in the next room over, "Why in the hell is Jesse Dayton writing a book?"

As the kids say today for their online relationship status, "It's complicated." For a working-class kid from the Texas/Louisiana area of Beaumont, Texas, I'm probably one of the only "Beaumonsters" (a term that I may have coined one drunken night at a wrap party of a horror film I directed, but now affectionately use to refer to all people from my hometown of Beaumont) who's had these types of brushes with people I would refer to as artists. That's not a brag, just a lonely fact, considering where I'm from.

1

My hometown is not the same place it was when I grew up there. More retail shops, more college grads, more people, and more of everything, like the rest of the planet is now. Then it was known for breeding high volumes of oil roughnecks, offshore rig workers, petrochemical plant workers, a few pro athletes, rodeo cowboys, notorious criminals, a few country singers and blues musicians, and some of the best damn working-class folks on the planet. And it's still that way today. But I knew at a young age I'd have to move to Austin to find like-minded weirdos. Most Texans who move to Austin are in fact weirdos who at some point stopped feeling like we were "home" in our hometowns. On some of the gigs or jobs in this book, it's true that I didn't always feel like I was worthy of these situations, but I was raised well enough by my mama, Glenda Faye, and daddy, Robert Earl, to shut off the "Shitty Committee" in my head (that's what I call my inner critic, which is more like a whole chorus of critics, and they suck) long enough to man up and do what I think was, most of the time, good work.

Just for the record (as I say often throughout this book) about what even I think is a bizarre career, I've somehow kept my expectations low enough and my standards high enough to not completely shit the bed while working with folks I've admired, some since childhood. Ultimately, that's what this book is about. Admiration. There's no one in these pages whom I throw under the bus, except myself. So, if you're looking for "dirt" on famous people, you won't find any here. What you will find are my own stupid mistakes and my sometimes squirrely, sometimes failing horribly, occasionally clean striving for greatness.

As someone who's been directly involved with some of the greats and up-and-coming masters of American music, film, politics, business, and barroom philosophy, but has never once thought of himself as one, I got the notion that a book of behind-the-scenes stories might give the folks, as we say in Texas, something to chew on.

This book came about via my online rants. My friend, and now literary agent, Rynda Laurel, was the first one who noticed my online stories about folks I've worked with, takes on political, social, and cultural issues, and of course baseball, and God-knows-what-else and said, "You need to write a book, JD." Throughout my life I've written plays, short stories, film scripts, the online rants, and most important, songs, day in and day out, so it wasn't completely out of the question. Writing is blue-collar work, and I get up pretty much every morning and put my tool belt on and just do it. Just write. Tip for all you grinding hustlers out there: don't dumb your voice down on social media or, to use that god-forsaken word, "content." Don't neuter your voice. If it's real (being good is something else), those "friends" you lose you'll make up for tenfold with new "friends" and hey, ya may even get offered a book deal.

I didn't cowrite this book with the help of another writer, although I'm sure there will be some writers who think I should have. By the way, writers are very similar to guitar players and actors. They all have that voice in the back of their head saying, *I wouldn't have done it that way.* I know because I'm a guitar player/actor/writer who is constantly telling that voice, sometimes screaming at that voice, *For Christ's sake, would you just shut the fuck up?* After thirty-plus years of making my mortgage and monthly nut, and saving enough at my local credit union in Austin, Texas, as a traveling minstrel and chronicler of life as I see it, well, I've built up enough alligator skin to at least sleep well enough through the blessings of my "let the chips fall where they may" meditation mantra. That seems to help me postpone my ongoing fight with my brain, at least until the next morning begins.

Yep, that ain't no bullshit when folks say, "The struggle is real." It's real for all of us, and even for the legends in this book who seem to have simultaneously had a charmed existence and what

Buck Owens called "A Tiger by the Tail" at the same time. And because I've seen and admired how others have handled it all, this book is a lot more about fighting through my shitty internal monologue and trying to make lemonade out of lemons than it is a tell-all book about "famous people." And while some of the folks in the book were merely passing through my life and some have remained good friends, all of them were and still are an inspiration to me when it comes to knowing how to navigate through this temporary journey we're on.

And my journey is far from over. I'm still currently involved in making musical and artistic memories with all walks of creative life. Besides my beautiful family—my wife, Emily, and only child, Sam—working on various projects is still what gets me out of bed in the mornings. Every day I try to better myself, show up on time, and do what I can to stay in the light and do honest work. It ain't easy. A big part of why I'm writing this is because I hope some of you who read it will say what I've been saying damn near my whole life: "Well, if he or she can do it, hell, I probably can too." And you can. But it takes a veritable shit-ton of work (that's a technical Beaumonster measurement, meaning more than 10,000 hours) and a lot of turning thousands of nos into a few dozen yeses if you're lucky. And it never gets any easier. For me at least, I've just found that the more rigorously honest I am with myself about what I do, how I live, and who I am, the less mental slavery bullshit I have to endure and the more present I can be.

It might be helpful to you, the reader, to know that my life and career have been full of a revolving cast of characters, some of whom reappear over and over again and become part of a long history and some of whom disappear forever. But either way, for the sake of this book, you'll hear me cross-referencing them in different chapters and jumping around a bit timeline-wise.

OK, that's enough of that. Hope y'all enjoy the ride, and if you can, try to put yourself in my incredibly lucky, sometimes ridiculous, sometimes asinine but hard-earned and well-worn shoes. It ain't that bad of a path to walk, and hopefully there's just enough redemption in each single journey to help get you to the next one.

Onward,
JD

SITUATIONS GROWING UP IN BEAUMONT, TEXAS, IN THE '70S

Eight years old, riding around town in a four-door, shit-brown 1969 Impala covered in whiskey dents with my drunk uncle, who keeps slamming on the brakes to barely not hit the car in front of us, and seeing all these Jack Daniel's bottles flying out from under the front seat around my small Converse high-tops. Then upon returning, seeing my parents' faces go from horrific worry to complete relief, hugging each other in the front yard as we drive up the long oyster-shell-covered driveway, luckily cheating death and returning home safely.

Another uncle of mine (warning: there are going to be a few uncles in this book) shooting a Brahma bull in the head that went completely crazy and charged his brand-new Chevy pickup truck that three or four of us little-kid cousins were all sitting in the back bed of while he drove us through his pasture, the bull coming out of nowhere, knocking me out of the bed of the truck onto the ground, nearly killing me. Then a few seconds later, going from seeing stars and being completely knocked out to coming to and seeing my uncle grab his 30-06 deer rifle from the back-window gun rack and drop the bull with a bullet to the head a few feet away from me. Not a great experience for a five-year-old.

Playing with my cousins at my aunt's and seeing another uncle's KKK uniform, a white gown and mask hanging in the closet, and thinking, Is that what I think it is?

My nanny, an elderly African American woman named Ms. Victoria, unsuccessfully holding back tears while listening to a recording of Martin Luther King's "I Have a Dream" speech on the *Sunday Golden Triangle Gospel Radio Show* on low volume on a small handheld transistor AM radio that sat above the stove while she made buttermilk fried chicken, collard greens with ham hocks, and sweet potatoes for our supper after church.

My mama crying after getting one of those middle-of-the-night phone calls informing her my cousin had committed suicide by shotgun in their family barn. Then a few weeks later, my mama crying again and waking me up to hold me for what I thought was no reason, but later finding out it was because that same cousin's father, my uncle, went to the same barn, to the same place, with the same shotgun, and committed suicide too.

Sunday fried-chicken dinners with wild game that we'd hunted or fried catfish that we'd caught with the whole family, then watching

Roy Clark or Jerry Reed tearing up their guitars and watching gorgeous, big-boobed hillbilly women sitting on the porch singing on the television show *Hee Haw*.

The entire family piling into a massive Buick LeSabre with a large picnic basket full of ham sandwiches and potato chips, then driving up Highway 95 listening to an 8-track of Willie Nelson's *Red Headed Stranger* to the Huntsville prison rodeo to see which inmates with absolutely nothing to lose survived the bull riding.

Playing day games with our integrated baseball team against the "all-white sundown town" of Vidor, Texas (which was next to my hometown of Beaumont), because the KKK Grand Wizard lived in Vidor. Day games because Black people (who were called a much worse name than Black people or African Americans) weren't allowed in Vidor after dark. There was a huge billboard sign on the side of Interstate 10 in Vidor up until the early '90s that said, "Don't Let the Sun Go Down on You in Vidor, Texas!"—a warning to all Black people. I remember seeing Geraldo Rivera on TV doing a news story on "the most hate-filled town in Texas," showing cross burnings and KKK marches through downtown Beaumont, and yelling at my mother in the other room, "Hey y'all, come see this, I think Geraldo is in my friend Kelly's front yard!" So goddamn awful and strange.

Having my only wealthy, oil-rich relatives come see us for the holidays from Houston and them being terrified of eating seafood gumbo because they'd never had Cajun gumbo or even been to Louisiana, which was only twenty minutes down the road from Beaumont. They asked, "Is there alligator and snake meat in this?" Crazy, huh? New-money folks are the same everywhere. (OK, there might've been some gator in it.)

Sneaking into the Palace honky-tonk to see Johnny Paycheck and David Allan Coe with a dip of Copenhagen snuff tobacco in my mouth, then being held down and having my baby mullet hairdo cut off with a folding buck knife by three older drunk rednecks because I had a black Thin Lizzy concert T-shirt on and was being called a "long-haired faggot." That's how redneck that shit was in Beaumont in the '70s. Even though I had a dip of snuff in my mouth at a fuckin' David Allan Coe/Johnny Paycheck concert, because my hair was a little long and I had a black Thin Lizzy shirt on, those mental giants still held me down and cut my baby mullet off.

Wondering why these old white men on TV kept saying the word "Watergate" over and over and interrupting my regularly scheduled after-school programming of *Ultraman* and *The Jetsons*. I knew those old bastards were lying, even back then. And I know they are still lying.

Sneaking into Lady Long Legs roadhouse to see Zydeco greats like Rockin' Dopsie (whom I would later record with in Houston), Clifton Chenier, and Beau Jocque, and being shocked at seeing interracial couples dance together for the first time but no one cared. Music was the answer.

Sitting in Mr. Arceneaux's sixth-grade class at Stephen F. Austin Jr. High and the principal trotting in these poor Vietnamese kids who didn't speak a word of English and had just arrived off the boat as Vietnam War refugees. That same year their parents' fishing boats were blown up with dynamite by the KKK between Bolivar Isle and Galveston Island. But their families not only survived and outworked the rednecks and Cajuns but eventually became local leading seafood distributors on the Gulf Coast, and later those same poor kids would drive into our high school parking lot in brand-new bitchin' Camaros.

Sneaking into the Foxy Lady nightclub and seeing blues greats Johnny Winter (who grew up a few blocks over from me), Barbara Lynn, Cookie and the Cupcakes, and Jerry LaCroix and the Boogie Kings, and getting the same exact goosebumps that I got listening to the music at a Pentecostal tent revival I went to off Interstate 10 in Vidor with my ex-wife. The devil's music had taken hold of me! Hallelujah! Catholics might've had the market cornered on Cajun food, drinkin' wine, smokin' cigarettes, dancing, and partying, but the Pentecostal churches had a hell of a band. In fact, I'd meet many a displaced Catholic musician at Pentecostal churches who would pretend for two hours they were Holy Ghost believers just because they had a killer band with drums, bass, guitar, B-3 organ, horns, and a full gospel choir. Hillbilly and Black gospel music was in my blood.

Getting in fights with racist rednecks on a monthly basis for no good goddamn reason whatsoever and thinking to myself, I can't wait to get away from these mean bastards. Looking back on it now, those idiots made me who I am today, and they're why I'm writing this book in the weirdest most progressive part of Texas, where I live now in South Austin. I owe a great deal of gratitude to every asshole I've ever encountered for reminding me I was my daddy's son. He taught me I didn't have to suffer the same BS behavior that people with less backbone did. Because of this I spent hours alone in my room by myself drawing, painting, writing stories, and playing music, and to this day I still know people who can't be by themselves for five minutes.

Jumping trains from Beaumont to Houston with Robbie Fonteneaux to see bands that everyone in Beaumont hated and clutching the buck knives we had in our pants pockets when the hobos in the train cars tried to shake us down for money. Most of the hobos were nice old pathetic drunks who just needed a dollar for some

Thunderbird wine, but about 1 in 5 were meth heads, and that's where I learned firsthand you can never trust a jittery speed freak.

My first time seeing long-haired bikers do cocaine and speed in 1978 in a dark room full of black-light posters and older girls with tube tops on while the song "The Needle and the Spoon" by Lynyrd Skynyrd played on the turntable. This would later influence what songs I needed my bands to learn in order to get paid and make it out alive playing biker parties in southeast Texas. Biker-party shows were terrifying, but the money was good enough to pay the bills for a few months. I just played my last MC (motorcycle club) party only seven years ago for a club we all know. While I'm still as obsessed with riding motorcycles as I was when I got my first minibike at ten years old, and I still love going to bike shows and occasionally playing them (I played the epic Born Free show with Willie Davidson there not long ago), I can't play for the biker clubs anymore. It's too dangerous.

Telling tent revival preacher Brother Venerable he should "read a science book" at the Piggly Wiggly grocery store when he said, "You need to use that Holy Ghost power you got on that guitar for Gawd, boy." He was no different from those old weirdos on the Watergate hearings, except maybe more dangerous because he was a true believer in the superstition he was selling on Sundays. One Sunday he slammed his fist so hard on the pulpit stand that he cut the side of his hand wide open and blood went all over the front row, on our faces, suits, and dresses. He wrapped his hand up with a handkerchief, we wiped our faces off, and he kept preaching. This gave a whole new slant to the popular fundamentalist expression "covered in the blood of Jesus."

Hiding the fact that I was reading voraciously and secretly going to the Beaumont library from pretty much everyone except my mom, who would take me there. She was the first one to go to college and was teased for it and called "uppity" by our redneck relatives. But the real obsession with reading took off after thumbing through a copy of *Rolling Stone* that my older brother brought home, and me seeing Ralph Steadman's bizarre and violent smeared artwork and then reading Hunter S. Thompson's sexually charged, drug-enhanced, subversive words below it. Until then I didn't know that literature and the act of reading could feel so punk rock.

This was the life of a Beaumonster growing up on the bayou in the '70s. By age fifteen I had already played drums and bass in little country, rock 'n' roll, and Zydeco bands. Piano lessons were mandatory 'cause of my mama, thank God; although I did take massive shit from all my baseball buddies for studying piano, it helped me understand how music theory worked. After meeting two Black guitar players when I was around fifteen, I became hooked on guitar and my life would never be the same. The first older Black guy I met was named Granville Cleveland (who I heard played with Edgar and Johnny Winter's White Trash band from my town of Beaumont), and he showed me a D chord, a G chord, and an A chord, which for some weird reason I could play almost immediately. Then he taught me three songs that would completely change the way I thought about music, and basically since then I've been doing variations of those same three songs my entire career. These three songs are what he called the "Three Heys," but more on that later. The other much older African American guy was Lil' Mack Minor (cousin to Mance Lipscomb and Lightnin' Hopkins), who showed me how to play twelve-bar blues, which I also got the hang of almost immediately. When I say "immediately," I mean that I could change chords and even play single-note melodies faster than most of the older guys around me who had been playing for a lot longer, but I still practiced. Just to clarify, while I could put in 10,000 hours surfing or playing first base on a baseball team and be marginally passable, the guitar was different.

Lil' Mack was an alcoholic who used to sit out under a big magnolia tree outside of Snook, Texas, and drink Mad Dog 20/20 and Boone's Farm wine all day. A cowboy friend of mine, Les Bullard, told me who he was and said that in order for him to show me stuff on the guitar (which was really just watching him up close), I had to supply the guitar and bring him a bottle of whatever liquor I could get from someone older. I have a VHS tape (that I really gotta transfer to digital 'cause it looks amazing) of a very young me playing guitars on a trailer porch and Mack is singing "Good Morning Little School Girl" and I'm paying him $5 to do it. Mack had to be pushing eighty when I met him, so I'm thinking as tore up as he was all the time, he must've died not long after that. When Mack got really drunk, he would cry and talk about "the farms" he worked on as a kid and how the owners used to whip him and his whole family. Looking back now, this had to be in the early 1900s. And while slavery ended in 1865, the system was still alive and well in East Texas for long after that.

Being a kid in Beaumont back then was simple. As soon as we got out of school we jumped on our minibikes and went straight to the Brick Yard Pond or to the bayou and started fishing. Until I was introduced to the guitar, it was fishing, riding minibikes or motorcycles, go-karting, reading comic books, drawing and painting alone in my room for hours at a time, and playing baseball. That was all I did. The whole motorcycle obsession started after my sister's boyfriend Randy took me around the block on his Harley-Davidson and I was gobsmacked. I put motorcycle pictures torn out of *Cycle* magazine all over my bedroom walls, and finally three years later I got my very first minibike. On the same day I got it I remember hitting a homemade jump running about thirty-five miles an hour, sending me crashing into some trees and my minibike off into the depths of the murky, black, snake-filled bayou behind our house. My buddies helped me pull it out, and the engine was completely locked up and totally ruined. So I managed to talk another kid in the neighborhood out of an old '60s minibike frame that had the crude stop brake for the back wheel. Then we took a five-and-a-half-horsepower Briggs & Stratton engine with no governor on it from an old lawn mower and got a friend's older brother to weld it onto the frame. Then we got him to weld a Schwinn bicycle sprocket onto the mower engine where the blade went and popped some links off the same bicycle's chain to make it tight, and that was my transportation for the next two years until I could get a Honda Trail 70 from mowing yards all over town that summer. Redneck ingenuity at its finest, and my introduction to a life of being fascinated by motorcycles that I still ride to this day. I'm not monogamous with motorcycles. I can usually find something that I love about any brand. Right now I own a Harley-Davidson, a Triumph, a BSA, and a Honda, and I'm working on buying a Moto Guzzi and a Norton.

These things were all first and foremost on my daily agenda until somehow an old Silvertone acoustic guitar showed up in my older brother's room. I had been playing my brother Bruce's Ludwig drum set constantly up until that point as well while he was out throwing papers to pay for the drums. He would set traps on the drums and leave tiny pieces of paper on them to make sure I didn't play them, but I was super careful to take them off, beat the hell out of his kit, then reposition the papers in the exact spot he left them. He would hide his drumsticks, so I bought my own and kept them hidden. It was a big gotcha game, and when he caught me on his drums, I usually took a serious ass-whoopin'. By the way, that's another thing I'm grateful for: my brother, Robert Bruce, whipping my young ass toughened me up big-time.

We also had a baby-grand piano that my sister, who was a brilliant piano player and cellist, practiced on constantly. I hated the mandatory piano lessons the kids in my family all had to take because I wanted to play Jerry Lee Lewis's song "Great Balls of Fire" and this square teacher was shoving beginner classical songs, church hymns, and children's tunes down my throat. The guy would yell at me every lesson, "You're never going to be a musician with that bad attitude you have, Jess!" Then I would go home and practice boogie-woogie stuff until my mom would come in and say, "Is that really what we're paying hard-earned money for you to learn?" I would think to myself, *Yep, I guess it is!* But I would always tell my mama, "I've already practiced, now I'm just having fun!" This was the story of my life.

At first the music thing was pure escapism. Hell, it's still escapism. But early on I would play whatever instrument I could get away with and play with whomever wanted to play with me just to be around the music I loved so much. My first paying gig was for $5 as a drummer with a bunch of old-timers who had a country band that played in retirement homes. I was told to not use any cymbals and to just play the kick and snare drum on the one and the three with brushes, no drumsticks that were too loud. This was big-doings getting a whopping five bones for playing along to Hank Williams songs like "Hey Good Lookin'" or Lefty Frizzell songs like "I Never Go Around Mirrors."

Later I would come to obsess over these old country records, but at the time I thought the music was real square because I was all of thirteen and listening to "Trudie" by the The Charlie Daniels Band and ZZ Top's "Brown Sugar," which were on my older brother's 8-tracks. Punk rock had not hit my hometown yet (and honestly, never really did), so Southern rock and country music ruled. A few years later MTV would show up on our television and turn me on to a whole world of alternative rock bands, punk bands, and even rockabilly and ska bands from England—music all my buddies hated. Also, heavy metal was starting to hit the suburbs of America and Beaumont, which was a big B-market tour stop. I remember hearing the first Metallica record and thinking it was a punk record because I had no one around to tell me otherwise. Early metal bands like Iron Maiden, Judas Priest, and Scorpions would play the Beaumont Convention Center, but I tended to dig the pre-metal hard-rock acts that opened for them like Nazareth, Trapeze, Rick Derringer, and Thin Lizzy, who might've been losing ground in the bigger markets but were still huge in Beaumont. ZZ Top were gods in Beaumont and I really dug those hard-and-heavy guitar bands before the new ones came on the scene and all started dressing like chicks, doing bad impressions of Van Halen, and singing power ballads. A bit later, Joe Strummer would save me and a whole bunch of other people my age (who might not admit it) from bad metal power ballads.

Really, there was no real "scene" to speak of except for all the '70s hard-rock bands, country bands, and of course the Zydeco and blues music that was constantly seeping in from Louisiana. We had twenty-four-hour all-Cajun music stations on our AM radio with Cajun DJs speaking broken French. Looking back, that was pretty exotic stuff compared to the rest of Texas. The whole state had left-of-the-dial twenty-four-hour Tejano and Norteño Mexican radio stations, but only small towns like Beaumont and Orange on the Gulf Coast had Cajun radio stations. As a kid, Mexican stations never hit my radar and, embarrassingly when I think about it now, sounded like circus music to me. But as I got older I came to realize that the best singers on the radio were Mexican vocalists like Vicente Fernández doing "Volver Volver." Fast-forward a few years and Grammy Award–winning accordion player and the pride of San Antonio, Flaco Jiménez from the Texas Tornados, who was played constantly on those stations where I was growing up, would play on my first two solo records. But I was young and oblivious because I was too busy rebelling against everything at that point and listening to rock 'n' roll bands like the Clash. I say rock 'n' roll because the term "punk" had barely entered the Texas lexicon outside of Dallas, Austin, and Houston. My friend John Cook bought a single called "White Riot" and we jumped up and down on his bed with tennis rackets as guitars and I was in heaven.

Anyway, life growing up in Beaumont, good and bad, made me who I am today. The Cajuns, the Pentecostals, the biker crank parties, all the cool Black folks I listened to and hung out with, my Mexican friends, my older redneck-rock brother and my hippie sister and my slightly progressive parents who were surrounded by the most backward-thinking, racist folks on the planet. I'm thankful for all of it, the good and the bad. That's why I play the way I play, vote the way I vote, read what I read, and later why I would pray and meditate the way I do.

The risk factor in doing what I've done could have been insurmountable. I could've just stayed in Beaumont, went to Lamar College or even to the University of Texas for a few years, or maybe got on at the petrochemical plant and blown college off. I could've married a hot Cajun gal, had some kids, settled down with a new pickup truck, a three-bedroom house on an acre of Piney Woods, and never missed a weekend of fishing in my Glastron bass boat or even still played music with my buddies on the weekend. Not a bad life. But the rest of Texas was calling me, and it was a big state. It was like Houston and Austin were screaming my name and if I didn't answer, I would've been miserable. This same story has been happening to Black and white working-class musicians since the inception of jazz, country, blues, and folk music in America. This is my truth. And so it goes.

THE THREE HEYS
AND A TRUNK FULL
OF RECORDS

When I was fourteen, about to turn fifteen, my folks told me that I had to come with them to Colorado on the summer vacation we'd taken many times before. We were the classic Texas family trying to escape the devil's armpit known as the Texas summer for a respite up in the cool mountains. My mom had summers off from teaching public school, and my old man had business meetings in Boulder, so they'd drag us kids up to the Rocky Mountains for some fresh air and a vacation. Usually, up until this point, I would've been so excited to go, but my older brother, who was driving his '75 Chevy step-side pickup truck with a gun rack, 8-track player, and oversized mudder tires, was now old enough to stay home. Since I was the youngest kid, I was forced to go with my parents and miss the blowout keg parties I heard my big brother was planning to throw at our house while we were gone. Major bummer. My sister had already headed off to college, and that left me, the youngest, alone and out of the picture. Hmmm, let me see, beer kegs, weed, loud music, chicks, and hell-raisers in our big backyard, or a Holiday Inn in Boulder with my parents and sight-seeing with my mom while my dad works? Ultimately, the decision was made by my parents that I was too young to stay with my brother. So there I am, bored out of my ever-loving mind, no kids anywhere to hang out with, sitting in a pool chair in Boulder at the Holiday Inn by the swimming pool, when one night this cool-looking older Black guy comes in and is just sitting by the pool playing his acoustic Alvarez guitar and singing songs. It was only us two out there and I was mesmerized by what I was hearing, so I finally walked over and said, "Hey, I'm Jesse from Beaumont, Texas, what's your name?" He surprised me and said, "Beaumont, Texas? Do you know Johnny and Edgar Winter?" I said, "I don't really *know* know them, but they always say hi to us at the Dairy Queen and the guitar shops and they live a few blocks away from me." His face lit up and he said, "Well, Jesse from Beaumont, pull up a chair, I'm Granville Cleveland and I love those guys!" Looking back, I'm sure my East Texas/south Louisiana hybrid accent was through the roof at that point, but he didn't seem to care. Just for the record, my accent is still running off a few uptight folks who aren't from the South, and it's a hell of a lot less intense than it was when I was a kid.

Granville immediately went into his cooler for another Coors yellow-belly, handed me his guitar, and said, "Here, play me one while I open this beer." I said, "Well, I don't really know how to play. I mean, I worked out the bass line to 'Tush' by ZZ Top, but I don't know how to play chords or anything." He said, "Guess what Jesse from Beaumont? You're about to learn how, 'cause I'm gonna show ya!" I have no idea why this grown-ass man, who was just a badass-looking guy with sideburns and a faded jean shirt and baby bell jeans and boots on (think a western-dressed Lenny Kravitz), took any interest in me, but he did. He showed me, as I mentioned earlier, how to play three chords. An A chord, then a D chord, then a G chord. I was shocked when I was able to play those chords really quick. He then told me to work on changing chords because he had to go to his room to make a phone call (this was way before cell phones).

Granville came back about thirty minutes later and I was changing chords not half bad for a first-timer. Then he said, "Now I'm gonna teach ya the 'Three Heys.' Ya ready?" I said, "What's the Three Heys?" He said, "Don't worry about it, let's get going." Then he showed me "Hey Good Lookin'" by Hank Williams, which I had heard and even played before in the little country old-timer band. He said, "You got that thick Texas drawl in your voice, so you gotta learn a good country standard first." I was so excited about learning an actual song, I didn't care that it was something off my grandaddy's old record player. And I gotta say, I took to it like a duck to water. Then he said, "OK, I'm gonna show ya an A-minor chord, 'cause we're in Colorado and you need to learn a good hippie folk scare song." That A-minor chord blew my mind because I could immediately sense what a dark and mysterious sound the guitar was capable of making. All those minor Hank Williams songs and Mexican songs that I had grown up around started flashing through my mind, but I didn't say anything and just concentrated on where he was telling me to put my fingers. Then he showed me "Hey Hey, My My (Into the Black)" by Neil Young. Now, this was a true revelation, because Neil was all over the radio in those days and I thought he had hung the moon. I wanted to run up to the room and call my older brother to tell him I'd learned how to play a song by NEIL FUCKING YOUNG, but again, I just stayed focused on what this generous stranger was showing me. He said he had to walk to the store for a beer run but that I should work on changing those chords until he got back.

While he was at the store, I noticed that I was instinctively humming along with the chords so I knew where I was in the song. I wasn't aware of it until Granville got back and said, "OK, play it for me." Not realizing that I was humming, he grabbed the neck and put his fingers over the strings, stopping me, and said, "Oh, you wanna sing it too?" I started turning red with embarrassment. I said, "Ah man, I can't sing." He said, "Well, you're already doing it, little man!" I said, "I don't even know the words," and he said, "Don't worry 'bout that, they'll come later." Then he said, "OK, I'm gonna show ya one more tune, then I got shit to do. You can't learn the guitar without learning a song by the greatest guitar player of all time." I said, "Who's that, Jerry Reed?" He about fell out of his chair laughing and said, "No, you little country-ass motherfucker, it's Jimi Hendrix!" I said, "Look man, I'm just learning; I'm not ready for Hendrix yet." My brother had brought me to the Gaylynn Theater in Beaumont on Eleventh Street to see the film *Woodstock* and after we saw Hendrix doing "The Star-Spangled Banner," we didn't even know if Jimi was from the same planet as the rest of us. He was a god, and everyone bowed and worshipped the guy. Granville said, "You know who Jimi's favorite guitar player was? It was Johnny Winter from Beaumont, Texas. From your hometown!" Not believing him I said, "How do you know? Did you know Hendrix?" He said, "Hell no, I didn't know Jimi Hendrix. I read it in an interview Jimi did that was in *Guitar Player* magazine!" OK, note to self, after you get a guitar, get a subscription to *Guitar Player*. (I also got subscriptions to *Maximumrocknroll, Creem,* and *Surfer,* even though I was and still am a terrible surfer.) Then he showed me the chords to "Hey Joe." Not the intro or the lead or all the little cool licks that Jimi does, just the chords. Then he said, "OK, young gun, that's the Three Heys, and now you're on your way!"

After meeting Granville a great sea change overcame me: I distinctly remember the sinking feeling of not having a guitar to play. I immediately ran up to our hotel room and started telling my folks (almost yelling, I was so excited), "Y'all, I just learned how to play the guitar and I'm gonna be a guitar player and y'all gotta get me a guitar!" For the next four years my parents never saw me again without a guitar either strapped around my neck or in my hand. It was beyond the word "passion." It was part of my body. It was like my parents had lost their old son, because I had overnight been assimilated into this guitar cult, constantly playing. This was at least eight hours a day before and after school, ten to twelve hours a day in the summers when I was off from school—just nonstop learning. And while I was never that great of a surfer or a first baseman on the baseball field, I was a natural when it came to guitar. It was literally just something I could do, just like when I could immediately play those first three chords. I learned Jerry Reed's "Amos Moses," the intro and lead to "Hey Joe," you name it: Andrés Segovia, Peter Tosh, Elvis, the Clash, ZZ Top, Jimmy Reed, Jazz standards like "Sweet Georgia Brown" and "How High the Moon," all the rhythmical funkiness of Zydeco, anything I could get my hands on. I became a student of the guitar game for life and everything else I had been doing before disappeared. No more sports. I even told this big redneck coach I had with such pride, "I'm quitting all sports and I'm gonna start a band one day." He said, "Well, I hope you're a better guitar player than you are a ball player, son." Guitar was it, and that humming I was doing to accompany the chords was starting to turn into a real but annoying singing voice.

I loved working with singers in bands and just playing guitar, because at that point I hated my voice. And usually no one else wanted to sing, so I got stuck with it. The word got out, and older bands who had seen me sit in with people were calling me to play with them. I started to go over to Lake Charles, Louisiana, to sit in with Cajun and Zydeco bands for free. I played every single chance

I got, no matter where or for whom, often for no money. I did this for years and years and years and learned hundreds of songs and how they were arranged and learned how to play with every kind of fucked-up cranky weirdo addict band member without rocking the boat. I would join or start little rock bands for short periods of time while still playing with other old-timer groups and not telling the band I was with. These bands that were usually with my friends never lasted, but everything I learned helped me later when I got the chance to play with focused and disciplined musicians. It was all one big school of music, and I was serious as a fuckin' heart attack about it. I'd get thrown into the fire onstage in some weird key or strange time signature and I could always find my place or my part to play without stepping on the other musicians. I'm still doing the same shit today when I sit in with people.

Within months I had a little combo band and we were playing a show at the Boulevard Club in Beaumont when the Texas Godfather of the Blues, promoter Clifford Antone, showed up to watch me play. My brother knew Clifford from Austin, and let me tell ya, this was a big deal, at least back then in Beaumont. But even though Clifford was originally from Port Arthur, the next town over from Beaumont (our families knew each other), he had gone on to worldwide acclaim for starting a legendary blues club in Austin called Antone's Home of the Blues. Antone's was a popular venue for national touring acts, and all the Chicago blues giants, like legends Buddy Guy, Muddy Waters, Junior Wells, and James Cotton, played there. In the process Clifford had also given all these Austin blues greats, like Stevie Ray Vaughan, his brother Jimmie Vaughan and his band the Fabulous Thunderbirds, Denny Freeman, Derek O'Brien, Marcia Ball, Charlie Sexton, Lou Ann Barton, W. C. Clark, and Angela Strehli, a place to play regular shows.

That cold December night, Clifford pulled up to the Boulevard Club in Beaumont sitting in the backseat of a big black Town Car with a driver/bodyguard who was a massive six-foot-eight hulk of a man dressed in a long fur coat. His name was Sugar Bear. I heard Sugar Bear was a lineman for the Houston Oilers before he got hurt and lost his career. When I saw them get out of the car and start walking toward the club, I ran inside and got the band going on a 6/8 Gulf Coast dance song called "Matilda." Luckily, this all worked out perfectly. As soon as they walked into the small night-club, the dance floor was packed and I was doing my best Jerry La-Croix and the Boogie Kings impression. (I would later find out this was Clifford's favorite band growing up.) We did five sets a night, switching back and forth with a DJ who played old-school songs like "Before the Next Teardrop Falls" by Freddy Fender and "Crazy Mama" by J. J. Cale.

Clifford, who was from a successful Lebanese family but looked straight-up New Orleans mafia with dark hair, olive skin, and a black overcoat on, started walking to the stage toward me during our first set break. "Hey kid, follow me to my car," he said. I was intimidated, but I followed him and Sugar Bear through the seedy club crowd of rednecks, Cajuns, bikers, and hippie girls with halter tops and hip huggers, out the front door, past the pickup trucks and Harley-Davidson MC choppers, to the long black car. I was so nervous when Sugar Bear popped the trunk, not having any idea what they were gonna show me or do to me. When the trunk door sprang open, it was like a heavenly choir of angels harmoniz-ing around one note that went off in my head. I saw rope lighting wrapped around the inside of the trunk, deep and high white shag carpet on the bed of the trunk, and what looked like a full-blown blues music section of vintage records like you would see at a real record store. After I realized I wasn't gonna get thrown in the trunk or see anything I could never unsee, I looked closer and the records were all labeled in standard blue typewriter font. Names like Junior Wells in the "J" section and Slim Harpo in the "S" section. Clifford told Sugar Bear, "Grab the kid some records, Shug . . . give him

Buddy Guy, Lazy Lester, Muddy, Otis Spann, and Freddy King."
These were all original copies of these albums and I still own them
to this day. Sugar Bear handed me the records, and Cliff (what I
would call him later) said, "You got talent, kid, and I love guitar
players. Learn these songs on all these records and call me in Austin. I'll get you up onstage at the club to play with the house band."
He and Sugar Bear closed the trunk, Clifford fired up a joint, took
a couple of big hits, handed me the joint, got in the big Town Car,
and was driven off. As I stood there in the dark parking lot with a
joint in one hand and five of the greatest blues records in history
in the other hand, I watched the big, long car fade into the Gulf
Coast humidity and out of sight. I was fifteen and knew right then
and there my life would never be the same.

ROAD KING GOES TO AUSTIN

The late '80s/early '90s was a strange time in America. The AIDS pandemic was still in full force, and I had two gay friends (a painter and a sculptor named Ron and John, both of whom we called one name, "Ron-John," after the famous surf shop Ron Jon). They lived in the Montrose in Houston and withered away and died right before our eyes. I remember those first conversations with people who were oblivious to it, but those of us who knew it wasn't just a "gay disease" also knew that unprotected casual sex was still Russian roulette. In England, Margaret Thatcher was going on her third term, so there was still some angry post-punk music coming out of the UK that also spoke to lots of bored American kids in the suburbs. Fox News had just started, and I remember seeing it for the first time and thinking, Why are they talking about how perfect the Bush family is all the time? Is this

Russian state-owned propaganda? It was very odd. Up until then journalists and especially military folks didn't so explicitly pick sides. Also, these things called computers started popping up in all my friends' houses.

I left Beaumont the day after I graduated high school and played in a few bands of no real note, then started a little rock-abilly band called the Road Kings in Houston, and we set out to play around Texas. Houston, Dallas, and San Antonio might've birthed more legendary musical history, but there was no music scene anywhere like there was in Austin in the late '80s and early '90s. So I moved there with my then-wife, Christie, and got a studio apartment. I had traveled around a bit, so I knew there was a small rockabilly, country, and cow-punk scene in Los Angeles that was amazing, but it was still overshadowed by the punk scene and Sunset Strip metal scene. Nashville had a thriving bluegrass scene then, and a few rockabilly and cow-punk bands like Jason & the Scorchers, but let's face it, for the most part, it was still dominated by the mainstream country music radio scene. Nothing could beat Austin's thriving country/rockabilly/punk scene in which everyone seemed to know one another and openly accepted their differences. Sure, people were competitive, but way less than they were in music-industry cities. London, Nashville, New York, and Los Angeles might've been where you went to get discovered, but Austin was where you went to find out who you were and to create and discover yourself.

During that time, when I went to other major music cities, all the "scenes" in those cities felt disconnected and separated, and to be frank, the people in their own respective scenes didn't really like people in other scenes. Did that make sense? In short, there was a lot of snarky backbiting. But the scenes in Austin kind of all melded together. The punks would hang out with the rockabillies and the honky-tonk people would hang with the ska people. On certain nights of the week you could look around and see hippies, cowboy hats, pompadours, skinheads, mohawks, and liberty spike haircuts all together in some of the clubs in Austin, everyone smoking cigarettes, drinking Shiner beer, and talking. I think this is a big reason that the whole cosmic cowboy/outlaw country thing started in Austin in the first place.

Waylon Jennings once told me that the first time he ever played the Armadillo World Headquarters in Austin he peeked through the curtain and saw all these long-haired rednecks with cowboy hats on and said, "Oh Lord, Willie's playing another practical joke on us. I'm gonna kick his ass!" Of course, everything went great and everyone loved Waylon and he figured out after the first couple of songs that Austin was different and all those hippies and rednecks were, in fact, not going to kill one another. Anyway, hairstyles and scenes had never meant as much to folks in Austin as real talent, and just being able to hang out and be cool seemed to be what mattered most. I say this because looking back there were so many great guitar players in Austin, you had to be pretty dang good and have some humility just to get a gig. My son, Sam, was born and raised in Austin, and every time he's traveled to other cities for work or pleasure he always says, "Yeah, it was great but not as real as Austin is, Dad." Of course, he grew up in a very different Austin than the one we have today. I know this will inspire some eye-rolling, but it's my book and I have to state for the record that anyone who has moved to Austin after the year 2000 has no idea just how cool it used to be in the '70s, '80s, and even the '90s.

The first night I walked into the Black Cat Lounge on Sixth Street, drummer Tom Lewis from the Wagoneers had his 1960 gold Cadillac parked out in front, with about twelve or fifteen Panhead and Knucklehead Harley-Davidsons lined up behind it. These bikes (which are now worth a small fortune) were all owned by one-percenter bikers, "1%" originally being a patch that hard-core motorcycle club members (that is, gang members) earned—quite the opposite of the 1 percent we refer to now in politics as the elitist global families who set world banking rates and own Wall Street and have more wealth than 99 percent of folks on the planet. There were no lawyers or accountants on bikes at the club who didn't know how to change their own oil on their brand-new expensive spaceship Harleys back then at the Black Cat, and the motorcycle gang contingent was in full force and made sure nobody got drunk and acted like an idiot . . . Unless it was them, that was OK.

The very first night I walked into the Black Cat Lounge, the place was so packed that the fire marshal was out in front stink-eyeing the doorman, an old, long-haired, patched-up, gray-bearded biker, not in the least impressed by the guy with the badge counting heads. Everyone at the Black Cat had a scene-identity look. Eighty percent of the crowd wore the classic Austin retro gear—'50s/'60s pearl-snap western shirts were a must. There were no hipster clothing companies making new pearl-snap shirts back then, so the only ones available were the real ones at resale shops, which meant every person in there had either bought them at one of the very few vintage clothing stores or dug through the bins and racks at Goodwill or Salvation Army. Today, all those places have been picked clean, but back then it was absolutely amazing what people were throwing out. There were piles upon piles of amazing ranch clothing from the '40s through the '70s. The next part of the uniform was the straight-leg Levi's with a big '50s-style rolled-up cuff on the bottom, usually worn with a black western belt with desert roses on it topped off with one of the classic western belt buckles we all collected. They were plentiful back then, and we collected all kinds, like Lone Star beer or Pearl beer belt buckles, championship rodeo belt buckles, buckles with sayings on them like "Damn right, I'm a Texan!" or town names on them like "Only in Waxahachie!" or "West Texans Do It Better!"

Then, of course, the last part of the classic Austin country outfit was a pair of pointed-toe cowboy boots. Drummer Tom Lewis, who was in the Wagoneers at that time but who would go on to play with Junior Brown, me, and lots of others, had told me to go back and watch the Paul Newman western film *Hud*, the how-to bible for all great western style, including clothes, furniture (we all bought that 1950s Roy Rogers ranch furniture with the spoke wheels and stallions on the couches, lamp stands, and matching chair sets), and of course boots. The go-to boots were the Mexican-made '60s black leather pointed-toe cowboy boots. Everyone had a pair. They were like what Beatle boots were to the Piccadilly scene in London, and everyone in our scene had them. It was weird to see square-toed or round-toed boots unless you were a biker, but you would see lots of custom boots that scenesters had found at ranch estate sales and garage sales that were absolutely unbelievable. Like 1940s western swing-era two-tone or three-tone ranch boots with names like "Billy Jack" or "The Big X Ranch " or leather fringe down the side, or black-and-white calfskin or shiny steel pointed tips mounted on the toe. Boots were a big conversation piece back then, the way George Cox creepers were for the punk scene in London or trashy New York Dolls clothes were for the rock scenes in L.A. and New York.

A lot of the musicians in Austin back then wore full-blown 1940s–1960s western suits with bolo ties or western neck scarves. No detail was ever left out. Look no further than an early picture of Austin legend Joe Ely to see what everyone wore. Of course, Ely would go on to tour all over the world with the Clash in their heyday and would influence the Clash's look and their romance with Texas and the Wild West. As far as the rest of the crowd, it was usually punk rockers or ska folks who had straggled over from across Sixth Street, from the Cave Club, where the Big Boys, the Offenders, or the Butthole Surfers were playing. Again, the MCs, the 1% motorcycle guys, were everywhere. Since the University of Texas was right up the street and Austin was a college town, from time to time we would see some frat boys slip in every once in a while, but they usually didn't hang out that long and they looked incredibly out of place. Eventually, when Austin exploded in the national consciousness and the rent on all the places on Sixth Street skyrocketed, all the cool clubs closed, driven out by high rent, the frat boys and college kids took over all the cool dive bars. The old live-music meccas turned into cheesy shot bars that hired cover bands. Not that it was the frat boys' fault per se, but most of them didn't exactly care about the scene or the music that came out of it.

But for a while, Austin had been what felt like the greatest American roots–music utopia. Everyone in this little cluster of clubs was dressed to the nines, and there were a good five hundred to six hundred people out on any given Monday, Tuesday, or Wednesday night. The Black Cat Lounge owner, Paul Sessums, was a trip, but he curated a lot of cool original music there and wouldn't let the bands play any trendy radio cover music. Like the Continental Club, Antone's, and the Broken Spoke to this day, it didn't matter how popular your band was or how many people you could bring through the door, if the owners didn't think your band was cool, you absolutely couldn't get a gig there. That's the difference between the old Austin and all the other music cities. Not to mention, it's counterculture central, and weirdness is not only embraced but highly encouraged. Our kids, all raised in Austin, have been brought up to respect and frequent live-music venues and outdoor festivals. I'm glad my son, Sam, has grown up in the live-music culture. I was shocked when, as an adult, he called me while I was on tour and said, "Hey, Pops, Clay from C-Boys is letting me run sound tonight for Jimmie Vaughan and I'm pretty nervous." I told him, "You should be nervous. He's only the greatest living white blues guitar player." Sometimes it's good not to sugarcoat things for your kid. Let them be nervous; it keeps them engaged and not checked out on their phone.

The first night that I walked into the Black Cat Lounge, I saw pretty much everybody from the Austin country, punk, blues, and rockabilly scene hanging out. Charlie and Will Sexton, along with Alex Napier, were lighting one another's cigarettes in the corner. Future mayor of South Congress and owner of the Continental Club, Steve Wertheimer, was with Austin scene royalty Wayne Nagel drinking a brand of beer that I'd never seen before called Shiner Bock. Songwriting brothers Bruce and Charlie Robison were in their Guy Clark blue-jean work shirts, bent-up Open Road hats, and scruffy ol' ranch boots. Blues gods Jimmie Vaughan and Kim Wilson from the Fabulous Thunderbirds were looking like a million bucks in sharkskin suits with bolo ties, talking to the hottest girls in the place. Classic country stars the Wagoneers— Tom, Monte, Craig, and Brent—were all there, sitting with Kelly Willis, who had a rockabilly band called Kelly and the Fireballs. The Wagoneers were all wearing custom Manuel western suits that A&M Records had flipped the bill for. Future rockabilly stars Kevin Smith and Shaun Young from High Noon were sitting on the indoor bleachers with musicologist and upright-bass god Mark Rubin, and next to them were drummer Mike Buck and guitarist Don Leady from the LeRoi Brothers. The greatest white blues bass player to ever live (OK, if not the greatest, definitely the coolest), Keith Ferguson, from the Fabulous Thunderbirds and Tail Gators, was sitting backstage, covered in tattoos, wearing eastside Mexican cholo clothes, looking scary. He actually turned out to be really nice. I even spotted Brian Setzer from the Stray Cats there, and he didn't even live in Austin. Everyone was there to see their friends and to dance to a band called Two Hoots & a Holler that was on-stage setting the place on fire.

Two Hoots & a Holler, quite possibly the greatest three-piece band name ever, was led by singer/songwriter/guitarist Rick Broussard. His bandmates were bass player Vic Gerard (who is still one of the best bass players to ever come out of Austin and would eventually wind up playing with the Derailers and Rosie Flores), along with drummer Chris Staples. Rick was a wild Cajun punk rocker/rockabilly poet front man who looked exactly like Eddie Cochran in 1958 and who could jump super high in the air, do windmills à la Pete Townshend on his guitar, and was like a cross between the Cramps and Johnny Horton. His original songs like "Step Fast," "Good Used Heart," and "Blues in the Night" were (at least for me) the pinnacle of textbook Austin music at that time. When my friend Brian Lux and I walked to the front of the club, Rick looked down and motioned me backstage as he walked off. I had never met him or talked to him before, and my young, insecure mind wondered what on earth he wanted. Two Hoots & a Holler ended their classic instrumental song "No Man's Land" and walked offstage toward the small dressing room to thunderous applause.

As I cautiously followed the three sweaty band members into the small dressing room, Rick sat down in a chair, cracked a Lone Star beer, his guitar laid across his lap, fired up a cigarette, and without introducing himself or anything said, "Hey man, take my guitar, go out there and play some songs with Vic and Chris."

I said, " I think you're doing great already. Besides, I don't even know what to play with them. By the way, I'm Jesse."

Rick was going outside in the back alley to do what musicians do in the back alley. He was by far the wildest front man I've ever been around, and he was known to have a crazy temper, a massive thirst for alcohol, and took drugs like they were candy. I don't want to say exactly what he was up to in the alley, but use your imagination. Again, this isn't a kiss-and-tell book, and to be honest, most of us—well, definitely me—were all drinking hard, and later I would go down some of the same roads.

Anyway, Rick stood up, put his Telecaster strap over my shoulder, and walked out of the room. Two Hoots bass man Vic Gerard looked at me with a big smile and said, "Come on, man, we

gotta go back out there. They're cheering for us and the natives
are restless." I realized this was obviously not the first time this
had happened, because the rhythm section wasn't fazed at all. So
I followed Vic and Chris up onstage and plugged Ricky's mid-'60s
Telecaster with the Bigsby tremolo arm into the silver-face Super
Six Fender amp. I looked over at Vic and mouthed, *What are we
playing?* I heard Mark Rubin yell out, "Play a Sonny Burgess song!"
But I didn't know any Sonny Burgess at that point. So I played
five Buddy Holly songs in a row, and although the crowd was disappointed because they definitely were not there to see me, I did
a passable performance for twenty minutes and we got through it
until I smelled Ricky's cigarette two inches from my face and he
was grabbing his guitar off my shoulder. I was wondering why the
crowd had all of a sudden come alive, and it was because Ricky had
walked onstage behind me.

That was my first time onstage at the Black Cat Lounge, and
although I wasn't great, I didn't suck, and I learned a whole lot
in those five Buddy Holly songs about what was expected onstage
in Austin, where the cool contest was through the roof. I remember the songs we played because I had just recently played them
for a Buddy Holly tribute show in College Station, Texas. They
were "Midnight Shift," "Blue Days, Black Nights," "Modern Don
Juan," "Rave On," and "Not Fade Away." Looking back, it's still
weird to me that we didn't play anything else but Buddy Holly,
and trust me, this crowd was full of vintage-record collectors, so
they knew every one of those tunes like the back of their hand.
The owner, Paul Sessums, came up to me with a very dry look
on his face and said, "Do you want to play here next Wednesday
night?" I said, "Yes, please!" He said, "Watch your volume, don't
play any bullshit cover songs unless they're cool old ones, and be
prepared to play as long as I need you to play." There was no discussion about money or even if I'd get free beer. I felt like I'd just
won the Texas lottery.

I drove home that night with Brian Lux in his '56 Chevrolet feeling like a god among men and also feeling grateful that I didn't fuck up those five Buddy Holly songs. It could've been a total train wreck if the Two Hoots & a Holler rhythm section hadn't known every tiny nuance that the Crickets had played. Trust me, I've shit the bed onstage with players who would start off in the wrong key, where somebody's tuning was a half-step up or down, where someone couldn't get their guitar in tune, where the amp or PA starts fucking up, or the drummer can't hold it together because he's too drunk. There's a million ways to make clams while playing a song.

Looking back, this would be another one of those nights that would inform the rest of my life. I would get trapped in a bubble, this subculture that was born in Austin, for years. And I gotta say, I loved every minute of it. I met so many folks who at the time were just hanging out on the scene but who would later become legendary. That night I smoked a tiny roach joint with songwriter Blaze Foley, whom I didn't know and thought was a hobo, for all of two minutes, and I walked down the street with Butthole Surfers front man Gibby Haynes, who told me, "You need to play more shows. You look stiff up there." And he was right. Then we walked into the Cave Club and he jumped up onstage with some band and ruled the crowd.

Later, when my band, the Road Kings (longtime friend Eric Tucker on drums and Brian Lux on upright bass, soon to be replaced by Jason Burns) played the Black Cat Lounge, bass player Keith Ferguson, whom I met that first night, invited me to his house and played all these amazing prewar blues vinyl 78s and explained the pictures on his walls of him and Muddy Waters while we snorted Peru. The blow back then was not as supercharged as it would become. I stopped snorting coke in 1997, after I realized that since I was the singer in the band, everybody and their brother who came to my shows would be offering it to me for absolutely free. I knew if I kept that up, I'd die, so I stopped. I'm lucky to not have the addictive gene that so many of my friends had, and still have. It seemed like my whole adult life was plagued with seeing some of the coolest people lose everything after getting strung out on blow. Quite a few ended up having those four a.m. heart attacks with no one around to help. Having a healthy fear of drug and alcohol addiction (family gene or not, anyone can succumb to addiction if they do enough) keeps me humble enough to not fall into the macho party guy/girl trap. I've been to the macho party guy/girl funerals . . . it's sad and unfortunate and no fun.

All of these musicians I met kept talking about gigs they had at this venue in Austin called the Continental Club. It wasn't easy getting a gig at the Continental. Owner Steve Wertheimer, who would later become a friend, was not easily impressed by cool clothes and attitude, but he eventually booked us to open for Two Hoots & a Holler because he needed a opener Ricky liked and that wouldn't cost much. We played for $150 that night and thought we had made it! The crowd liked us OK—nowhere near the response that would come later—but it was good enough for an opening act. Then Rick and Two Hoots came out and did something unexpected that taught me a huge lesson. As the stage lights dimmed and the silver ball started spinning and shooting crystalline lights all over the crowd, Rick and the boys came out and opened with a laid-back western Japanese instrumental song called "Sukiyaki," and the whole place started dancing. It was so beautiful that my eyes started welling up, but I made sure no tears fell.

I had seen Rick walk onstage and do these high-energy punk versions of "Love Me" or Johnny Horton's classic "Battle of New Orleans" and blow the roof off the place, but never something this slow and dramatic, yet with the same intensity, and *still* able to completely own the crowd. It was performances like this that informed everything I did in my own shows later. "Amateurs borrow; professionals steal." (In other words, amateurs are derivative and professionals are thieving magpies who rob everyone blind.) No one knows who originally said that. It has been attributed to everyone from Picasso to Stravinsky to T. S. Eliot to John Lennon, but it is true. So yeah, I was and still am pretty inspired by Rick Broussard and all those amazing shows back then in Austin. The guitar pickers then were nothing like the Telecaster string poppers in Nashville or the power-chord punks of L.A. and New York. There have been several times as I've looked back on seeing guitar players in Austin when I thought: I can't believe what I saw.

I remember seeing Junior Brown wailing on his Guit-Steel guitar, an instrument that he had a dream about and then built with a table steel on the bottom and a Telecaster on the top mounted together, at this place called Henry's. It was a life-changing show, and after seeing him throw Jimi Hendrix licks and Buck Trent banjo-tuning licks and Hank Marvin licks all in the same song, my mind opened to what the guitar could do. A few weeks later, Junior was playing to an empty Continental Club. This was right before he became a big deal, and there were, like, five people in the place and two of them were Neil Young on one side and Elvis Costello on the other, both watching him like hawks. I saw Jimmie Vaughan playing at the tiny club Ginny's Little Longhorn one night for maybe ten people, with a bass player and drummer, and it sounded exactly like he did on those Fabulous Thunderbird records . . . no foot pedals, no effects, all in his hands. I saw guitarist Denny Freeman (who played with Bob Dylan), who's pretty much considered the best around town, play a set at a half-full Saxon Pub that made me shut myself in my room for a week practicing. I heard Don Walser yodel at the Broken Spoke with a completely empty dance floor and thought, Why aren't there more people here? This guy can sing better than anyone in the world! Austin guitar masters David Grissom and David Holt had a band called the Booze Weasels that would set the roof of the Continental Club on fire. As a kid I had seen Stevie Ray play with the Austin band the Cobras, fronted by Paul Ray, at the Old Beaumont Café in my hometown, but by the time I got to Austin, Stevie Ray was played on every jukebox in the country as much as Zeppelin or Skynyrd was. But I did get to see him onstage with the house band at Antone's once, and I left thinking the same thing that I thought when I saw him in Beaumont as just a sideman: That guy can wipe the floor with any of those British rock stars.

The late, great, and young Nick Curran was around a lot, playing the best jump blues licks ever, then two nights later you'd see him playing straight punk rock at another club. Charlie Sexton had a band called Mystic Knights of the Sea with Speedy Sparks and John X that was mind-blowing. I remember when Redd Volkaert moved to Austin and freaked all the other guitar players out with his sophisticated hillbilly jazz licks, and I saw guitar players Gary Clark Jr. and Eve Monsees tear up plenty of stages playing blues standards when they were both still in high school yet played like fifty-year-old bluesmen. Van Wilks, Danny Barnes, Ian Moore, Sean Mencher, W. C. Clark, Eric Johnson, and Lloyd Maines were all playing around town constantly. There were so many amazing guitar players that you had to not only be great to get one of the slots at one of the best clubs on any given night of the week, you had to play your own style too. I think club owners in Austin really took it upon themselves to foster and develop all this talent because musicians were not in Austin to "make it," they were there to find their own voice and get really good at what they did.

After my band, the Road Kings, started playing at the Black Cat Lounge for months to barely anyone, people finally started trickling in through the door to see us. Nothing big. It wasn't sold out, but it didn't matter. We were young, dumb, and bulletproof and playing the music that we loved in a town that, before computers and cell phones, was the coolest place on Earth to find out about all these great records and then hone your chops learning how to play them.

Eventually the Black Cat Lounge burned down. Some folks say it was an electrical fire from the new ATM machine, but who knows. I heard a band had left all their gear in the club that night and lost everything. Hard-core biker Paul and his wife, Roberta, had started the club around 1984, and Paul's kids "Martian" and Sasha kept it going.

Sometimes, I think about that scene and miss the $2 Pearl beer, wild two-step dancers, crazy punks and Oi skinheads, the bikers who made sure no one started any shit, the free hot dogs we needed so desperately when we were too hammered at the end of the night, and seeing Two Hoots & a Holler pack the joint every Monday night and blow the roof off the place. What a time to be alive in Austin, Texas! By the way, know how many locals it takes to talk about how cool Austin used to be? Apparently every damn one of 'em. Look, all I do is travel the world, and still to this day, no matter how many McMansions have popped up in what used to be my working-class neighborhood, no matter how many people from California have moved here (I'm OK with my Cali friends being here; that whole "Don't California My Texas" slogan is some ignorant bullshit for folks still living in 1973 who haven't realized we have almost 8 billion people on the planet now), no matter how many historical live venues have shut down or how many software nerds have moved here and exponentially exploded the cost of living so normal working-class families can't live here as abundantly as they used to . . . well, I still love it. And I couldn't be a luckier guy for meeting my wife, Emily Kaye, who put a figurative gun to my stupid young small-town head eighteen years ago and said, "OK, big boy, put aside all your silly hand-to-mouth ways, because we're buying a house like normal grown-ups." Let's put it this way: our place is worth a lot more than the $108,000 we bought it for, and I take absolutely no credit whatsoever for being smart enough to buy it back then. It was all Emily. Oh, and guess how we found the house? Remember the drummer friend of mine, Tom Lewis, who played with the Wagoneers and Junior Brown? He found it and called me one day and said, "So there's this old woman who's selling this cool house. I think you should check it out!" Thanks, Tom, and thanks Austin, Texas.

There's no place like home, y'all.

ASTROS, DOUG SAHM, AND CLIFFORD ANTONE

Doug Sahm might be a legend in Texas, but in Austin he's a god.

Unlike other musicians from Austin (yeah, I know he's from San Antonio . . . I'll get to that) who've gone on to international acclaim in their respective scenes, be it country, blues, garage rock, or whatever, Doug was loved because he was a part of *all* of those scenes. Doug had country tunes that he wrote during the birth of the outlaw country scene in Austin that most musicians from that scene would've given their souls to write. He had obscure blues songs by Guitar Slim that he would pull out live onstage at Antone's Home of the Blues during the height of the blues scene in Austin that would blow the mind of a young Stevie Ray Vaughan, who was just learning who Guitar Slim was. Today Doug (if he were still alive) could walk into the Psych Fest scene in Austin with all its psychedelic and garage-rock bands and bang out "Two Headed Dog" because he originally produced that song in the studio for the king of that scene, Roky Erickson. Folk music? Bob Dylan played on Doug's records and loved Doug. And everyone from Jerry Garcia to Boz Scaggs in San Francisco thought Doug was a musical messenger, which is as "folk" as it gets. Tex-Mex rock 'n' roll music? Doug basically was one of the originators of the genre in his hometown of San Antonio. This is something obsessive musicians and insider Austin music fans have known forever, but the news of Doug's deep-pocketed, multi-genre talent is continuing to get out to hipster kids and mainstream audiences only now because most folks just know Doug from his oldies like "She's About a Mover" or his blip on the country radio charts as the singer for Texas Tornados hits like "(Hey Baby) Que Paso?" or "Who Were You Thinkin' Of?" There's so much more to Doug. It's completely mind-blowing how much he had to offer the universe. And yep, he was definitely trying to tell us something. In fact, he was screaming at the top of his lungs for us to open our minds, get away from our so-called genre loyalty, and take two and a half minutes to listen to his latest foray into blues, country, Tex-Mex, garage rock, Cajun, you name it. But when an artist is larger than life yet still fighting the competition of corporate pop noise, uncool music business executives, and genre wars, well, only some of us were able to hear him through the noise. Now, thankfully, more and more folks are getting turned into "Dougheads," as they are called in Austin.

The first time I heard Doug was when I was a kid at a Cajun festival in Port Arthur, Texas, and I saw the whole crowd going absolutely buck wild when the Sir Douglas Quintet broke into their Tex-Mex garage-rock hit song from 1965, "She's About a Mover." But the first time I really explored Doug's music was when I did a recording session at the legendary SugarHill Studios in Houston (once called Gold Star Studios, though not to be confused with the Gold Star Studios in Los Angeles) with one of Doug's producers,

Huey P. Meaux. I was playing rhythm guitar for Huey on a Zydeco session in the smaller B-room studio, and there was a picture of Doug's record *Mendocino* up on the wall. I asked Huey, "What's the deal with that Doug Sahm record?" Huey, in his thick Cajun accent, snapped back at me and said, "I produced the only hit on dat reckid," and then went back to complaining to the engineer that the bass was never loud enough on the song we were doing: "Why y'all so skerd to turn up da bass brah?!"

After the session the next day I went over to Cactus Records in Houston and bought *Mendocino*. I played the title track over and over and then finally listened to the rest of the record. The song "Texas Me" would become a regular staple I'd play in honky-tonks around Texas, and I recorded the song "At the Crossroads" for a Record Store Day vinyl release in 2020. So yeah, Doug Sahm was a huge deal in Texas to us musicians who were in the know and to his massive cult following all over the world.

When I first moved to Austin, I would randomly see Doug out on the town. He would jump up onstage at clubs like the Hole in the Wall or the Continental Club a lot and sit in with bands, and I always saw him coming and going in and out of Clifford Antone's office at Antone's Home of the Blues. Doug would say hi to me in passing (always very '60s soul brother, like, "Hey, young brother, what's happening?") but we weren't formally introduced until later. Back then I was virtually unknown to everyone except Clifford Antone, who treated me like gold 'cause I was "that kid guitar player from Beaumont." Doug would usually end up onstage those nights at Antone's singing something like "Blessed Are the Tears" or some Bobby "Blue" Bland song, and Clifford would be standing on the side of the stage wiping actual tears from his eyes with a towel. Seeing Clifford Antone openly and publicly crying (and I mean tears of joy running down his cheeks that reminded me of Ms. Victoria listening to the MLK speech) and giving zero fucks what anyone thought was almost as moving as Doug Sahm's performance. It had a major impact on me, and I knew right then that Doug was something way more important than the party band I saw as a kid doing "She's About a Mover."

Another thing that blew my mind was that Doug had zero musical boundaries. He would break into a Gulf Coast swamp-pop song in 6/8, then a hard-core Texas honky-tonk shuffle song, then rock the crowd with one of his high-energy Tex-Mex San Antonio–style rock 'n' roll songs. Musical styles were only a tool for Doug to get at the truth. If you weren't a top-40 cover band and were hard-core about your own music, most acts in Texas, and all over the country, played just one kind of music. We're a country band. We're a rock band. We're a Cajun band. We're a blues band. And so on. But being raised on the Texas–Louisiana border, I saw how genres could be more integrated because of all the different ethnic musicians who ended up in the same bands and writing songs together. Blues, Zydeco, country and western, and rock 'n' roll were all thrown around in one set by all the bands. Doug Sahm just confirmed what I had already been thinkin'.

Doug's band, the Texas Tornados, with his San Antonio buddies Freddy Fender, Flaco Jiménez, and Augie Meyers, was all over the radio at this point with songs like "(Hey Baby) Que Paso" and "Who Were You Thinkin' Of" and "Adios Mexico." Just like Doug's solo career, the Texas Tornados supergroup saw a lot of country music fans and a lot of rock 'n' roll fans and, of course, a lot of Mexican music fans at their shows. Singer Freddy Fender had already had a huge swamp-pop hit with "Wasted Days, Wasted Nights" and a massive international hit with the love song "Before the Next Teardrop Falls," both of which Doug's Cajun producer, Huey P. Meaux, had produced in Houston's SugarHill Studios. While we're on the subject, let me just say that although Huey P. Meaux was a genius in the studio, his personal life was a nightmare and things didn't turn out so great for ol' Huey. Huey's nickname and his record label was "Crazy Cajun," and he was definitely nuts.

In his early days he produced local, regional, and even big international hits like "You'll Lose a Good Thing" by Barbara Lynn (another fellow Beaumonster, who still lives in Beaumont) and "Talk to Me" by Sunny and the Sunliners, and even "Big Blue Diamonds" by rockabilly/country star Gene Summers, in addition to the aforementioned Freddy Fender and Doug Sahm hits. But in 1996 all of it went to hell in a handbag, and Huey's perverted secret life caught up with him.

A musician friend of mine, Brian Thomas, who had been playing pedal-steel guitar with my band, was living upstairs in the tape vault of SugarHill Recording Studios. One morning Brian was woken up by the Houston Police Department with a Glock-9 and a shotgun pointed inches from his face. The cops didn't let him even put a shirt on, and he and studio engineer legend Andy Bradley and a couple other folks were led into the warehouse area at gunpoint and told by the police to stay put while they raided and searched the entire studio.

Huey, unbeknownst to them, had a secret door in his office that led to a small room where the police found hundreds of pornographic Polaroid pictures of naked children, a doctor's office examination chair with stirrups on it, and cocaine. After waiting for a couple of hours in the warehouse in the back of the studio, Brian and the others wandered out with their hands up to find the studio turned upside down and the cops gone. They had no idea what was going on until they saw that the raid was all over the local news and eventually the national news and in all the big music-industry media outlets, who reported that Huey had been molesting kids in that secret room in the studio. Again, no one working at the studio knew anything that Huey was doing back in his private office because he made it very clear that no one was to go back there, and he kept it locked 24/7. Later that morning, as Huey was pulling out of his driveway, the police surrounded him and he was arrested. Huey was eventually let out on bail and went on the run to Juarez, Mexico, where the FBI finally caught him, by then a federal fugitive and on the Most Wanted list.

Huey Purvis Meaux from Wright, Louisiana, was sentenced to fifteen years in prison. He eventually got out but died shortly after that in 2011 at the age of eighty-two. This was shocking news for all of us who had worked with and known Huey. If you've ever done any recording in a big studio, they usually have two or three individual studios that different acts are working in, a reception area in the front, and a lounge to hang out in. People never really go back into the studio owner's offices or into the warehouse, or at least I never have. But we were all shocked to know that Huey was leading a double life. Goes to show, you never really know some people, do ya?

In 1995, I was at Willie Nelson's studio, Pedernales, recording my first solo record, *Raisin' Cain*, when I brought out a song called "Carmelita" (not to be confused with the song by Warren Zevon of the same name), and producer Randall Jamail said, "We should call Flaco Jiménez to play accordion on this track!" I was of course over the moon. I was a big fan of Flaco, who was considered the greatest Norteño/Tex-Mex/Tejano accordion player in the world. We called Flaco and he said in his thick Mexican San Antonio accent, "You'll have to come get me in San Antonio and bring me back afterwards. Oh, and by the way, I live about two six-packs away." So we went to the liquor store, bought two six-packs of Miller tall boys, and picked up Flaco, who regaled us with a story about how he hung up on Rolling Stones guitarist Keith Richards when Keith randomly called him to play accordion on the recording of "Sweethearts Together" on the album *Voodoo Lounge*. Flaco said, "There wasn't no way Keef was calling me, man. I thought it was a friend playing a joke on me, so I hung up on him. Luckily he called back!"

By the time we got back to the studio, Flaco had downed the last of the Miller beers and walked in and nailed the accordion part in two takes. It's amazing how many times this situation has happened to me in studios, whether it was me or some other musician. You spend all that time planning their calendar, planning all the logistics for travel and hotel and making the deal with the manager for how much you're going to pay the musician, then they travel all the way there, take an hour or so to set up, you get sounds you like and the producer and the recording engineer like . . . all this work, time, and preparation, and then: boom, the musician comes in and nails it in three minutes on the first take! OK, sometimes it's the second or third take, but usually it takes minutes to record but months/weeks/hours to prepare for that performance of one song in the studio.

I gotta say for the record, no matter how much it costs or how long it takes to set it up, I'd still rather be in the room with a musician while the recording is going down than have them email the tracks to me. All of my favorite old records sound so great because those people were all in the same room, moving molecules like people can only do when they're together. That's one of the secrets to all those recordings I love: you got to get it in the room while it's happening.

Both of Flacos's takes were so full of personality and vibe that we went around for days trying to decide which was the best. Flaco was probably at the studio for less than an hour, if that long, and we had a driver pick up some more Millers for the ride home and take him back to San Antonio. Flaco was so cool that evening that I wanted to hang out with him and drink and listen to his stories, but he had a gig the next day, so he had to split. We ended up seeing each other again at a Texas celebration concert at Cynthia Woods Mitchell Pavilion in Houston, and he sat in with me live on the song he'd recorded with us. Then we hugged and drank beer and talked about San Antonio music for the next two hours straight.

The next day after the Flaco recording at the studio, producer Randall Jamail said something that I had been hoping he would say: "This track needs Doug Sahm on it." Now I was really excited. Doug was a bona fide hero, and getting him on my record would be a dream come true. Randall, who was friends with Doug, had mentioned that Doug was a huge baseball fan. So before Randall called him I called my friend Rob Matwick, who worked for the Houston Astros, to see if I could get great seats for opening day so that we could talk Doug into coming into the studio to play on my record. When we called Doug, he said, "Yeah, I'll do it if you can get those Astros opening-day seats, but I need one for my buddy Clifford Antone too." Look, I'm sure Doug would've done it as a favor to Randall but I knew the baseball angle would add a whole other level of interest for Doug, who was probably getting called to play on people's records all the time. So I called Rob Matwick back and got three tickets instead of two. The game was scheduled for later that day, so Doug came in that morning, listened to the track, and pulled out an old vintage bajo sexto Mexican guitar and played. He nailed it in the first take, and *boom*: Doug Sahm was on my record.

Doug also suggested several arrangement ideas, which we used. We had a great morning and Doug told me all these crazy stories about the music scene in my hometown of Beaumont. And though I was a young record-collecting music nerd, Doug knew all this stuff about musicians from my beloved hometown that was all new to me.

Besides owning Antone's, where everyone from Muddy Waters to Stevie Ray Vaughan had played, Clifford Antone owned a baseball-trading-card shop, and he and Doug, like me, were obsessed with baseball. Later that day, Doug and I set out in my 1950 Ford Shoebox to go pick up Clifford Antone and drive the two and a half hours to Houston for opening day. Clifford sat in the front seat and Doug sat in the big backseat, and the first thing Clifford did before we even got out of the driveway was fire up a big, fat joint and pass it around. Doug was a big talker, and so was

Clifford. We must've smoked five joints on the drive to Houston, and I never got one word in edgewise. Listening to these two legends talk about blues music and baseball the entire way to Houston was like sitting in on a Harvard graduate-level class of American music and America's favorite pastime. Cliff and Doug would argue about who played piano on which Muddy Waters recording, Pinetop Perkins or Otis Spann, and this would go on forever, until one of them figured it out. This was pre-internet, when you really had to know your shit and be a true record collector and student of the blues. Here's an example. Clifford: "Magic Sam was playing Earl Hooker's guitar on all that Cobra Records shit, man!" Doug: "No, he wasn't, 'cause after he got the deal he went and bought that cream-colored Stratocaster!" This would go on and on and on, the whole time marijuana smoke was just filling the car. We passed several Texas Highway Patrol officers, and neither Doug nor Clifford gave two shits, whereas I was so paranoid we were going to get busted but didn't want to say anything because (A) I didn't want to look uncool and (B) I was so completely engrossed in what they were saying, I didn't want them to stop. Anyway, if I was gonna get busted for pot with anyone, getting busted with these two would be a badge of honor.

By the time we pulled into the Astros' stadium a half hour before game time, I was more stoned than I'd ever been in my life. (I know I've said this a few times in this book already, but I sincerely meant it every time!) We walked into the ballpark completely baked and reeking of weed, and Clifford acted like he owned the entire stadium. I followed Doug and Clifford to our seats, which were right down in front of home plate near the players' wives and where George and Barbara Bush (who were also hard-core Houston sports fans) were sitting. We sat down, Clifford ordered us beers and said, "These are great seats, kid. The umpire's gonna be sweating on us!" I would like to have been more relaxed, but truth was I had forgotten my sunglasses in the car and was so paranoid from smoking so much pot. My eyes were beet red, and I knew people were looking at me and this big *Godfather*-looking figure in a suit jacket and a Yankees ball cap (Clifford), and this other old hippie with his Cleveland Indians ball cap, long hair, and Willie Nelson concert shirt from 1975 (Doug). The talking never stopped. It was constant. Clifford would say, "Bagwell and Biggio got their work cut out for them, 'cause they didn't look that good at Kissimmee for spring training." Doug would counter with "Well, they signed Johan Strauss as an amateur free agent, so he's got something to prove if Terry Collins will let him play." After about three hours of being totally silent I finally chimed in while they were both taking a midsentence breath and said, "The San Diego Padres' (who we were playing that day) Trevor Hoffman's on fire and we already lost Ken Caminiti to these assholes." Doug and Clifford looked at each other with a smile, and Doug said, "Uh-oh, I think he's one of us!" After that I didn't give a shit about being so visibly stoned and was just happy I was finally in the conversation, although I think that was the only sentence I got in the entire game.

After the game we went to Etta's Lounge in a rough section of Houston called the Third Ward and listened to Grady Gaines and the Texas Upsetters play the blues. I had been there before as an underage guitar player with Houston club owner Rory Miggins, who owned the Local Charm blues club on Telephone Road. Rory was actually shot by a gangster coming out of Etta's a week later (it went straight through, no vital organs), but he was back at Etta's the next week listening to blues. I had met all the rap superstar Geto Boys there—Bushwick Bill, Scarface, and their crew—so I think Clifford was impressed that my car practically drove itself to this old juke joint. We ended up later at Rick's Cabaret and Clifford was throwing money at the strippers like it was raining. He told a beautiful Creole girl, "Dance for the kid until you get tired please, my dear." I don't know how much money Clifford spent that night, but it was a lot, and those strippers loved him. Finally, Doug and Clifford and I jumped in my old flathead Ford and drove back to Austin. The blues-and-baseball conversation never stopped, and neither did the pre-rolled joints that Clifford had in his coat pocket. They talked about Houston blues record labels Duke and Peacock and owner Don Robey until we made it back to Austin at four a.m. After a day recording with Doug and then going to the game in Houston with him and Clifford, I was in heaven.

Later Clifford would get busted and sentenced to four years in prison for drug trafficking (lots of marijuana) and money laundering. Cliff had got busted before in the '80s for 1,000 pounds of marijuana and got his time cut by putting on a big benefit concert featuring the Vaughan brothers. But this time he got popped for five tons of pot and trash bags full of cash. Even legendary lawyer Dick DeGuerin—who was a big friend to the music community of Texas; who had defended Waco cult leader David Koresh; who would later defend NYC real estate heir Robert Durst, who had a documentary made about him; and who would even get Texas outlaw singer-songwriter Billy Joe Shaver off for shooting a man—still couldn't keep Clifford out of prison.

Later, when I went to visit Clifford in jail, he looked at me with a big smile and said through the glass, "You didn't think the blues paid for all of that, did ya, kid?" Later, in 2006, right around my birthday in May, I got the call that Clifford had died unexpectedly at the young age of fifty-six. My ex-wife and the mother of my son, Christie, had been the president of Clifford's blues label Antone's Records, and my brother, as I said in another chapter, was old friends with Clifford from our home area of Beaumont/Port Arthur. His death hit all of us hard, and I still can't bring myself to delete his number from my cell phone. He was the first one who had any real juice to say, "I think you got the talent to be a real guitar player, kid."

I would stay friends with Doug Sahm as well. One day Doug called me up and said, "Hey, brother, I need to use those red, white, and blue George Jones–lookin' cowboy boots you wear." So I dropped the boots off at Antone's Records, and a few months later they ended up on the cover of Doug's Grammy-nominated blues album *The Last Real Texas Blues Band*. The last time I saw Doug I was in Los Angeles at Ocean Way Studios playing guitar on a session there. He was talking about how much he loved being up in Canada to escape the brutal triple-digit Texas summer heat. A few weeks later I heard the news that Doug had died of a heart attack in his sleep in a motel in Taos, New Mexico. When I say Doug was one of the coolest cats I've ever known, I mean it. He was the embodiment of Texas cool. I still see Augie Meyers and Flaco Jiménez around sometimes and Doug's two sons. Shawn Sahm has been fronting the Texas Tornados and his other son, Shandon, was playing drums for the Meat Puppets. I miss Doug, but didn't know him as well as I did Clifford, who was always there for me if I needed to call him for advice. Texas will never be the same without them, but man, what a gift they gave to the whole world.

KRISTOFFERSON
TO WAYLON

The first **Wednesday** of January 1996 was just another show for me at the world-famous Continental Club in Austin, Texas, the night Nashville music executive Evelyn Shriver walked through the door. The club was somewhat full of local diehards, but not packed. At this early point in my career (if you want to call it a "career"), I had moved on and realized that I wasn't going to die in a fiery car crash like Eddie Cochran, so I did what all young rockabillies from Texas and the South do: I left the teenager music behind and completely reimmersed myself in the classic country music I'd heard growing up. As we played, I saw this out-of-place-looking woman in a business outfit staring at me. After my set she approached me and said, "Hi, I'm Evelyn. Listen to me, you definitely don't sound like modern country radio, but I'd love to get you on this TV show in Nashville and get you in front of some people."

Evelyn was a powerhouse publicist/manager and onetime major record label executive, and she had a lot of juice in the music business at that time. I also have to say she was cool and knew how to talk to musicians—not your typical self-absorbed, square businessperson. I'll try to say this the most elegant way I can without sounding like I have a chip on my shoulder ('cause I really don't), but a lot of music businesspeople I've met have no earthly idea how to talk to musicians. They're constantly making comparisons to other musicians and throwing out unwanted, and usually awful, opinions about "what you can do better," and usually when they open their mouth, they say something that immediately reminds the musician of how horribly out of touch they are with what the musician is trying to do. Evelyn was the opposite of that, and she was a great hang. Two days later she called and said, "You need to come to Nashville. We're going to start you off on a national country television show called *Crook & Chase.*" Not exactly *The Tonight Show* (which I would do later with John Doe from the band X), but for a young gun like me, I could still call the folks back home in Beaumont and tell them to watch. There was a fine line I always had to walk when dealing with businesspeople. If they wanted me to chase them they would be shit out of luck. Desperation ain't a sexy look. If you're the talent and know you're good, then the businesspeople should be chasing you. That's not ego, it's just knowing your worth and not wasting your time jumping through hoops "networking" at cheesy events. Not taking things personally when people don't get what you do is like a superpower. Alligator skin can be eventually built up after you've turned a thousand nos into one yes. But most of the music businesspeople you meet who have a cool factor, at least in my experience, are older and not chasing trends, not easily influenced, not terrified about losing their jobs or status from signing the wrong person. Evelyn Shriver had a cool and easy way about her, and I knew I needed to get my ass to Nashville ASAP.

So I drove my beat-up 1982 Ford F-250 crew cab pickup truck the twelve hours from Austin to Nashville and checked into a Motel 8 out in the bricks, far from the lights of lower Broadway and far from the business offices on Music Row. Hell, that Motel 8 was all I could afford for a whopping $26 plus tax. It was full of truckers and lot lizards selling sex and whatever drugs you wanted. The *Crook & Chase* show, on the other hand, was squeaky clean and pretty square, but it was the only national show that featured country music stars nightly, so I was excited. Seeing a big black limo Town Car with a chauffeur pulling up in front of a ratty Motel 8 to pick me up was pretty much my first lesson in the smoke-and-mirrors game of the music industry. Even though I was a broke guitar picker who couldn't afford to stay near the scene in a decent hotel, perception was and still is everything in the entertainment business. The look on the faces of all the hustlers and dealers and ladies of the night who were hanging out in the parking lot was definitely *Who in the hell is this guy?* So I made the chauffer wait on me a minute while I went up to my room and grabbed my suitcase so it didn't get stolen while I was out pretending I was in the big leagues.

By the way, I think riding in a limo alone is creepy. It just feels weird. There's no one there with you to enjoy it, and raiding the mini bar for drinks alone is just kind of sad. After that trip I remember calling my best friend, Lew Temple, and telling him how pathetic it felt, riding in this huge empty limousine alone. A few years later, when Lew became a successful actor, he told me he would drive his beat-up pickup truck to his movie premieres in Hollywood and that one night Denzel Washington told him, "You know the studio will send a driver and car for ya, right, my man?" Lew said, "Yep."

So I arrived at Opryland to the TV studio, and it was pretty much what I thought it was going to be. There I was, the Texas guitar slinger with my 1961 Custom Telecaster (which I about killed myself working to buy but which would later be stolen from a backstage dressing room in NYC. For the record, there's a special place in hell for guitar and horse thieves). Picture me with my black pompadour and sideburns and tattoos that weren't that big in the early '90s rehearsing my song "Kissing Abilene Goodbye" (which had shot to number 1 on a brand-new thing called the Americana charts) with a house band of killer Nashville musicians who had been neutered from playing with any real heart. They all had those mullet haircuts and silly modern country pastel-colored western shirts à la Garth Brooks. Ugh. They all looked at me and smiled when we played this upbeat tune as if to say, *Damn, that felt good.* Unfortunately, the producers didn't let the talent bring their own bands. Typical cheesy TV-executive move to keep the show "running on time." Hey, I get it. It's live TV, but so many other TV shows like *Top of the Pops* and *The Tonight Show* or *Conan O'Brien* figured it out with rock 'n' roll bands, who, let's face it, are usually way more dysfunctional than modern pop-country singers. Of course, Hank Sr. or Johnny Paycheck showing up in their prime would've probably been a train wreck to deal with in terms of booze and pills and making it to the gig on time, but this was long after Nashville corporations had sucked all the cool out of country music and found a way to sell it to housewives in New Jersey who liked line dancing, pop choruses, and "country music that doesn't sound too twangy." The whole thing felt cheesy. And I go out of my way to not give in to my punk-rock attitude, trying not to be the ungrateful guy with the chip on his shoulder. I've been in bands with guys like that, and 99.9 percent of the time they self-sabotage every opportunity that's given to them and end up bitter and working some day job they hate. But all these preconceived notions about the hosts, who looked like Christian Broadcasting Network people, and the sets and furniture that looked like it was something my grandmother would have, well, all these thoughts were about to change.

I was sitting next to Nashville radio/TV legend Ralph Emery as he was getting his makeup done. He was a legend in country music, and I plied him for stories about *The Porter Wagoner Show,* and he happily obliged but wondered, "How does a kid your age know about a banjo picker like Buck Trent from Porter's band?" Right about then, Evelyn Shriver showed up knocking at the dressing-room door with none other than Kris Kristofferson in tow. Evelyn said, "Hey, Jesse. I'd like you to meet Kris. He's going to be on the show tonight as well." I was shocked. Everything just went from L7 to being, as we say in East Texas (all in one word), "coolernhell." Kris was super nice, very low-key, and in that incredible speaking voice said, "Good to meet ya, Jesse. Hear you're from Texas too." I was shitting my pants, so I said, "Uh, yeah, I mean yes sir . . . uh, yes Mr. Kristofferson." He laughed and said, "Call me Kris, brother." Coolest guy on the planet. Later I would get to know Kris and his daughter Casey and get to play with him more at festivals and TV tapings, but as a young gun I could've died happy meeting an original country outlaw during my first trip to Nashville.

Another odd coincidence is that later, Kris's ex-wife, the super talented Rita Coolidge, and I would end up on the same record label. When I was introduced to Rita at our South by Southwest (SXSW) showcase, she immediately bypassed me with her arms out wide and said, "Oh, Emily!" and hugged my wife. Turns out that Rita used to babysit Emily when she was growing up on Maui. Small world. Emily's father, Chuck Kaye, was the head of Almo/ Irving Publishing at A&M Records in Los Angeles, where Rita was signed along with Joe Cocker, whom she sang with.

Back to the Nashville TV show: I went out and did my song with the house band and I was asked over to the couch by Lori-anne Crook and Charlie Chase, who looked just like televangelists from the 1980s. Very nice folks, but as I mentioned before, the set looked like Jim and Tammy Bakker's show. They asked me some pretty silly questions for two minutes, cut to a commercial, and that was that. Oh, well. At least I got to shake Kristofferson's hand. Kris went out and sang "Help Me Make It Through the Night," and after the first verse of "Take the ribbon from your hair" he stopped the house band on live TV and said, "Oops, put my capo on the wrong fret." He moved the capo down a fret and started the song over . . . on live TV! The producers and the house band were freaking out, because you're not supposed to start a song, stop the song, then start it again on a slick national TV show! You're not supposed to do that on *any* live television show! (Ask yourself, have you ever seen that before on Conan or Kimmel?) And of course Kris, the coolest guy there, couldn't have cared less.

After they brought him to the couch to talk, out of nowhere he said, "How 'bout that kid Jesse from Austin?" I was shocked. Kris came backstage, and before I could say thank you, he said, "Hey, wanna go to the Gibson guitar factory?" I said, "Sure, man, but it's ten o'clock at night, isn't it closed?" He said, "Not for us it's not." So Kris, Evelyn, and I headed over to the Gibson guitar factory in a black Town Car, and Kris and I smoked a joint on the way. Evelyn gave me a Kristofferson tour ball cap that I put on, and we immediately started talking about books. Vonnegut, Bukowski, Hunter S. Thompson . . . basically all my favorite writers. I was blown away with how much Kris knew about these writers because, duh, he had actually hung out with them. He also told me that Hollywood was really banging on his door to play Abraham Lincoln in this film, but he didn't feel like the script was tight enough, so he kept turning them down. That's the mark of a true artist, someone who turns down big movie money because the script sucks. Kris might've been from Brownsville, Texas, but he ended up going to Oxford University in England and becoming a Rhodes Scholar in English literature.

We walked into the Gibson factory (I was baked out of my mind) and got the grand tour from the shop manager, who was so happy to see Kris. I played some acoustic guitars from the late 1890s that Orville Gibson himself had made. It was like I could feel the wood of these old handmade guitars breathing in my arms. I've been fortunate enough to play some priceless vintage acoustic instruments in my day, and even owned a few virgin vintage guitars that were original and straight out of the box, but there's only been a few times in my life I got to play an acoustic instrument that actually resonated and vibrated like that. Another time was playing a gut-string flamenco guitar from Spain that had been built for the greatest flamenco and classical guitarist ever, Andrés Segovia, that my friend Randall Jamail owned. I used it to record on two Ray Price songs. Anyway, Kris and I took some Polaroid pictures together (as seen on page 4 of the insert), the limo dropped him off at his tour bus, and Kris shook my hand soul brother–style and said, "Gotta gig in Memphis, brother. See ya down the road!" I got back to that ratty Motel 8 and thought to myself, That was cool while it lasted! I finally crashed out after lying in my dingy, dark motel room watching the ceiling fan spin shadows on the wall with the faint sound of the night people out in the parking lot. Quite a feat, trying to take it all into my li'l Beaumonster head.

The next morning my phone rang at nine and a familiar voice on the other end said, "Hey hoss, saw you on TV last night. I cut my hand in the kitchen last night cooking with Jessi and want you to meet me over at Woodland Studio and play guitar for me." I just held the phone out for a second and stared at it. Nah, no way. Then I heard, "Hey where'd you go?" So I stuttered back, "Um, is this W-Waylon Jennings?" The voice said, "Yeah hoss, see you at the studio in two hours." OK, so all these questions start running through my head: (A) How did he get this number and know where I was? (B) Was this the thing my friend/producer Randall Jamail hooked up and didn't tell me? (C) There's a million great guitar players in Nashville, why would he ask me to come down?

(D) Where's Woodland Studios? (E) What song does he want to record?

Soon I checked out of the motel, drove over, and pulled my banged-up pickup truck into the Woodland Studios parking lot next to a really nice Jaguar. I was standing there with my trusty Telecaster case. I knocked on the door, and the Man in Black himself, Johnny Cash, opened it! My jaw hit the floor. Sorry, but this next sentence deserves the severity and intensity of a good ol' F-bomb. On the outside, sure, I'm just trying to reel it in and try-ing to be cool, but inside, I was *freaking the fuck out*! I have a whole chapter later dedicated to my hyperventilation.

I walked into the studio and immediately a film crew pointed their cameras and lights at me. Waylon was sitting on a stool in front of a vocal mic and casually said upon meeting me for the very first time in person, "Hey hoss, grab that Martin off that stand and let's go over this song. Oh hey, I'm Waylon, good job on that thang with Kris last night." I kept telling myself *Just keep your mouth shut and give them what they want, JD.*

We began to work up what I soon realized was a unique arrange-ment of Willie Nelson's song "I Never Cared for You," and Waylon was singing the shit out of it. Cash was just sitting there in the control room with producer Randall Jamail and the engineer, and Cash was not saying a word, just watching and listening. If you Google my name along with Cash's and Waylon's, a YouTube video will pop up of us working on the song. I look incredibly young, and at that point these two legends were constantly being filmed for posterity. Between takes, Cash and Waylon were cracking jokes nonstop. Waylon would say to Cash, "Hey John, remember that time the cops pulled me over in Bucksnort, Tennessee, for writing a check for cocaine?" Cash said, "Yeah, and they didn't even arrest you, just took your stash, said, 'Waylon, don't write checks for that stuff,' and sent you back to Nashville! Did you write 'drugs' on the memo line of the check?" And they just laughed their asses off. They were getting such a rush out of making each other laugh, it was hard not to think, These two men have been through things that the rest of us mere mortals can't even imagine.

We got the song down, Waylon said thanks, I took more pictures with him and Cash, and as I was walking out the door Waylon said, "Might call ya 'bout some more recording, hoss." I drove my old truck back to Austin a changed man. I went home and obsessed on Jerry Reed guitar licks and just tried to get better by returning to my early guitar discovery days and practicing ten hours a day again. Eventually, Waylon did finally call Randall to say he was doing a new record called *Right for the Time* and he wanted me, Pete Anderson, and Mark Knopfler on it—two guitar players I am completely in awe of. Later I got to work with Pete Anderson in the studio he shared with Dwight Yoakam in Los Angeles. Pete not only made country guitar cool again but got it back on the radio. He actually produced a song I did for the record *Young Guitar Slingers Texas Blues Evolution*, an Antone's Records release. Pete and I are still friends to this day.

I flew back to Nashville, showed up at Woodland Studios, and Waylon walked in and said, "Pete and Mark are not going to be on the record." This was going to be a dream come true being on a record with them, but also completely terrifying for a twentysomething kid. Waylon loved Dire Straits. I've talked to Shooter about it since then, and he confirmed: that first Dire Straits record is more than just a masterpiece, and even though it's a rock record, it significantly influenced a lot of the writers and guitar pickers in Nashville. After being in my little clique in Austin, that whole experience opened my mind. I started embracing all genres of music and opening myself to whatever moved me without allegiance to any particular genre. I was always open to all kinds of music because that's the way I was raised, but I was becoming my own man and not letting scenes dictate what was cool or uncool. It's real common with young people who are easily influenced, but let's face it: a lot of people never grow out of that stage of listening and end up missing out on a whole lotta cool stuff. Any song, from any genre, from any great performance was what I was looking for. And I gotta say, when a young person, like I was at the time, breaks down all the walls and the rules and starts to open their arms to the universe, amazing shit happens.

Let me set the record straight, at least for my book, and say that in my mind, Waylon was the coolest of all the outlaws. Willie was and still is operating on a universal Zen level. He has a Dalai Lama–esque approach to life, and only a wise old survivor—a seer, if you will—can vibrate at that frequency. Kris is literally a genius in terms of being a Rhodes Scholar and is also one of the best-looking people you'll ever see in your life. I see him as a poet in his heart of hearts who is on par with all the literary greats. He also happens to be a movie star on top of it all. Johnny, after finally tempering his addiction issues, became a champion for the underdog and had a glowing spiritual aura surrounding him. Maybe it was easier to pick up on Cash's deep spiritual vibe because of the era when I met him? He was a humble and gracious man who made me think about working on myself. Even so, Waylon was, and will always be, at least to me, the coolest man to ever sing country music. Yep, I know, Hank Sr. had all these qualities and he was only twenty-nine when he died. But Waylon was like part Elvis, part outlaw Josey Wales, and part the wildest horse that even the most experienced ol' cowboy could never tame. By the time I worked with him, he had calmed down quite a bit, but you still felt like that side of him might show itself at any minute.

On the flip side, all he wanted to talk about was his son, Shooter. He talked about Shooter and Jessi constantly. The true loves of his life. He loved being Shooter's dad, and they would listen to records Shooter had, like Nine Inch Nails and even Marylin Manson, and they stayed up and watched '80s horror movies together. Now, besides all the classic outlaw stuff, how cool is it that he took that much interest in his son's life? I know comparison is the thief of joy, and I'm definitely not comparing, but most of our dads, especially our country-ass daddies, wouldn't be too big on sitting around listening to Nine Inch Nails, even with their young son. Yet another lesson to remind me to keep my mind open.

Waylon was hilarious too. One day he walked into the recording studio while the engineer and I were talking about recording guitar parts. Waylon looked at me and said, "Well hoss, they want me to play *The Lola Falana Show*." I said, "That's weird. Like, the hot chick who was a dancer from the '70s?" He walked out mumbling, "I don't know what the big deal is." Ten minutes later his manager, Nikki, walked in and said, "Did he tell y'all? Waylon's doing Lollapalooza!" Turns out James Hetfield's daddy was a huge Waylon fan, so Metallica wanted Waylon on the bill with them. Waylon called it *The Lola Falana Show* from then on out on purpose, and we died laughing every time he said it.

Speaking of Metallica, in a *Guitar Player* interview, Hetfield said he really dug my lead break on Waylon's cover of Paul Simon's "The Boxer." That was a weird day in the studio. Waylon said, "We're gonna do a song by my friend Paul." All the musicians in the band looked at each other like *OK, our mental Rolodexes are frantically thumbing through the P's*. Willie's drummer, Paul English? No, he wasn't really a writer. Paul McCartney? Probably not. There's no way it could be Paul Simon? Yep, it was Paul Simon. Crazy, huh? Also I used Waylon's black-and-white leather-bound Telecaster to cut that lead 'cause Waylon handed it to me in the control room and said, "Here, use mine and make it funky." I ran the guitar through his '70s silver-face Super Six Fender amp with two curly cords and a wah-wah pedal, and he dug it. Listening back on that song, he definitely *Waylonized* it.

I was on tour in San Francisco in 2002, walking up Clio Street, when I saw through the front glass of a bar a TV with CNN on that said WAYLON JENNINGS DEAD. I immediately started crying right there on the street, which is way out of character for me, but I couldn't help it. I wasn't sobbing uncontrollably, just tears started streaming down my face. I remember people walking past me, which reminded me I needed to pull it together. I was in the middle of a tour, but I was so sad that I didn't know if I could play the show that night. I knew Waylon wouldn't have wanted me to cancel, and my friend Dallas Wayne (who is now a top DJ on SiriusXM Outlaw Country radio) was opening the show. We ended up playing a bunch of Waylon songs that night and we bonded big-time. Dallas and I still call or text each other every year on the day Waylon passed away. That night onstage I wore big black sunglasses and didn't face the crowd much. Again, I wasn't bawling, but I had to play those songs and I knew when I got to the song "Dreaming My Dreams" that a few tears were gonna fall. Waylon had believed in me and was one of the most principled and soulful musicians I've ever worked with. Even now, while I'm writing this, my eyes are welling up.

Looking back on playing with Waylon, it all seems like a dream. There were times when he truly felt like just one of the guys hanging out, talking about some '80s horror movie he watched the night before with Shooter or some restaurant that he and Jessi went out to. But then he would go in and sing some incredible high-harmony vocal on one of his own tracks, without rehearsing it, and nail it in one take. Or put a little electric-guitar riff on a track that changed the whole vibe of the song and that you wouldn't be able to get out of your head. He wrote little hooky musical parts that are the stuff big songs are made of. Sometimes, at first, he would go into the recording room and start doing something with his guitar or with a vocal part and you wouldn't really have any idea what he was going for. It's not like he ever explained himself—he was

Waylon Fucking Jennings—so he just told the engineer, "Punch me in right here." And then he'd come back into the control room, play it back, and everyone else would look at one another like a lightbulb just went off in our heads, as if to say, *Oh, I see what he just did!* Waylon could do subtle little things in his music and in his real life, things he would just barely slip in, and it would later make you say, "Wow, I didn't even realize what he was doing or talking about when he did it, but now I do!"

I miss Waylon as a fan, but I also miss him in the sense of having had the honor of being let into his world, if only for a short time, and getting to make music and hang out with him. But he did give me Shooter as a friend. As a spiritual man myself, I think Waylon is with Shooter and Jessi everywhere they go. I know my own father is with me at every turn, for every decision. I'm sure Waylon is with Shooter when he wins awards and also on the road out in the middle of nowhere on the back of his bus.

All these spirits we meet along the way seem to become part of our future, whether they're physically with us or not. When little pieces of fragmented memories show up years later in our minds, seemingly out of nowhere, it's not just some déjà vu trip. It's almost like once another spiritual being has that profound effect on your life, they become a part of you. Lord knows, there's so much I'd like to tell my old man about, so sometimes I just do it anyway. Talking to people who've passed away doesn't mean you're crazy. Sometimes, you're just writing a book, like this one, and you realize that as the dim light of your laptop beams in the corner of your dark room, there's probably someone else in there with you, guiding you. Hippie-dippy bullshit? Nah, it doesn't hurt to open yourself to these concepts. The fear of not doing things I'm fearful of has become greater than the fear of doing them.

I still have this sticker that I got from Waylon that he used to put on all his road cases that says THIS IS NO DRESS REHEARSAL. WE ARE PROFESSIONALS, AND THIS IS THE BIG TIME. I think about that

sticker a lot, and it took me years to really understand how profound it is. Not just about music or show business, but about life.
All the stories in this book might have some famous-person component to them, but really they're about me finally growing up and
getting my shit together, which is the plight of every human being.
Some of y'all get your shit together quicker, and some of us, well,
not so quick. One thing that'll make you grow up quick is playing
guitar with Waylon Jennings when you're a kid.

THE MAN IN BLACK

When I knocked on that studio door at Woodland Studios in Nashville and Johnny Motherfuckin' Cash opened the door and smiled at me, he said, "Are you just gonna stand there with your mouth open or come in and pick that thang?" I lost my mind. Or may I say, I lost my mind inside of my mind, and tried hard to cover up how I was in fact losing my mind, if that makes any sense. And then, to top it off, he stuck his hand out and said, "Hello, I'm Johnny Cash." I mean, HOLY FUCK! Looking back on it now, I wonder how many people he did that to, just to completely freak them out. I mean, for all intents and purposes, if you grew up in the South, or out west, or in Texas like I did, and grew up around older people who listened to country-and-western music nonstop, there was Jesus Christ, and then Johnny Cash was a close second. He wasn't God, he wasn't the Son of God, but he was *right* under the Son of God. Now, I say this half seriously and half jokingly, because when I met John (that's what everyone around him seemed to call him, just John, so I did too), he had morphed into a deeply spiritual person, and I mean spiritual, not merely religious. After years of strife and woe with drugs and alcohol, the menacing stress of a roller-coaster ride of one of the craziest careers in the music business, he had finally found God and seemed to be beyond comfortable in his own skin. What small amount of time I did get to be around him, he wasn't at all like one of those old, pushy, religious people. And let's face it, there's a lot of old, pushy, religious country guys who get into their sixties and seventies and jump on the Bible bandwagon in full force and start testifying to anyone who will listen. I know, I grew up with those folks. Especially the Southern Baptist and Pentecostal fundamentalists. But John was nothing like that.

I'll just say this, and I don't care how hippie/Eastern/woo-woo it sounds, at the stage of Johnny Cash's life that I met him, he had a spiritual aura that surrounded him. I think if you were looking for it, you could see that spiritual aura as plain as the nose on his face. Even if you weren't looking for it, and you got within six feet of the man, you could probably feel something that was otherworldly about him but not understand what it was exactly that you were feeling. I know anyone who has any inkling to believe in a power greater than themselves can hear it on those old spiritual songs John cut later in his life on the American Recordings albums. For full transparency's sake, this is probably because I romanticized the guy from all the way back when I first heard him singing "Folsom Prison Blues" in my cousin's pickup truck when I was, like, six years old. Besides my parents playing Willie Nelson's *Red Headed Stranger* on 8-track, this was my second memory of hearing a country song and wanting to hear it over and over and over.

I remember my cousin David singing every word while the song poured out of the old Delco truck radio as we drove down a dirt road in the middle of nowhere through the black night with zero light pollution. As a young boy I thought the line "I shot a man in Reno, just to watch him die" was as badass as any Bruce Lee movie, James Bond film, or Muhammad Ali fight. Thinking back now, driving down that dark road with that song cranked feels like a dream. And at the time I had no idea that the dream would continue and I'd be two inches from him standing in front of the studio control board with this guru-like person who seemed to have a direct line to God.

I had heard all the stories about John's friendship with Billy Graham and how he and June studied the Bible. I grew up like that, too, in the church, going to Bible study, singing all the old-timey hymns in the church choir. I know, it sounds cliché, but just about everyone in Texas and the South was like that, and we Beaumonsters were no different. But there were also a lot of things that tipped me off to Johnny Cash not subscribing to the usual teetotaler fundamentalist church thing, and one was his wicked sense of humor. And I'm not talking in the square sense of clean, country *Hee Haw* humor either. (I loved *Hee Haw* growing up, but I also loved Richard Pryor, and I knew the difference.) If there were no ladies present, and it was all friends, he'd throw out a cuss word, not for shock value but if the story demanded it. This is the same thing my grandfather did, Jesse the first (I'm Jesse the second, named after him), when he would tell a dirty joke outside with the menfolk, maybe even sip a little flask of whiskey every once in a while. But if my grandmother came out to see what they were up to or tell him dinner was ready, he'd hide the flask and clean his act up immediately. I don't think John was sneaking any whiskey after his sordid past with booze and drugs, but good Lord he was hilarious! I laughed so hard one day. I'm talking about some laugh-your-ass-off stuff. And it wasn't any bullshit where it's like "Oh, the legend said something funny, we all have to laugh now!" Nope, I've seen that, too, and it was nothing like that. It was just goofiness and brilliant timing.

Here's one example:

We were in the studio one day and were just hanging out. Me, Waylon, the engineer, and Johnny Cash. We were waiting on the producer, Randall, to come back with one of his crazy high-end Neumann microphones. I was in the kitchen/lounge area, and I heard Cash on the microphone in the vocal booth talking to the engineer, and John's saying, "Have y'all ever seen that movie *Aliens*?" Waylon said, "Yeah, I think me and Shooter watched it." John said, "I love it when that guy starts losing it, man, uh, saying . . . 'We're all fuckin' doomed, man!'" I made my way to the control room and we all looked at one another and just started laughing. Then Cash started really getting into trying to imitate Bill Paxton's character from *Aliens,* and was laughing over the mic and told the engineer, "Put a bunch of reverb on my voice and I'm gonna nail this sucker!" So the engineer drowned it in reverb and Cash started yelling, "Hey man, we're all fuckin' doomed, man! Game over, man! Game over!" By this time Waylon is spitting out his coffee and the engineer and I have tears in our eyes we're laughing so hard. Of course, it sounded absolutely nothing like Bill Paxton (God rest his Fort Worth, Texas, soul, RIP) but sounded exactly like Johnny Cash saying Bill Paxton's lines from the film. Cash saw us laughing and couldn't do it anymore because he was laughing so hard at us laughing. Funniest shit ever. Like Richard Pryor funny. Like being on mushrooms with your friends and you're laughing so hard that you get mad at them and tell them to shut up because your side is hurting funny.

Years later I talked to Shooter, and he told me that John and Waylon had some kind of falling-out. Nothing bad, just a misunderstanding among friends kind of bullshit about whether Cash was in or out on some Highwaymen shows. Cash was in the middle of a comeback with his American records that he did with Rick Rubin. Just a few years before all this, he was playing at a half-full theater in Branson, Missouri, where Rick went to see him. These things happen with careers, they go up and down, peaks and valleys, and it's just part of the deal. People in the music business were shocked when Cash lost his record deal with Columbia. He had sold millions of records for them and they just let him go. I remember seeing Dwight Yoakam call out John's old record label for dropping him on national TV during an interview with Ralph Emery and thinking, Damn, this Dwight guy is a real rebel. So basically, before the Highwaymen got together (a supergroup consisting of Kris, Waylon, Johnny, and Willie), John was just playing his smaller-theater shows and living his life. It's not like he had anything else to prove. In retrospect, it's not like he was looking to reinvent his career and win a ton of awards, or gain a whole new younger audience. He was just making a little record with this weird hippie-looking guy named Rick because it seemed like it would be a cool thing to try. Anyway, after the Highwaymen became a huge draw, then John's solo career blew up all over again out of nowhere. So back to the story: That day in the studio Waylon and John hadn't seen each other in a while because of whatever had happened with scheduling for some Highwaymen shows that John couldn't make. You gotta remember, Waylon, Willie, Kris, and Johnny were/are like brothers, so they fight sometimes. From what Shooter told me, Waylon and Johnny were really happy to see each other again, and of course, like brothers, let bygones be bygones. Man, looking back on it now and knowing that, I can't imagine how good it felt for them to laugh that hard together (and it was hard), after probably missing each other's company for a while.

Most days in the studio or on tour, these guys had film crews following them around everywhere. It was no secret that they were getting on in years, so documenting what they were doing seemed to be very important to everybody but them. They were probably laughing at a whole host of things, but especially that they'd cheated death and prison and were still alive to laugh about it all.

Just think, when John and Waylon were roommates at one point John was so strung out on speed that Waylon had to do an intervention to get him cleaned up. Waylon brought it up and said, "Imagine being so strung out that they get me of all people to talk to John! Hell, I was doing as much speed or more than he was!" Cash chimed in quickly, "More . . . you were doing more." Waylon started to explain how they used to steal each other's stash. Johnny said, "I had a few good hiding places in that old apartment that you never knew about, but I always found your stash!" This was memory lane, and not the one you see on VH1's *Storytellers*. This was warts and all, and it was just us in the control room.

Thinking about being there while these two legends traded old war stories about each other makes my heart smile even now. I think Johnny Cash was a deeply complicated person. In fact, I would say he was a lot of different things to a lot of different people. The working-class listener saw him as the man's man country star. Women loved him because he seemed very vulnerable, easy, confident, and gentle in one way and straight up whip anybody's ass in the room in another way. He was deeply in love with June, and one day when June came over to the studio, as soon as she walked in he put everything on hold and went up to her and gave her a hug and a kiss on the cheek and said, "I've missed you; so glad you're here." Now, these two people had been together for an extremely long time and they were elderly at this point, but there was still a deep, burning love between them. This memory chokes me up just writing it. But there were a whole lot of other people besides working-class country fans and women who loved and still love Johnny Cash. In fact, I would go as far as to say that the people who loved him the most were the people he was standing up for. Johnny Cash was much more of a protest singer than anyone in the Nashville music industry would admit. His friends Bob Dylan, Pete Seeger, Judy Collins, and Jimmy Carter all knew he was a protest singer. They knew he was sent here to spread a bigger message than just being an outlaw country legend, and they knew his mission was searching for capital-T Truth. There were thousands upon thousands of prisoners locked away within the industrial prison complex whom everyone had forgotten about or written off except Johnny Cash, and they loved him for it. There were tribes and tribes of Native Americans scattered all over the rural areas and reservations across America and Canada who loved Johnny and his rendition of "The Ballad of Ira Hayes" and the benefit concerts he did on their behalf. Johnny stood up for them when no one else would. He shined a light on their problems by singing protest songs and dedicating gospel hymns to them on television shows and at concerts in front of large audiences.

I can tell you one thing, Johnny Cash would not like what is going on in politics today. He was a man who took it upon himself to carry a torch and shine a light on those who were struggling, and he would not be happy about the current tribalist political divide America has now. He made sure that the lyrics of his songs addressed everything: homelessness, war veterans afflicted with PTSD, hungry children, racism against Native Americans and African Americans, basic human rights for prisoners, and especially the poor working folks who were and still are basically indentured servants to a bunch of tax-dodging multinational corporations who've stolen these folks' chances at a dignified way of life. This guy knew the scriptures and tried to live in the light of those words. Even when his American records reignited his then-dormant career and made him one of the biggest stars on the planet all over again in the '90s, John never forgot his poor/working-class upbringing, and he dug in on those issues even harder. I must have heard him and Waylon say "beats pickin' cotton" a dozen times in the studio, responding to something that would take a little more effort or work. They both had actually picked cotton and were both from cotton country. Littlefield, Texas, and Kingsland, Arkansas, were both known as nothing but cotton fields.

All this drives home my philosophy that country music is not merely a genre but an actual place. I grew up around a lot of country folks in East Texas, and it still blows my mind just how universal the message of that place, the country, is in these OG outlaws' music. Unlike me, people around the world don't have to be born in the country or spend lots of time in the country or even be raised by folks who were from the country to really and truly understand where these country music pioneers were coming from. The words and feeling of their music are so powerful that they could put some kid in the slums of Bangladesh smack-dab in the cotton fields of Littlefield or Kingsland. My granddaddy Jesse always said, "I picked cotton so your daddy didn't have to." But those early childhood days of spending all my time out in the woods, hunting and fishing and just being out in the country with not one building, car, or paved road in sight still have an effect on me to this day. That's a feeling that I can hear in people's voices when they sing country music.

My granddaddy Jesse loved Ernest Tubb and Johnny Cash. Ernest was John's musical idol, among a few others, but he loved Ernest. So it makes perfect sense that most of the older Ernest Tubb fans eventually turned into Johnny Cash fans. One year we went to a family reunion out in the country and two of my older cousins kept calling my granddaddy Uncle Doc. Finally I asked my granddad, "Why they calling you Doc?" He said in the early '60s, he and his brother were hunting deer out in the woods. They drove for miles and miles down an old dirt road, pulled over in the middle of nowhere, and parked their truck. They grabbed their guns and gear, jumped over the ditch, and struck out into the deep piney forest to hunt the evening, then pitch a tent, camp out overnight, get up at sunrise, and hunt some more. They didn't see any deer that first night, so they built a small fire, cooked some food, had a little bit to eat, and then zipped up their sleeping bags and went to sleep. In the middle of the night my uncle whispered, "Jesse, there's something in my sleeping bag." He had to say it, like, four times 'cause my granddad was snoring. Finally my granddad woke up and said, "What's wrong?" My uncle said it again in a low voice: "Jesse, there's something in my sleeping bag." So my granddaddy got up real slow and walked over to my uncle's sleeping bag. My uncle said, "It's in the bottom, by my feet." So my granddad started to slowly unzip my uncle's sleeping bag, and when he got down about to my uncle's knee, my uncle gnashed his teeth and said, "He got me, Jesse, he got me!" A big, thick diamondback rattlesnake about five feet long rolled out of the sleeping bag and squirmed off into the bushes. My granddaddy told my uncle not to move and try to stay calm, then tied a bandanna around my uncle's leg, right above the bite, as tight as he could. He picked my uncle up (if he would've walked himself, the poison would've spread quickly all over his body to his heart and probably killed him) and carried him a few miles, over the ditch, to where the truck was parked. He put him in the truck and hauled ass to the hospital and saved his life. When my grandfather fired up the old International pickup truck, Johnny Cash's version of Ernest Tubb's hit song "So Doggone Lonesome" came over the radio. My uncle was getting very weak. My granddad was trying to keep my uncle's mind off of what had happened and said, "That damn sure ain't Ernest . . . Who is it?" My uncle said, "I don't know, Jesse." Then the DJ came over the radio and said, "That's newcomer Johnny Cash doing 'So Doggone Lonesome!'" My granddad looked over at my uncle, and his head was starting to lean back like he was passing out, so he floored it. That's the first time my granddaddy heard Johnny Cash and why he was called Uncle Doc. I told Johnny Cash that story, and he loved it. He listened so intently and told me about snakes out in the cotton field and in the barn at his parents' place in Arkansas. I felt like we were just friends talking, because that's what we were at that place and time.

The best memory I have of John is him telling me, "You're different, so be patient. It might take you a little longer, but you'll
have a longer career because of it. Don't change, just be you, Jess."
When he and Waylon asked me if I had a girlfriend, I said, "No,
but I got a wife who's trying to leave me right now." They looked
at each other and smiled, and John said, "Been there, done that.
Write some songs, son!" and they walked out of the room.

My first wife did in fact leave me, and while I was experiencing
an incredible high working with these heroes of mine, I was simultaneously hiding a low-grade depression over the breakup of my
marriage. Looking back now, it's amazing the interest they took in
me during that brief span of time we got to be together. I'm sure
when John was younger he was restless and tortured, but when I
met him he seemed so incredibly centered that it rubbed off on
everyone around him.

I am a believer in God, because I choose to live my life that
way. I'm totally fine with you if you're not. In fact, I seem to get
along better with folks who are not making every decision in their
lives based on some "faith"-driven rhetoric. Sure, I'm a science guy
and don't believe in talking snakes or raining blood or zombifica-
tion disappearing acts, but I do believe there's something bigger
than me out there. So therefore I have to think that Johnny and
June knew their bodies were temporary vessels and that their souls
would mesh and carry on forever. Take a second and think about
that. Think about how liberating it would be to love someone else
so much that you believe when you both roll off of this mortal coil,
you'll somehow find each other and continue your journey with
that person. You can look at it one of two ways: that it's antiquated,
fairy-tale thinking, or that it's a pure form of love that's setting an
intention that just might work if you believe in it. In this day and
age of so much cynicism, so much negativity, I think we could all
use a little more of what Buddy Holly called "True Love Ways"
kind of thinking. Not only does it make us feel better, but it always

gives us a responsibility to treat one another more kindly because we know there are more repercussions to our behavior at the end of all of this than just becoming worm food.

The most interesting thing about being around Johnny Cash was seeing how kind and thoughtful he was to everyone around him. He was not the wild outlaw we see in those early pictures and film clips, although that vibe was still part of him. He was quick to put a hand on your shoulder, quick with a smile, and quick with a remedy to move things forward and keep things positive. We can all only hope to be that free of cynicism when we are that age. Johnny Cash had taken quite a long, hard road to get to that place of freedom and light, but when he got there, he tried to shine that light on everyone he came in contact with, as if to help make their journey a little easier than his own.

WILLIE'S AMPLIFIER

My earliest memories of music are of my parents playing Willie Nelson 8-tracks in the car on vacation while I dozed in and out of sleep in the backseat. Willie created the soundtrack to the lives of most Texans my age, and this was a few years before the outlaw country thing really took off outside of Texas. So I was a little rug rat then, but still, I remember hearing "Phases and Stages" and thinking, What the hell is he talking about?

By the way, there have been a bunch of records in my life that made me ask this question. I had no idea what the Clash were talking about when I got their record *Sandinista!* With no easy internet answers from Siri on the iPhone, I had to go to the public library and hunt things down through the Dewey decimal system, or worse, wait till one of those rock magazines I subscribed to showed up in the mail. But long before I got turned on to rock magazines, I just listened to whatever was playing in our family car or in the living room, and that was usually Willie Nelson records.

I can still remember the whole '70s country-rock scene that blew sky-high with Waylon, Jessi Colter, Charlie Daniels, David Allan Coe, Hank Jr., Leon Russell, and Kris and Rita before Willie Nelson became a god everywhere outside of Texas. His hair wasn't very long, but I do remember seeing the hippie with the bandanna and red beard showing up on TV shows and awards shows and thinking, Is that the same guy who had short hair and a suit on my grandparents' records? But then the outlaw thing hit like a tidal wave and completely flooded the country.

During the outlaw music explosion, a whole host of other Southern-based genre-bending blues and rock artists like the Allman Brothers, ZZ Top, the Marshall Tucker Band, Wet Willie, Elvin Bishop, and Asleep at the Wheel all started melting into one big country-rock festival scene, and the mecca of festivals was the Charlie Daniels Volunteer Jam. The hippies and the rednecks finally found a way to come together and tolerate one another long enough to create one big festival-attending supertribe, and Willie Nelson was the chief, the alpha and omega who started it all. Before that, these two groups were archrivals. Remember, when I was younger I was chased down by rednecks for my not-so-long baby mullet, which was crazy, because outside of listening to Thin Lizzy and Cheap Trick, I wasn't that different from the guys chasing me. But once the outlaw country scene hit Austin, it not only changed the concert scene forever but changed the dialogue on the way people all over the world viewed country music. Sure, Bill Graham in San Francisco had eclectic live-music bills, but a night at the Armadillo World Headquarters in Austin in the '70s would be similar to those lineups, with a whole other hillbilly component that was not just a novelty act to book, but acts that were sold-out sellers every bit as much as the current rock and pop acts of the day.

It would be something like this: Early show, Miles Davis. Middle show, Frank Zappa and the Mothers of Invention. Midnight closer show, Willie and Waylon. Regardless of what Waylon's song says about how "it don't matter who's in Austin, Bob Wills is still the king," after the outlaw scene in Austin blew up, Willie Nelson was and will always be the unequivocal king of the great state of Texas. Willie was our Beatles and our Stones. And when everything he touched turned to gold (be it records, movies, television appearances, or concerts), all of his early fans in Texas, like us, romanticized him like he was some modern-day outlaw that even your grandmother loved, even though he always seemed to be surrounded by beautiful women, took pictures with Lone Star beers in his hand, and openly chastised the Texas police with his public weed smoking.

Punch forward from 1975 to 1995, and I'd just gotten my first solo record deal with a label out of Houston, Texas, called Justice. The label had Willie Nelson, Billy Joe Shaver, Kris Kristofferson, the great New Orleans jazz trumpeter Kermit Ruffins, Louisiana blues guitar prodigy Tab Benoit, and Houston's heir apparent to Janis Joplin and Barbara Lynn, an explosively talented young girl named Carolyn Wonderland. The label owner was a guy named Randall Jamail (who we've talked about before), whose father, Joe Jamail, was the wealthiest trial lawyer on the planet and was actually in the Guinness Book of World Records. He won a lawsuit mounted by Pennzoil against Texaco that accused them of improperly buying Getty Oil. This was some real old-school Houston, Texas, oil shit for sure. This high-profile case made Joe a billionaire.

The rumor was that Joe took a private jet from Houston to Las Vegas to celebrate winning the case, put a million bucks down on a craps game at Binion's and won another $10 million more off that one hand. Joe was also close friends with Willie Nelson and University of Texas football coaching legend Darrell Royal. "Coach" as Royal was referred to, along with Joe Jamail, put together shows for their friend Willie when he moved back to Austin after being frustrated with Nashville. Nashville had tried almost every possible way to get a hit song with Willie singing the song himself (he had already written hit songs like "Crazy" for Patsy Cline and "Hello Walls" for Faron Young), but the only thing they wouldn't do is let him use his own band and do his songs his own way.

So Willie and his band would play James White's legendary Broken Spoke dance hall on South Lamar Boulevard in Austin, and Coach and Joe would invite the entire UT football team, their families, and their dates and make every damn one of 'em pay. So as you can imagine, these three tried-and-true Texans, Darrell, Joe, and Willie, were super tight. Supposedly the song "Good Hearted Woman" was inspired by Joe Jamail's wife because of all the bullshit she put up with during those crazy nights back then. After a hard run of partying, Willie and Waylon would ask, "Joe, how can you stay out so late without your wife getting mad at you?" Joe would always say the same thing: "Well, she's a good-hearted woman."

Needless to say, the Jamail family opened a lot of doors for me and were very supportive of my career. Randall, Joe's son, owned the Justice Records label and spared no expense for his artists. When I was asked who I wanted to play on my first record, *Raisin' Cain*, they were surprised when I said, "I'd like Doug Sahm, Flaco Jiménez, Johnny Gimble, and Doug Kershaw if we can afford them." So I ended up getting them all, and some others as well, like drummer Kenny Aronoff, who played on so many hit records it's crazy.

The sessions were cut mostly live, with all of the players in the room at the same time. My young voice hadn't dropped yet, so my singing still sounded like a rockabilly kid, but luckily my songs, which were my only real saving grace, shined through. I'd been writing up to four or five songs a week for years, and I still feel like those songs hold up. Even though the record wasn't a big mainstream radio success, it went to number one on the Americana

charts (thanks to Rob Bleetstein, who really believed in me, and radio promoter Al Moss, who relentlessly pushed it on everyone), and
it helped me build a widespread cult following in the United States
and especially Europe. Some folks still think it's my best record,
but I can't listen to it. Despite the performances and the songs, my
voice sounds like I'm twelve. But hey, it was a start, right? The first
day we arrived to the studio I met Willie and his two small sons
Micah and Lukas. These two little boys turned into amazing musicians and civil rights activists and eco-activists. I think the world
of them both. In fact, I was on the Willie Nelson Outlaw Music
Festival Tour with Ryan Bingham and saw Lukas and Micah just
a few months back, and their sets with their own bands were fan-
tastic. Lukas sang his new song "Turn Off the News (Build a Garden)," and the song blew my mind.

Anyway, back to the studio. We did some amazing experimental
stuff, and it was all fueled by this Lebanese coffee that our producer brought that we called "Christian crank" and lots of Willie weed. After that first day with legendary Texas fiddler Johnny
Gimble playing on some tracks (remember the fiddle on "Amarillo
by Morning" by George Strait? That's Johnny Gimble), I walked
outside later that evening to get some fresh air and Willie and Poodie (his longtime tour manager) were standing outside, and they
just kept talking and handed me a joint. Willie said, "How's it going in there?" I'd never met him before. It was like God himself
had just handed me a jazz cigarette and I was just trying to not
freak out. I said, "Great so far." Then the effects of the Willie weed
started setting in and I just clammed up and listened to them talk
about some flight arrangements for a TV show. I was in heaven.
Not bad company for a young Beaumonster. They said, "See ya on
the golf course," and walked off. I didn't realize what this meant
at the time because I was higher than a lab rat, but the next day
I ended up playing nine holes with Willie and Poodie on Willie's
private golf course. Once again there were joints going nonstop on

the golf carts, and I got so incredibly high I have no idea how I played. I'd never golfed much, but I did have a tiny enough natural athletic ability that must've carried me through on my long game to get the ball up on the dance floor. Larry Trader, who ran Willie's golf pro shop next to the studio and golf course, gave me some great pointers that kept me from totally sucking and slicing into the trees. What a day! I can honestly say that's one of the top ten highest times of my life (as you've probably already noticed this top ten list keeps getting longer). Willie was a master golfer who played every single day that he could, but I never understood how he could play golf or perform a concert or record a song in the studio while completely stoned. If you try to keep up with Willie when it comes to smoking weed, you will fail miserably. After that day, if I had something I needed to show up for later, I would always take a couple of hits and when the joint came back around just say, "I'm good," and pass it. I've never had that kind of tolerance, and I think Willie respected people who admitted it or even said "no thanks" altogether. I've heard story after story of musicians going on Willie's bus and coming out so high that they thought they were gonna die. Good news is, they weren't ever gonna die, they just got too high and became paranoid. As Willie would say later, after he started his legal marijuana company, Willie's Reserve, which would become massively successful, "The only way marijuana will kill ya is if you let a bale of it fall on your head!"

The only time weed every really hindered me was one time when I was on the back of Asleep at the Wheel's tour bus smoking with Wheel bandleader Ray Benson, and I heard a band start playing an instrumental. I said to Ray, "Wow, that's pretty cool . . . that band's playing a Buddy Emmons instrumental song. My guys used to play that song all the time." Ray laughed and said, "That's because it's your band . . . think you're supposed to be onstage right now, Jess." I got tore up on that joint with Brother Ray, forgot that there was a daylight saving time change the night before, and my band had

started without me. We were out playing with George Strait on his
Strait Fest tour at University of Alabama's Bryant-Denny Stadium,
which was a big deal, so I flew off the bus, ran through the parking
lot about half a mile toward the stage, dodging cars, high as a kite,
and ran up onstage and started my show. After the show, the tour
manager walked me back to the bus and poured me a margarita
and said, "Well, you were a little late but you made it!" If it had
been any other business, I would've been fired. The news spread
quickly throughout the tour and a couple of other musicians (who
are a lot bigger names than me and might not want to be called
out about smoking weed) came up to me and said, "Don't feel
bad, same thing happened to me on Ray's bus too. Space and time
ceases to exist on the Wheel bus, if ya don't watch out!"

Back to the story. We had been hard at work on my record all
that week at Willie's recording studio, and the weekend was coming up and I had to go play this Americana music conference in
New Orleans at a venue called the Howlin' Wolf. Before we left the
studio to go to the airport, the producer of the session said, "I'm
not sure if the venue has backline, so take one of those amplifiers
from the studio and fly it with you." The studio had all these badass vintage amplifiers, like 1950s and '60s Blackface Fender amps,
mid-'60s AC30 Vox amps, a few Matchless amps . . . all kinds of
stuff. Knowing how expensive and rare those amps were, I didn't
feel comfortable taking one, so I took this old beat-up Baldwin
solid-state amplifier thinking no one would freak out if the airline
destroyed it. It was in this old brown wood tour case that had a
massive old sticker on it from the '70s that said in big letters WILLIE
NELSON FOR PRESIDENT! This was a classic bad stoner idea, where
my heart was in the right place, but my head was clearly inserted
up my ass.

So the bass player, Steve Bailey, and drummer, Kenny Aronoff,
who was at that time in the process of leaving John Mellencamp's
band to go off and play with everyone in Nashville and L.A. and

would leave Austin soon after we made the record to play with Frank Sinatra, and I all got to the Howlin' Wolf in New Orleans at the same time for load-in. I remember walking in and hearing Buddy Miller sound-checking the song "That's How I Got to Memphis," and it blew my mind. It seemed like everyone eventually cut that song (including me) after Buddy reintroduced the Tom T. Hall–penned classic to the world all over again. Buddy started out playing guitar and singing harmonies for one of my songwriting heroes, Jim Lauderdale, but now plays and produces records for everyone from Emmylou Harris to Solomon Burke to Robert Plant. Buddy is one of the tastiest guitar pickers on the planet, meaning he can write these great, simple, hooky parts that stay in your head but don't cover up what all the other musicians are doing on the track. There's an art to that. Sometimes when players who are used to playing too much and end up spewing all over the lead vocals become self-aware, then they go in the opposite direction and play way too safe and boring. It's a real high-wire act to play just the right parts, in just the right places, with just enough fire. Buddy Miller and older guys like Steve Cropper are masters at it.

That night was the first night I met New Orleans trumpet legend Kermit Ruffins. He walked backstage and fired up the biggest Jamaican-style joint I'd ever seen. Kermit and music biz insider Rob Bleetstein and I smoked out and talked about what musicians were going to be in town that weekend playing. Yeah, I know, this story has a lot of weed smoking, huh? Welcome to the world of musicians with lots of free time. It bears being repeated, we're only onstage usually two hours, so it's the other twenty-two hours where the trouble sneaks in. Anyway, the show went great and afterward Rob introduced me to Dwight Yoakam's guitarist/producer Pete Anderson, who said, "Let's get in the studio together!" At this point in my career I worshipped Pete Anderson and every guitar lick he played on those early Dwight records. Pete single-handedly made country guitar cool again and probably turned more suburban rockers who didn't grow up on country music on to cool country guitar playing than anyone since Don Rich from the Buckaroos and Clarence White from the Byrds a long time ago. Pete and I did end up in the studio about two years later, where we did the song "Give Me Back My Wig" by Lightnin' Hopkins for a blues compilation record that came out through Sire called *Young Guitar Slingers*. That track got some attention from some record-business folks and got some radio airtime as well, and I almost went in that direction musically, but I was writing country, folk, rock, blues, and all kinds of different songs, and didn't want to paint myself into the blues corner. That night, the show went great and of course afterward we did what you do when you're in New Orleans: went out and partied our asses off.

The next morning, as our plane lifted off the NOLA runway to fly home to Austin, I sat there thinking about the night before. I vaguely remember doing a snake dance and following a bunch of drunk Black people up and down the stairs and through the rooms of an old two-story house, high on cough syrup for the first time and God knows what else, and within this train of folks is a full second-line brass band of young and old Black men with Saints football jerseys on. We wound through the streets of a rough neighborhood called Treme at four a.m. This was no small event. The band was made up of trumpet players, trombone, tuba, one guy with a big bass drum, and another with a snare drum and cymbal, and they were playing traditional New Orleans jazz music at full volume. I have no idea how I made my flight on time, but I crashed hard and woke up abruptly in Austin to the wheels of the plane hitting the runway.

That day we pulled up to the studio and walked in through the back door, Willie was in the kitchen. He said, "Hey, did you take my Baldwin amp?" I was stricken with fear. I realized right then that's just what I'd done. He wasn't raising his voice or looking pissed off, he just asked in a kind of matter-of-fact way. I barely got the words *Yes . . . I guess I did* out. Willie said, "We got all these amplifiers here, and you take mine?" I said, "Oh my God, I'm so sorry. I thought if I took the old one that wasn't as nice as those Fenders, it would be OK." About that time one of Willie's roadies rolls the old road case into the kitchen and says, "Look your Baldwin is back." I was mortified. Willie said, "Well, Merle dropped by last night and we ended up recording and I didn't have my amp, so . . ." Merle as in MERLE FUCKING HAGGARD! My stomach dropped to my feet. I'm sure Willie could see the lines of sweat that started rolling down my face, so he said, "Well, no biggie. Damn, that old amp case has seen better days though, hasn't it? You need a case for your amp?" I didn't realize it at the time because I felt so bad about taking his amp, but Willie was talking about his original '70s road case with the huge Willie-for-president sticker on each side. I said, "Yeah, thank you so much I'd love it, and yes, I do need a case!" Willie smiled at me like he knew I needed a case (and a whole lot more) and walked out of the room. I nearly shit myself and fell to my knees and just caught my breath. Poodie walked by, saw me on my knees in the middle of the kitchen, and said nonchalantly, "Oh wow, scored ya a cool amp case, brother." Ugh.

Years later I would get to play guitar and sing harmonies with Willie on some recordings that he and Johnny Bush did together and on some recordings that he and Ray Price (aka Father Ray) did as well. I also played the Willie Nelson Fourth of July Picnic with my solo band four times and as a guitar player for Ryan Bingham, and with Willie's daughter Amy Nelson's group, Folk Uke, that she has with Arlo Guthrie's daughter Cathy. One night, not long before Merle Haggard passed away, Willie and Merle were onstage doing a show at the Whitewater Amphitheater when Willie's daughters and good friends of mine, Paula and Amy, grabbed me, Kinky Friedman, and actor/friend Jake Busey, to get up onstage and sing background vocals on Willie's gospel medley at the end of his show. If you've ever seen Jake Busey, you know he's the spitting image of his father, Gary. As Amy and Jake and I walked by Willie and Merle, Willie leaned over to Amy and said, "Damn, Gary Busey looks amazing!" Amy told her dad that it was Gary's son, and both of them started laughing. Then, later in the song, I remember Kinky Friedman leaning over to me and whispering in my ear, "Look how fuckin' cool Merle is." And he was the coolest of the cool.

Earlier in my career I had met and opened some shows for the Hag at Rockefeller's in Houston and after my show, he asked me, "Where ya from, son?" I said, "Well, I live in Austin." Hag said, "I didn't ask you where you live, I asked you where you're from." I said, "Oh, sorry Mr. Haggard, I'm from Beaumont, Texas." He said, "I used to hang out in Beaumont when Lefty Frizzell lived there and Elvis had blond hair." Now, I'm not sure if this meant that he liked that I was from Beaumont, but he did go out of his way to make small talk with me. Looking back on it, if you would've told this young Beaumonster that any of this shit would take place, I'd have laughed your ass right out of Jefferson County. But it did. Years later, I played the South By Southwest Luck Reunion show at Willie's western town outside of Austin with his daughter Paula and her band. (Paula is a DJ and has a great radio show on SiriusXM.) I remember talking to one of my songwriting heroes, Steve Earle (whom I met when I was a kid at a Guy Clark show in Houston. Steve doesn't remember this, but there's probably a lot Steve doesn't remember), and writer/actor Turk Pipkin backstage when Willie showed up in a beat-up old Chevy pickup truck for the show. This was a typical Willie entrance. No limo, no entourage, just Willie in a banged-up truck with his beat-to-hell cowboy hat on. He got out of the truck and started walking through the throngs of people who were just trying to get a peek at the biggest country superstar on the planet. Steve split, Turk backed up, and I was standing by the stage trying to just stay out of the way. As Willie walked by, he looked at me and said, "Is my amp here?" and smiled. Let's face it, older folks do start losing their memories at some point. It happened to my daddy and his daddy before him. And considering the amount of weed Willie has smoked throughout his life, well, you would think that it would've had some effect on his memory. But twenty-something years later, when he looked at me he probably saw that same scared kid standing in the kitchen at his recording studio with flop sweat rolling down his face.

SET BREAK: HANGING OUT IN HOUSTON WITH GUY AND TOWNES

In 1994, I met Guy Clark in a tiny dive bar in Houston called Live Bait. He was sitting in the corner alone drinking whiskey, with his guitar case in the chair next to him. No one knew who he was, and that's probably why he was at that bar. I walked over and said, "Hey, are you Guy Clark?" He rolled his eyes and said, "That depends on if you're buying me a drink or not." Very gruff. Very unimpressed. I said, "Sure, I'm grabbing a beer now." He said, "Only Paddy whiskey for me." He might've said two words for the first ten minutes I sat with him, until I mentioned that I was reading James Joyce's *Dubliners* for the first time. We then proceeded to talk books and drink double Jamesons for two hours straight.

Finally after covering Beat poets and Irish and Russian authors, Guy said, "My buddy's probably out front waiting; I have a gig." At that point I wanted to see the show. I walked him out and asked if I could catch a ride with them to Rockefeller's, where he was playing. He told his friend, "Jesse Garron is hitchin' a ride." (Jesse Garron was Elvis Presley's twin brother who died at birth, and this was a joke about my pompadour.) He and his friend, who never told me his name at the time, talked about an East Coast tour the entire way over. After a good six doubles, I was hammered but holding it together, and Guy seemed totally normal. We got out of the car and I walked through the backstage door of Rockefeller's with Guy. Before he split to do the show I said, "Hey, man, how do you remember all the lyrics after that much whiskey?" He said, "You oughtta see the guy I'm tradin' songs with. He makes me shine like a diamond." The guy was Townes Van Zandt, and I met him after the show and he was way more of an open book than Guy had been. He wasn't as drunk as I'd seen him at other local shows at Anderson Fair or Fitzgerald's. We hung out for another hour backstage, Townes bummed a couple of cigarettes off me, then they got paid and drove off into the night.

HONORARY
SUPERSUCKER

My first solo record had gone to number one on the newly emerging Americana radio charts and I was underwhelmed by how white-bread and safe that whole scene was, although I will say it had certain types of music that I was into, be it songwriters like Townes Van Zandt and Guy Clark or the punk-rock elements of new bands like Whiskeytown or the outlaw country stuff. But I felt completely alienated in my home state by the brand-new "Texas Music" scene that was on the rise with all these frat boys who were part of it, and frankly, it just didn't click. It seemed like overnight there were about twenty young college guys who started taking over the whole live music scene in Texas who were Robert Earl Keen sound-alikes but looked like they worked at a bank. They had the button-down preppy dress shirts and the khaki pants and gave off a straightlaced Republican vibe. For the record, I was a big-time Robert Earl Keen fan, but I don't think any of his frat-boy audience members knew or cared who Townes Van Zandt or Guy Clark was, and that's who Robert was a direct descendent of. I had seen Robert's early shows at the Front Porch in College Station, and his songs were great. So this was all happening in Texas in the mid-'90s, and on top of it I was going through a messy divorce. I was young, and my life with her was becoming too unmanageable and I was like a wild bronco trying to bust out of my stall. I felt like I didn't fit in anywhere. So, in comes one of the most dangerous bands on the planet, the Supersuckers. I met them backstage at a club in Dallas called Trees. I remember leader and front man Eddie Spaghetti walking up to me in cowboy boots that had duct tape holding them together. The first thing I said to him was, "Man, you need to get some new boots." Then he said, "That's quite an accent you have, Tex. Wanna do a bump?" Eddie railed out a couple of lines of Peruvian marching powder as guitarist Dan Bolton, drummer Dan Siegal, and fill-in guitarist Rick Sims walked in. I think Rontrose Heathman was either in rehab or on a drug sabbatical, but I would meet him a few weeks later in Los Angeles. That night all I wanted to talk to Eddie Spaghetti about was punk rock, and all Eddie Spaghetti wanted to talk to me about was country music.

I don't think the rest of the Supersuckers were into country music that much at that point, but this would soon change. I know a lot of talking went on that night because we snorted a ton of blow, and that's what you do when you're on that shit. Before the end of the night Eddie said, "Hey, why don't you come on tour with us?" And by the way, every time in my life I end up getting lots of new fans for this cult following I've built up usually starts with the words "Hey, why don't you come on tour with us?"

Not too much had happened, culturally or musically, between country music and punk rock at that point. Country rocker Joe Ely from Lubbock, Texas, a total legend in my neck of the woods, did a whole world tour opening for the Clash. I saw that tour in San Antonio and Houston and it changed my life. Joe Ely and Joe Strummer were heroes to me, and a lot of folks from those two respective camps thought that was weird. Now it's no big whoop, even common, but back then I didn't know many folks who were simultaneously into Joe Strummer and Johnny Paycheck. By the way, that's Joe Ely singing all that Spanish stuff on the Clash's biggest single, "Should I Stay or Should I Go." Dwight Yoakam had also opened some shows for X around L.A., and a few scattered tour dates around the states for the Blasters, one of which I saw in Houston. Dwight's band was in a 1960 Cadillac pulling a U-Haul trailer. John Doe and Exene of X were singing a couple of country duets in the late '70s, as was Mike Ness from Social Distortion, who had been doing "Ring of Fire" by Johnny Cash since the late '70s. But other than that, the two worlds pretty much hated each other. Rick Rubin changed all that with the release of the Johnny Cash American Recordings, but for us longtime country fans who had seen Johnny just five years before he met Rubin, we were all very suspicious of these new punk fans wearing Johnny Cash's picture on their shirt flipping the bird. Looking back, God bless Rick Rubin. That record definitely planted the seed in the minds of a lot of new listeners and changed the entire game.

So here I am with this number-one Americana record and getting some great press, and no one in the Nashville country music world will take me out on tour because I'm too rock 'n' roll for country and too country for rock 'n' roll. My record label had no idea what to do with me, and actually put me on a tour of Walmarts a year before with these sappy Nashville country acts who sported mullets and wore pastel shirts, and I basically got treated like a circus freak who played that "old drinking music" with our pedal-steel guitar, an instrument that was being ignored by mainstream country music. It was one of the worst tours I'd ever done, and I wanted to strangle those Nashville acts who were riding around in their tour buses that their labels were charging to them and who were all listening to this guy named Garth Brooks non-fucking-stop, 24/7. I realized then that Garth had written a great rodeo standard with "Much Too Young (to Feel This Damn Old)," and now I realize that "Friends in Low Places" is like Hank Williams Sr. compared to the god-awful right-wing kiddie pop coming out of Nashville now. But none of my friends in the Austin country scene were sitting around listening to sappy Garth Brooks ballads that, at that point, sounded more like Kansas or Styx than they did Hank Williams or Ray Price.

After a long, hard night of a dozen bourbon shots, never-ending rails of blow, and lots and lots of marijuana joints, I parted ways with the Supersuckers in Deep Ellum in Dallas, knowing that wouldn't be the last time I would see them.

It was only a couple of weeks until my band started driving out to meet the Supersuckers for our first night of the tour at the Dragonfly in Hollywood. When I got there I saw a shivering, long-haired guy in cut-off jean shorts with a blanket wrapped around himself, and a lady holding him. It turned out to be Ron Heathman, aka Rontrose, the original lead guitar player for the Supersuckers, evidently kicking some kind of heroin comedown.

Rick Sims, who originally played in the Gaza Strippers, was still hanging out. It was weird. I wasn't sure if Ron was on the tour or not, and I wasn't sure if the Supersuckers knew if he would be either. Lo and behold, Rontrose went up onstage later that night and slayed the place. They did all their classic MC5 moves, Ramones-power-chord-inspired songs, bringing all the heaviness of Motör-head. No offense to Rick Sims, who was a cool guy, but it was a way better band than I'd seen in Dallas now that they were back with Ron Heathman on guitar. At that time these guys were the most dangerous rock 'n' roll band happening.

Eddie Spaghetti walks up to me with a big smile and hands me a beer and says, "Are you ready to get it on, brother?" I must admit, I had done some hard partying but I didn't know what I was in for. We proceeded to do an eight-week tour across America. Every night was cocaine/whiskey/marijuana–infused pure debauchery, and lots of rock chicks who were absolutely crazy about the Suckers. None of us got any sleep. But after a while I got used to it. It became a badge of honor how long we could go without sleep and still recover enough to hit it hard again the very next night. We had youth on our side and thought we were indestructible.

Every night I would walk out onstage with my upright-bass player, Charlie, my drummer, Eric, and my pedal-steel player, Brian, my 1961 Fender Telecaster on, and bust into these high-energy classic-country sets. Many Supersuckers fans had never heard the George Jones songs that I would play, and frankly, I don't think the Supersuckers themselves had either. When I would first come out onstage the crowd would look at me like *What the hell is this redneck-looking guy about to do?* I would always open with some up-beat hillbilly train song, and the sound of the music would wash over them and freak them all out. They were definitely not used to hearing a pedal-steel guitar, which would later become almost like a swirling sound-effects instrument for these Americana rock bands who were more pedal-steel owners than they were students of classic pedal-steel players like Lloyd Green or Buddy Emmons. As long as I kept the tempo up for these punk-rock crowds, they fell for it hard. But every night during my forty-five-minute set when I played a slow country weeper, they headed for the bathroom or to the bar for a drink. Eddie Spaghetti and I started having more and more talks about country music, and he and Rontrose became very quick students of country songwriting and country guitar-playing. Rick Sims had disappeared after that first show, and Rontrose was back in full force. Rontrose was getting into playing these chicken pickin' Jerry Reed licks and was actually getting really damn good at it.

I came back from that tour a complete mess. I must've slept for two weeks straight and my then wife, who I found out was pregnant, was trying desperately to push the divorce through. One morning I woke up and found all my stuff piled in one big heap in the middle of the living room with a note on it saying, "You need to put all of this in your van and leave." I knew she was right and that we couldn't stay together because we were fighting so much, but I was still heartbroken.

I drove home to Beaumont, and my dad took me into the den, just us two, broke open a bottle of whiskey, and basically took the weight of the world off my shoulders by saying, "If your mother was as unpredictable as this woman you're with now is, you wouldn't be here. You'll always be this kid's father, so go live your life and get your own place." After my old man told me that, it was like all the depression and anxiety I had over it just left my body. I think it's because I thought he was going to be disappointed in me, and he wasn't. His whole schtick was carry on no matter what and don't sweat things you can't control. The big problem in my first marriage was never cheating or drinking or any of those classic things you'd think. Our biggest problem was that we were living totally separate lives and had grown apart, so we argued about anything and everything. Also, we were super young and not the most mature people on the planet.

The next morning at my parents' house in Beaumont I got a phone call from a person at my record label, who gave me Eddie Spaghetti's phone number in Seattle because Eddie wanted me to call him. I called him and he said that he had some country songs that he and the guys in the band had written and he wanted to come down to Houston to the legendary SugarHill Studios to demo the songs up. This was a much-needed diversion, so of course I said, "Absolutely, bring it on, Brother."

Eddie arrived in Houston and he, Brian Thomas, and I worked out the arrangements for all the songs on what would become the *Must've Been High* record. I still have the demos on cassette for all of those songs we cut that day in the studio. I should probably dig those up and digitize them at some point.

A few weeks later, my pedal-steel picker, Brian Thomas, the legendary harmonica man Mickey Raphael from Willie Nelson's band, hillbilly fiddler Brantley Kearns from Dwight Yoakam's band, and I all flew up to Seattle to make a "country" record with the Supersuckers. Sub Pop Records, their label, was definitely not happy about this musical transition, but the Supersuckers were very hot, and I hear Eddie really had to put his foot down to get the record made. The day I arrived at the airport in Seattle, punk-rock author/poet and Suckers manager Danny Bland picked me up in a vintage black hearse. Danny was this crazy, dark character who ran the Supersuckers empire and was pretty much an all-encompassing fifth member of the band. So I get into this crazy hearse at the airport that all the cops outside are stink-eyeing. I remember asking Danny if he had a joint, and with an insulting look on his face he said, "I'm a recovering heroin addict, why would I fuck around with that silly hippie shit?" But then he laughed and said, "Here's a leftover roach in the ashtray from one of the guys if you want it." I fired it up and took a few hits, and within ten minutes on the drive over I felt like I was on mushrooms. This was way before medical marijuana, and I was used to smoking only Mexican lettuce dirt weed in Texas. I was so high that it felt like I was waking up from a dream over and over on repeat and I couldn't make it stop. I told Danny, "Damn, this is some serious shit." He was laughing at me as we walked into the studio, and Ron Heathman immediately put a guitar in my hand. File this under another one of those times that I wish I hadn't been so baked. It had been a long-ass flight from Houston to Seattle, and I had to deliver the goods. The first song I played on was "One Cigarette Away," and I had no chart or anything. So I just went for it, and after I recorded the first take they wanted to keep it and not let me do it again or do any overdubs, and they were insistent. I told them, "Hey guys, I got pretty lit up on the way over here and I'm sure I could make it cooler once I learn the song a little better." They were having none of it, and they put me in a cab back to the hotel.

All that traveling to get there, just to record a three-minute guitar part once, and *bam*: done for the day.

It turned out my hotel wasn't just any hotel. My hotel was the infamous Edgewater Hotel that was built over the bay, and of course Danny Bland got me the exact same room where drummer John Bonham and Led Zeppelin road manager Richard Cole were rumored to have fished out the room's window, reeled in a few small sharks, and proceeded to use them to defile a Zeppelin groupie. (True story or urban myth? I've heard it over and over for years.) Even so, when I wasn't at the studio recording with the Suckers, I hung out there for, like, three days and fished out of this big window with a Zebco 808 fishing rod and caught some bay trout. I was trying to clear my head before I went back home and signed those damn divorce papers.

Rontrose Heathman and I became close guitar buddies. He showed me some rock 'n' roll licks and I showed him some country licks, and it was a great hang. A lot of them made it onto the record, as did some of the spaghetti-western guitar parts that I had written on the demos with Eddie and Brian in Houston. I got to be close friends with Danny Bland, who would eventually introduce me to my wife, Emily Kaye, but that's another story.

In no time, the new Supersuckers country record *Must've Been High* was out and we were on another never-ending North American tour together, playing every A, B, C, and D market known to mankind. The fans did not like the record when it first came out. Every night I would hear them yell things like "Quit playing that country shit and play some fuckin' rock 'n' roll!" Supersuckers guitarist Dan Bolton, who was probably the most angry punk rocker of them all, would shoot the finger to the audience every night and the whole crowd would flip the bird back. Eventually Danny Bland got a bunch of those big foam middle fingers (like the ones you'd see at sporting events) made and he would throw them out to the audience. This became part of their act, and to this day,

Eddie still takes pictures most nights on tour all over the world of the whole audience flipping the band off.

Eventually word got out that the Suckers had made an "outlaw country" album, and their audience slowly began to like this new punk-country sound. I remember two distinct events happening that changed the whole trajectory of that record. None of the skateboarders on the West Coast were into country music, and all the hard-core rock 'n' roll Ramones fans on the East Coast hated it, but something happened that turned the tables. Producer Randall Jamail and harmonica legend Mickey Raphael had somehow got Willie Nelson to sing on one track and play guitar on another. One night we were on tour, and Eddie came in and said, "Hey, we just found out we're going to do *The Tonight Show with Jay Leno*, and Willie Nelson is going to play with us!" As someone who had grown up in Texas and had probably seen Willie Nelson more times in concert than any other musician, I could not believe that these two worlds were going to collide in front of millions of people on national television. Ernie Locke, the harmonica player from the punk-blues band Tenderloin, was there with us as well. Eddie and Ernie and I looked at one another dumbfounded and were like *Well, let's celebrate!* We would celebrate over anything back then, but this was the big-time. Two nights later we watched the Supersuckers and Willie Nelson play Willie's classic "Bloody Mary Morning" on *The Tonight Show*. This turned a ton of rock fans on to outlaw country and got them to take notice of the record we made. There's a clip of it on YouTube, and it's amazing, raw, and unfiltered. Also Willie plays lead on it!

The second thing that happened that accelerated the acceptance of the merging of punk and outlaw country was a show we did in Minneapolis, where alternative music star Kim Deal from the Breeders and the Pixies sang the duet "Hungover Together" with Eddie. The song was written by Danny Bland, and it's basically Danny's dark past bottled up into three minutes of sex and pain. The audience was stunned. It was quiet for, like, five seconds after it was over, and then the place erupted into insane applause, hoots, and hollers. It was like watching a tattered zombie punk version of Conway Twitty and Loretta Lynn. This was a big change from when we opened for Iggy Pop at SXSW and the whole crowd was booing and saying, "Fuck country music, play that rock 'n' roll!"

I barely survived that tour as well. My last memory was Eddie and I had worn the same clothes every night for more than three weeks. We would sweat them out and roll them up into the back window of the van and sit there in our underwear and smoke pot and drink beer and play poker till we got to the next town. Again, I don't remember sleeping that much at all.

After the tour was over I got home and my divorce was still dragging on. I didn't realize it at first, but the never-ending tours with the Supersuckers gave me a cult following of people that no one in the Texas music establishment or the Nashville music industry had. To this day my rockabilly friends still come out and say, "Who are all these people at your show? I don't recognize any of them." Back then my playing shows with the Supersuckers and bands like X, who we opened up for the first two nights at House of Blues when Billy Zoom first came back to the band, exposed those audiences to something different. At the time I didn't have any idea that I would later go on to fill in for Billy Zoom on guitar and tour with X and also tour with Mike Ness and Social Distortion. I'm glad I learned how to tour low-rent punk rock–style from the Supersuckers, given some of the prima donnas I've been around since then, who whine about cheap hotels and not having their vegan chips backstage on their riders, and just can't hack living the life of a broke vagabond. To quote John Doe from X, "We don't have to do this, we *get* to do this!"

I would go on to play on several Supersuckers records, even after the band changed its lineup to feature Metal Marty on lead guitar and Chris Von Streicher on drums. I even produced and played all the guitar on Eddie Spaghetti's criminally underrated solo record *The Value of Nothing* on the Bloodshot label, featuring his cool rocker wife, Jessika, on the cover. It's amazing that any of us survived those years of insanity. Sure, we all get together for drinks and maybe burn one every now and then, but I personally quit snorting blow in 1998 because I knew that if I didn't, I'd probably end up having one of those five-a.m., alone-in-your-hotel-room heart attacks and die, so I just stopped and never touched it again. Sadly, Ron Heathman did go out alone in a hotel room. Ron and I had talked about Thin Lizzy and vintage motorcycles by text regularly, and I still think about texting him a couple of times a month when I see a cool '70s Bultaco or Husqvarna dirt bike. Addiction is ruthless, and Ron tried hard to keep it in check but just couldn't do it. I miss him big-time, and I'm still working on not being mad at him for checking out early on us. It's a process. Eddie has since gotten sober, and I still talk to him all the time and sit in with the Supersuckers whenever they tour through my hometown of Austin. Eddie was just on my Gimme Country radio show, and it was a hell of an interview, considering his crazy story as the front man for one of the most dangerous bands ever. Danny Bland, who now has well over a quarter of a century clean and sober, became one of my best friends and is now a published author/poet and full-time tour manager for acts like Dave Alvin, the Blasters, X, and Steve Earle. In fact, in about three weeks from the time that I'm writing this, the Supersuckers and our old friend Danny Bland will all be on the Outlaw Country Cruise with us. My liver used to be terrified of these music cruises because they're basically "a floating Sodom and Gomorrah of the sea," as Danny says. But Steve Earle, who's been sober a hell of a long time, too, did tell me, "If you ever wanna get away from the drunks on a cruise, just go to the ship's gym: there's nobody in there."

While I was never technically in the band, I feel like an honorary Supersucker. We both play a lot of shows every year and even still manage to tour together every once in a while. Playing guitar in the Supersuckers, still, to this day, feels like a rock 'n' roll dream. The kind that makes it all real for that twelve-year-old kid in me who was jumping around my older brother's room with a tennis racket to Thin Lizzy's *Jailbreak* record.

One last thing about this whole punk-meets-country thing. No matter how big of a bang this fusion of music styles makes, I don't think that these two worlds will ever truly understand each other. The punk rockers I know, like X and the Supersuckers, will always have their guard up against the county musicians, because they didn't grow up on country and they're always going to be suspicious of country's right-wing establishment history. The same goes for the country folks I know, who will never ever openly accept the radical left wing and anarchist values that punk was founded on. But there's a piece of both of those worlds that lives in me because of where I was raised and the times that I grew up in. I'm cool with it. I'm used to being the odd man out. I know I'll never truly be accepted in either camp, and I'm OK with that. My old man taught me early on that looking for other people's approval is a waste of time. "Be your own man . . . it gets lonely sometimes, but it's worth it" is what he used to preach to me, and he was right.

LIVIN' THE BLUES AND MEETING THE HOOK

My first wife, Christie, who was a Cajun gal from my hometown, and I had just lost our first child. Zane Dayton was born prematurely in Houston, and he held on for three days. It was absolutely one of the worst periods of my life, and our marriage was never the same after Zane passed away. Don't get me wrong, we had problems before that, for sure, but there was a depression that came over Christie that was impossible for my young mind to comprehend. Yes, I was depressed too—of course I was. But I didn't carry the child around for nine months in my belly. It's a completely different experience for women. Looking back now, just sitting here writing this, it makes me have so much more compassion for her and what she went through. I mean, no matter how vicious our arguing became and never mind that we were just a couple of small-town kids who probably should never have married in the first place, I see things a lot clearer now than I did back then. The real sad part of it was, I had the means to escape our surroundings because the record label was breathing down my neck to tour and support the record, and she was stuck at home alone thinking about our son. So five shots of Jameson and a couple of bumps of blow, then a joint to take the edge off before walking into an after-show party in Chicago or San Francisco was a much welcome diversion for me at that time. It wasn't like she was laid up in bed, not talking or eating, but she was definitely depressed and in major pain. While I was gone she dived headfirst into her job of running a record label (Antone's Records). Thank God Harry Friedman and Clifford Antone gave her that job and that Seymour Stein, founder of Sire Records, mentored her and kept her busy.

We were both in a ton of pain, but we were processing it differently. We had been together through all the early days of living in a $250-a-month garage apartment, with me barely bringing home enough money to pay all the bills. But we were young, so we figured it out. Those were pretty amazing days, too, in terms of not wanting or needing much and just the overall joy of having a young, easy, carefree life. Lots of partying going on then. But I gotta say, I don't want to romanticize it too much, because we were at each other's throats from the beginning till the end. This alpha Cajun woman was wild; she knew how to party and cook but was mainly a big-time ballbuster, and I absolutely couldn't wait to get back on the road and get away from her.

The one thing we had going for us is that we were young. With her job as president at Antone's Records in Austin, she had a lot on her plate to keep her busy too. She was making her own money and I was starting to finally make mine. So after weeks of nonstop crying and praying about the loss of our son, I was off to the West Coast for a short ten-day tour, and she went back to work. As I played my way through Phoenix, L.A., and San Diego and headed north, I started to come out of my shell. Copious amounts of whiskey and Mexican lettuce helped me, but it was also talking to my daddy on the phone and him reaffirming that I had to, as Bob Dylan's gospel song says, keep "Pressing On." My old man, Robert Earl, was a rock for me during this time. He was there 24/7 if I needed to talk, but he would also be quick to tell me, "Get your shit together and focus on your work, son!" Six days into the tour we were playing Slim's in San Francisco, a club owned by Texas legend turned San Fran resident and international rock star Boz Scaggs. Note: Things like playing a show at Boz Scaggs's legendary club matter to me, so it's with a heavy heart that I write I just got word the other day that Slim's has closed permanently. What a tragic loss. Although this closing was not directly due to the Covid-19 pandemic, it definitely didn't help. This catastrophe has destroyed so many legendary American live music venues, no one has any idea which ones will still be open after the smoke clears. Looking back now, I had played smaller places than Slim's that were very historic, like Buddy Guy's club in Chicago, or the Antenna Club in Memphis, and also went on to play much bigger places than Slim's. (George Strait's Strait Fest show at Texas Stadium had 65,000 attendees, and an outdoor festival in Houston had 200,000 people.) But for me at least, I don't really connect with the audience on a personal level in megavenues. I'm glad Freddie Mercury could own 30,000 folks, but that's not what I aspired to. My heroes, for the most part, played joints. And one of the most important joints was Slim's. The last time I played at Slim's, Chuck Prophet brought out Austin guitar slinger Charlie Sexton to see me. Charlie had played with David Bowie and now plays with Bob Dylan and is the pinnacle of cool in terms of Austin musicians. After the show, I saw Charlie and I told him I was glad I didn't know he was in the crowd because I probably would've gotten stage fright. He laughed it off, but I was serious as a fuckin' heart attack. There are a few guitar slingers who still make me nervous, and he's one of them. I'd recently had to learn all of Charlie's guitar parts for a Ryan

Bingham tour, 'cause Sexton produced and played all the guitar on
that album but then had to split for dates with Dylan. His guitar
parts were so hooky and soulful they rolled around in my mind for
days after the tour was over. And oh yeah, the great Jello Biafra,
the singer from the legendary punk band the Dead Kennedys, was
backstage. Never a dull moment with Jello!

So rewinding, we're onstage that night at Slim's, the place is going
crazy. There's a woman on the side of the stage who keeps eyeballing
the shit outta me with this kind of knowing look on her face. She
kept clapping in the middle of my lead guitar solos, which usually
only happens on certain special nights when the crowd is extraordi-
narily inspired and filled with guitar freaks. (By the way, I love to
get a round of applause after playing a particularly kickass lead guitar part, and I've definitely clapped after seeing mind-blowing solos
by Buddy Guy, Redd Volkaert, Kenny Vaughan, James Burton, and
lots of other pickers.) But this woman was just clapping all by her-
self on the side of the stage after every lead solo I played. Odd to say
the least, but it was San Francisco, and if there's one thing I learned
from San Fran, it's this: It's not that it takes all kinds, it's just that
there *are* all kinds. San Francisco is like New York or London or
other places I love, like Paris, Rome, or Madrid. I don't want to live
there, but I absolutely love being there, whether it's for work or for
play. I ended up making some great friends in San Fran, like Thee
Parkside bar owner Sean O'Connor and indie record label owner
Nick Tangborn, who are still pals today. But yeah, I just wrote this
woman off as another eccentric San Fran hippie fan.

Before the last song, this woman pulls on my shirt from the side
of the stage and whispers in my ear, "Really love your guitar playing. Wanna meet John Lee Hooker?" So I pull my shirt away from
her and look at her like *Did I just hear you right?* Then we kicked
into the encore. By now she's burning a fuckin' hole through me,
staring me down. People say crazy things all the time on tour
to musicians. I've heard some of the most whacked-out BS you

could imagine. "I'm George Jones's sister!" or "I work for Marlon Brando!" Just crazy talk. So people are clapping for an encore and I walk offstage and she grabs me again and says, "I'm not trying to come on to you. My boss is John Lee Hooker and he digs guitar players and I think you should jump in my car and let me take you to his house!" Could she have been a serial killer? Yes. Again, I can't even begin to tell you how many drunk full-of-shit people I meet on the road. Yes, I meet some of the sweetest, most inspiring, incredible friends I've ever made on tour, but there's also a number of folks who show up with lots of baggage and have this preconceived idea that they are going to your show that night to suck you into something—a master plan if you will.

Since I couldn't get a real read on whether she was crazy and I didn't really trust her, I took my bass player, Chuck, and my pedal-steel player, Brian, with me. Fuck it, surely she wasn't going to kill all three of us, right? And she didn't get weird when I brought along my two band members, which was a good sign that she wasn't just trying to get me alone. So, we all get into her car, and luckily she's not acting drunk and she starts driving us through the city and over the Golden Gate Bridge. She's playing blues music by Little Walter and Otis Rush on stun-level volume the whole drive over, and of course Chuck has a joint of some West Coast hydro going and we're all drinking our red Solo cups full of bourbon that we smuggled out of the venue. We were probably thinking, There's no way we're going to see John Lee Hooker, so we might as well make it a party, right?

Finally, we turn into a long driveway, and someone buzzes our car in through a big Graceland-type electric gate with musical notes on each gate. As we slowly cruise down the driveway, I see lots of beautiful custom pimp-style Cadillacs and Lincoln Continentals from the 1960s through the 1980s parked in the grass on either side of the driveway. I turned the music down, and the woman saw me looking at the ten or twelve soul brother sleds parked out there and said, "Oh, you dig cars, huh? So does Hook. Those are all his cars. You should tell him you dig his cars!" OK, this was starting to feel more real. Looking back, I'm glad I was with Charlie and Brian, 'cause those guys were world-class drinkers and party animals but never acted out of control when they partied. If you've ever just smoked a joint and had a few drinks and then been asked out of nowhere to do something "responsible," that was the vibe I got when I thought, Wait, are we really at this guy's house?

We parked at the end of this long driveway and walked up to this big house. We all sheepishly followed the lady in through the back door, and the place was bustling inside with kids, parents, and old folks galore. Maybe twenty African American folks in there watching TV in a huge living room and cooking and talking in the kitchen. I said to the lady, "Who are all these people?" She said, "John's family. Brothers, sisters, cousins, nieces, nephews, you name it." All of them were super welcoming, and one of the little kids (probably a six-year-old girl) yelled, "Hey, Granddad, there's some white boys here to see you!" We all busted out laughing. Out of the mouths of babes, right? So we followed the lady through the big house and down the hall, and she turns into one of the many bedrooms, and there's John Lee Hooker lying on the bed in a three-piece sharkskin suit with his custom dress hat on. (You know, the one with the little feather in his hatband.) He was obviously very old at this point, but he was dressed like a full-blown Chicago-style '70s pimp/bluesman. He didn't even look at me and said, "Come here, my man, hear you're a guitar player like me?" He put out his fragile hand and pulled me onto the bed to sit next to him and said, "My girl called and told me you're a real guitar man." I stuttered. I'd never stuttered in my life until then. "W-w-w-well, well, well, Mr. Hooker, I'm not like you, per se." He laughed and said, "I thought *I* stuttered. Ain't nobody call me mister, son. Call me Hook." At a loss for words I said, "Sure do dig those Caddies out there, Hook." He said, "Oh yeah, man, I gotta fire one of 'em up and drive on up to Portland. I gotta hot little gal up there who misses me!" I said, "I'll bet you do!" Now, this was preposterous, because he was very old and frail at this point and probably hadn't driven in years. But we both laughed and he said, "What is it with us guitar players and all these wo-wo-wo-womenfolk?" I had forgot that he stuttered. Not out of nervousness, it was just the way he said certain sentences. You could hear it in his songs a lot, too, but I always thought it was just his way of dragging out the lyrics to make them sound more emotional. Either way, it worked.

I looked across his room, and next to his bed on the nightstand is a picture in a frame with a youngish white guy. I said, "Hey, Hook, who are you with in that picture on the bedstand?" He said, "Oh, that's Sean Penn. He brings me spaghetti sometimes from this Italian-food joint I like up the road." I said to myself, *How cool is that?* I was already a fan of Penn's acting skills, but this impressed the hell out of me. Leaning up against the wall in the corner was this old 1940s black-and-yellow Sunburst Stella acoustic guitar. John saw me looking at it and said, "Pick up that guitar right there and play me something." So as I was reaching over to grab it, I said, "This thing is from the '50s, right?" Hook said, "That might be '40s; that's one of my first guitars, before I had any money." I about shit my pants. I said, "Hook, are you sure I should even play this?" I was totally frozen. He said, "Just play something, man." So I played a little bit of this Mance Lipscomb tune "Jack of Diamonds," and his face lit up with a smile. I didn't wanna shred or play anything too fast, I just wanted to play something I thought he would dig. (Yes, of course I was pandering to John Lee Hooker; he was a living, breathing blues God sitting two inches from me on his bed in his room.) Then I played a part of a Lightnin' Hopkins song, "Black Cadillac," and he smiled even bigger. He said, "Ah, you doing that Texas shit right dare young man. You got dat drone string workin'!" He was talking about keeping the E string playing the whole time you're playing the lean part on the other strings. Mance and Lighntin' (both from East

Texas, and not far from where I'm from) made that style famous. I told Hook that I had learned it in Navasoto, Texas, from Hopkins's cousin named Lil' Mack Minor. Hook said, "Never heard of him, but I knew Lightnin' and Mance a little bit."

OK, this was where the shit started really blowing my mind. Hook said, "We all used to play these colleges and folk shows for all these white people out east." The whole time I was noodling around on his Stella guitar, and he was looking at me with a smile. Finally he said, "Where you going next on your tour?" I said, "Tomorrow's a travel day, then we're headin' to Portland." He said, "Well, look, if you get up there and see a hot li'l gal named Tessa who's about forty-five years old, tell her Big John's coming back to town and wants to see her, OK?" He was totally serious. This guy was super old and could barely get out of bed, but he was still talking about chasing young girls!

I didn't wanna wear out my welcome, so we took a couple of photos and I said, "Hook, I know it's late and we don't wanna keep you up all night." He said "Well, I know y'all gotta go to Portland, and my kids get mad if I stay up too late." As we shook hands and said goodbye, he looked me right in the eye and said, "G-g-give 'em hell, young man." On our way out we used the front door, and when we got to the living room I could not believe how many awards he had. They covered every inch of every wall. Gold and platinum records, keys to several American cities, plaques from all over Europe, and handwritten notes from everybody from B.B. King to Bonnie Raitt to Muddy Waters to Carlos Santana. And of course there was a big glass case with all of his Grammy Awards on display. Let me put it this way, if I had walked through the front door instead of the back door on my way in, I would've been a hundred times more nervous than I already was when I met him. This room was one big sucker punch that said, *Wake up, young lion, you're about to meet an OG American blues star.* And I did. On the way to Portland the next day I listened to John Lee Hooker's classic record "Crawlin' King Snake" over and over and over. Hard to believe that Hook's first record, "Boogie Chillen'," came out in 1948, so I was wondering the whole way up, How old *is* John Lee Hooker? We didn't have iPhones or Google then, so it blew my mind he was willing to have a young white kid guitar player over to his house at eleven thirty at night.

I didn't run into his gal Tessa while I was in Portland, but I did play a show that night with guitar god Link Wray at the legendary punk venue Satyricon. I was in awe of Link Wray, and his song "Rumble" was an anthem for all things concerning tough and badass guitar tone/sound. "Rumble" was considered such a violent song when it came out in 1958 that lots of radio stations banned it, thinking it would escalate gang violence, which only helped it sell more records. This was light-years before square-ass Tipper Gore came along and helped sell millions of hip-hop records by putting "Warning: Explicit Lyrics" stickers on them. Same bullshit here with Link, whose song went on to sell one million records. You know an instrumental guitar record's gotta be tough sounding to sell a million.

It's amazing to me that even today the religious right is that out of touch. I mean, they have to know that every time they protest a rock or rap act, they're just giving them free publicity and legitimizing their street cred, right? When I was on tour with Rob Zombie, those knuckleheads in the Westboro Baptist Church would just follow us around. It was the greatest tour publicity for Rob Zombie ever. I got a Polaroid of that somewhere. Anyway, that night in Portland I told Link Wray that we had just met John Lee Hooker, and his wife, who I think was from Scandinavia, quickly responded with her thick accent, "Well, now you're meeting Link Wray!" Link actually cut in and said, "No, honey, meeting John Lee Hooker is a big deal." I wasn't trying to boast to Link. I was just making conversation. I was used to vibing with musicians and then sometimes having their girlfriend or boyfriend come in and inject weirdness. It happens more than you'd imagine. Maybe it's some kind of insecurity/

control thing. It's not easy being in a relationship with a public person. And then Link asked how I met him, and I told the story about his assistant hanging out at my show in San Fran. Around this time Link Wray and Dick Dale (another famous dude I would tour with) were both having big career resurgences due to film director Quentin Tarantino licensing their music for films like *Reservoir Dogs* and *Pulp Fiction*. Even though I was a fan before that, because I was a young rockabilly record collector nerding out by constantly scouring milk-crate bins in resale shops for what the kids now call "vinyls," I was just so happy that people were getting to hear original American guitar gods all over again.

Just one note about Dick Dale. I opened for him at the Belly Up Tavern in Solana Beach, California, that same year I met Hook and Link, and I broke strings on two guitars in two consecutive songs and I didn't have a third guitar to play, so I told our drummer to solo while I threw a string on. Dick Dale came over and threw a set of these massive 13-gauge guitar strings in my face and said, "Don't be a pussy. Play bigger strings and you won't break them! I told Stevie Ray Vaughan the same thing!" Even though he was a total dick about it, he was right, and I've played 13, 15, unwound 18, 36, 46, and 52 ever since, and I never, ever break strings.

Anyway, back to Link. That night Link brought my pedal-steel player, Brian, up to play a song with him, and after the show he went on and on about how much he missed playing country music. He loved our thick Texas accents and asked if I had any Native American Indian blood. I said that I didn't think so, and he said, "Well, I'm Native American. You should find out if you are, because it will help you to understand music in a whole new way." He was very serious when he said this to me. Fast-forward to 2017, and our friend guitarist Stevie Salas, who's played with so many rock legends like Mick Jagger and Rod Stewart, helped work on and release a documentary film called *Rumble: The Indians Who Rocked the World*, and it was then I realized what Link was telling me about "understanding music in a whole new way." If you haven't seen this documentary, I highly recommend it. I had no idea how much Native American blood our original blues heroes had in them.

After that night with Link in Portland, we pushed on to Seattle, one of my favorite cities to play, then down to Salt Lake City, and finished in Denver. I knew I was going home to face a depressing situation. I had called my wife at the time from the road and I could tell she was trying to keep her head up, but it was not working. When I got back, things were weird and we both spent most of our time working. If I wanted to write some great country songs, this was the best and worst possible way to go about it. I was still trying to live like my heroes, drinking a fifth of whiskey or more a day, smoking tons of weed, snorting blow, popping whatever pills you gave me. I wasn't looking for it, but the party always found me back then. I never felt like I was a young alcoholic/drug addict because I could put it down whenever I needed to, but I always had the thought in the back of my mind that I needed to be careful about how much I did and when. I'd get home from tour and dry out, but I was young and could bounce back pretty easy. Later in life, I didn't bounce back so easy. Thank God the "party" lost its luster. But back then, I would get home and we would try to make the best out of our failing marriage by going to therapy, or on vacation, or maybe back home to Beaumont to see our families. None of it worked. It's a very strange binary feeling to have so much cool stuff and so much bad stuff happening to you in your life simultaneously. When you're young and immature, your first thought is to play the victim and wonder, Why can't she just get along with me? Look at all the great stuff happening. But looking back I was a total train wreck every bit as much as she was. Gone all the time with my only mistress and only real true love . . . music.

But hey, I'm trying to be rigorously honest in this book, and I hope I don't come off like a prick, but there were many nights when my ex-wife and I would go to bed mad at each other, and the thing that kept me going was thoughts like *Fuck all this. I went over to John Lee Hooker's house and hung out with him!* I knew there was something happening with me—not so much my career, but with me and the people I was getting to meet and perform with. Hook, Link, Dick Dale . . . all of these good memories helped to make the bad memories tolerable, even now while I'm sitting here writing this.

My old man used to say, "Ever seen a hearse pulling a U-Haul?" None of the vintage guitars, motorcycles, and hot rods I've acquired really mean jack shit to me. Sure, they're fun, and it makes going to the grocery store a much cooler experience than, say, driving a minivan or a family car, but the money comes and goes and all we truly have is the hang, and then the memories. You can get the money back if you lose it, but you can't ever get the time back. That's why the hang is so important. And hanging with John Lee Hooker and having him tell me about firing up his Cadillac and driving up to Portland to see a "li'l gal," or having Link Wray drop some Native American knowledge on me, and even having Dick Dale throw some guitar strings in my face and yell at me, that's the most important stuff. The hang. The memories. That's why I don't do jack shit anymore if the hang isn't awesome. It took me forever to learn that one, and sometimes I'm a slow learner, but once I get it, I got it.

Another thing is, after a while, those memories, no matter what book they end up in, or who you tell them to that you might think can truly relate, after a while, all of the memories just become part of who you are and part of your story. No one who's ever had these experiences feels like they're name-dropping. . . . They just feel like I feel right now as I'm writing this, sharing some crazy shit that happened to me for reasons I'll never be able to explain. And I'm OK with that. I don't need answers to everything. Searching for those answers gets in the way of possibly opening yourself up to experiencing more of these unexplainable events. That's what I'm after.

EMILY KAYE

I saw her for the first time at Danny Bland's wedding at the Sit & Spin laundromat in Seattle, but it all started a few months before that at the SXSW *Spin* magazine party in Austin. I was playing the outdoor stage on Sixth Street with the Supersuckers and Iggy Pop. She was watching me play from one of the balconies where the *Spin* party was happening. As you may recall from an earlier chapter, the "country-punk" Supersuckers record called *Must've Been High* that I had just worked and played on was released to very mixed reviews. A large portion of the Suckers crowd at that show were booing these new songs. I had brought out legendary western swing fiddler Johnny Gimble (from Bob Wills's and Willie Nelson's bands) to play on my solo set, which the crowd was OK with because they viewed me as some kind of local novelty act. But they definitely didn't want to hear the Supersuckers play anything but their usual loud Ramones-meets-Motörhead-meets–Thin

Lizzy songs. Not exactly the same as when Bob Dylan got booed for going electric, but the Suckers did get booed big-time for going country. So there I was, sitting in with a band getting booed, and she saw the whole damn thing.

Next, Emily and I almost met when she unknowingly hired me to play guitar on a record by a punk blues band called Tenderloin that she'd signed to Jim Guerinot's label Time Bomb Recordings. Our mutual friend Danny Bland (who was like Cupid at this point) was managing Tenderloin and made a deal with Emily, who was the head of A&R for Time Bomb, to sign them. Danny said something to the effect of "you need to meet this country guitar player named Jesse Dayton; think you two would hit it off." Not a normal thing to say to a jet-setting rock music executive from Los Angeles who couldn't have cared less about some hillbilly from Beaumont, Texas. I played on the record but never got to meet Emily.

Well, that all changed at that live music/wedding event/laundry place in Seattle. Danny flew me up there to sing "Angel Flying Too Close to the Ground" at his wedding, which was a veritable who's who of the Seattle music scene. Grunge and punk rockers from all the big bands were there. (I know this is supposed to be a real book and all, but don't make me look up who played bass or drums or sang in those multiplatinum radio bands.) Sub Pop Records folks, legendary venue owners, and of course the band Danny managed, the Supersuckers, were all there. I went up onstage to sing that song by Willie Nelson, and standing directly in front of me was this tall, gorgeous, olive-skinned brunette in a tight dress who had a Hawaiian flower in her hair and who was burning a hole through me, staring at me. I sang the entire song, not looking at Janet and Danny, who were the ones getting married, but at this knockout of a woman. At this point I was going through a divorce and, frankly, after nine months of separation, exhausting touring, and living single, I was on the rebound big-time. There was a guy standing next to this woman who was obviously not very happy about the "wedding singer" and his date having eye sex with each other, but it really was like we were the only two souls in the crowded room.

After the official said "you may kiss the bride," I put down my Telecaster and darted straight over to her. The music was loud and we kept speaking into each other's ears and "accidentally" touching our lips on each other's hair and ears. Christ, she smelled so good. I was getting turned on in a big way just talking to her and the guy who was hanging with her was not having any of it. Finally, she said, "Why don't we all three go back to my hotel room so I can change out of these wedding clothes and we can all go grab some food and go to the Tractor to see a band?" "Great! I'm in!" I said. Sure, it was a little awkward, but I was in full conquer mode and she was reciprocating.

We got to her nice hotel suite and she went into the bathroom, so I straight-up asked this guy who's sitting there not saying anything, "So how long have you known Emily?" He said, "Oh, uh, Danny introduced us earlier today and I offered to take her to the wedding." Hmmm. So I said, "So you've basically known her a few hours longer than me, right?" Before he could answer I said, "Well, I'm going to do everything I can to lock this down tonight with her, brother." He said something like, "I'm not your brother." By the time she came out of the bathroom, wearing these tight jeans and a tiny Monster Magnet T-shirt, that dude was poof, gone. "Where'd he go?" she asked. I didn't answer her and just walked over and started kissing her.

We fell on the big bed and started tearing each other's clothes off. We never left that hotel room bed that night. We made mad passionate love and talked about everything imaginable: our families, our upbringing, our careers, what we wanted and didn't want out of our lives, where we lived, past relationships, past sexual exploits, and most of all our futures. Even though I did want to get in her pants, there was something completely magnetic pulling us toward each other. We stayed up the entire night. No booze, no blow, no weed, nothing. She was completely sober, which was a whole new experience for me, but I was so gobsmacked I couldn't have cared less. Just for the record, Emily was not one for one-night stands. Turns out she had gone an entire two years before that without sex or being in a relationship with anyone after breaking up with music-biz super-lawyer Stephen Finfer. She was working and flying around the globe nonstop. So was I. We both deserved a break together.

During our nonstop talk I finally found out more about her and her journey. Emily had grown up on the Hawaiian island of Maui and had pretty much the exact opposite childhood as me. She was raised by a divorced single mom who was once a TV/film actress, appearing in things like *In Like Flint* with James Coburn, and had been identified in more than a few history books as the Las Vegas dancer who worked for Sam Giancana's hotel as the lead dancer for Dean Martin and had had the big affair with Elvis after he finally broke it off with Priscilla. Emily's mother, Kaye Farrington, was a bombshell who used to room in Hollywood with Stella Stevens when they were both studio-hired actresses. Kaye eventually was married for a short time to Albert S. Ruddy, who produced *The Godfather*, then met and married Emily's father, Chuck Kaye, who came from a music publishing dynasty/family. They eventually divorced as well, and Chuck left them the house on Maui, jumped on his sailboat, and headed back to L.A. to start over. I had no idea about any of this or who any of these people were or what they did when I met her. She loved that I was this small-town guy with a thick East Texas/Louisiana accent who came from a wholesome family and whose parents still loved each other. Frankly, I didn't know anything about the entertainment business whatsoever and had been getting by on what I'd like to think was talent and charm. But this would all change, and Emily would become my teacher on many different levels concerning not just business but the spiritual principles of how I lived my life, and in some cases forgiving me when I failed miserably at living up to those principles.

As the sun came up around six a.m., we hopped in a cab and left her swanky hotel downtown and headed over to where I was staying at the Marco Polo Motel, known for being the place where Kurt Cobain and other junkie musicians hid out from the world. She left from there to head to the airport and fly back to L.A. I told her before she got in the cab, "You don't know this yet, but you're stuck with me from here on out." She said, "All right, when are you coming to see me?" I said, "Tomorrow." And I did. I bought a ridiculously overpriced plane ticket to L.A. at the airport, and that's how this whirlwind all started.

We immediately moved in together. We were both circumnavigating the planet touring and working, which made it all the more romantic when we did see each other. One day I thought I'd surprise her, so I showed up at our house by the beach in California with my baby boy, Sam. Emily was shocked and the first thing she said was "Can he walk yet?" Sam is now twenty-five. That's how long Emily has been Sam's stepmother. I have to say, after the chaos of her own crazy childhood, she made it her mission in life to become Sam's personal protector. They still to this day have an unspoken bond between them and they are thick as thieves. Emily's grandfather, notorious music business pioneer Lester Sill, the patriarch of the family, somehow accepted this outsider goy (as in non-Jewish me) from "down in Elvis country." Her father's brothers, Joel, Greg, and Lonnie, who are all in the music business, too, were all really supportive of our bizarre union.

I've seen Emily do it all, from starting the music supervision company the Chop Shop with our old friend Alex Patsavas to working for Sony Pictures and advertising agency GSD&M to producing my film *Zombex* to finally taking over as my full-time business manager. Yep, it gets hairy sometimes, but Christ we're still madly and passionately in love all these years later. Sadly, her father just passed away from complications due to Covid-19, at age eighty. When he wasn't working on music-publishing deals with John

Lennon, the Eagles, or Madonna, he was this swashbuckling sailor who sailed his own boats all over the world. Emily just got back from California, where the family spread his ashes on Catalina Island. She flew back to Austin two nights ago and came straight from the airport to my show. When she walked backstage, we immediately went to the tour bus and made out.

Even though we've been to hell and back together, we're still in love. Sometimes I can't believe we're still together. It's like a two-person cult. A suicide pact. Weirdos from two different backgrounds that don't necessarily look right on paper but are still working in real time today. Some people think I live with a woman who "works out a lot," but actually, I live with a competitive athlete who is constantly trying to beat her own time and level up. She's inspired me more than anyone to clean up my act and get healthy. This is the one chapter for me in this book that can never truly explain or reveal my love and gratitude. To say I'm lucky to have met Emily is beyond an understatement, but I truly believe it was written in the stars, preordained by the universe, and all we had to do was just show up. We're still living it and walking through it now. Together.

ROB ZOMBIE,
CAPTAIN CLEGG,
AND HALLOWEEN

My **best friend** in the whole world is a guy named Lew Temple. We came up together in a small scene of musician/theatre weirdos in Houston, and Lew went on to become a successful character actor. He has lived in Los Angeles for years now. Google "Lew Temple" and I guarantee you've seen him in a movie or TV show or something. It seems like he's been in everything.

If I got thrown in jail in Bangkok or Juárez, I'd call Lew. A few years back, IMDb reported that he is one of the top working character actors in Hollywood. Lew's story is pretty crazy. He started out as a Triple-A baseball player for the Seattle Mariners, and when he didn't get picked up for the big show by the majors, he started working as a talent scout for the Houston Astros. My all-time favorite team. He was doing really well with the Astros (big salary, nice car, high-rise condo) when he called me one day out of nowhere and said, "Hey, JD, they're shooting this new TV show outside of Dallas called *Walker, Texas Ranger* and Chuck Norris wants to put me in it. I think I might have to try this acting thing, brother!"

To be totally honest, I was completely against it. Not him being in a TV show, that was great, but just randomly switching careers seemed like a crazy move. After all, he was doing great with his career in pro baseball, and I tried to tell him how incredibly brutal the rejection could be in the acting game. But I was wrong. Lew went to the manager of the Astros and said, "I may never have another chance like this one ever come along again" and quit pro baseball. He then started doing theatre and studying acting and paid for it all by getting his ass kicked every other week as the bad guy on *Walker, Texas Ranger*. He attacked his acting parts with the same discipline he'd had playing baseball and was always carrying a book of Sam Shepard or Tennessee Williams plays around with him.

Our conversations changed from baseball to acting, and I gotta say, I was totally impressed with his focus and conviction, because I was doing the same thing with my music and saw a lot of folks who were all talk and no work. Lew, on the other hand, was always studying and working on his craft and blowing through his 10,000 hours (as Malcolm Gladwell calls it), performing in plays and going on auditions and taking classes. Since then he's worked in films with Sean Penn, Denzel Washington, Benicio del Toro. And he's done a whole bunch of TV shows, like his big role as Axel on the global phenomenon *The Walking Dead*.

Anyway, my ol' friend Lew got one of his first great parts as Adam Banjo in Rob Zombie's 2005 film *The Devil's Rejects*. One night at a party in Hollywood with Rob, Marilyn Manson, and Alice Cooper, Rob started talking about having a fake '70s country band do the soundtrack for the film. Lew immediately told Rob about me, and the next thing I know I'm getting a phone call from

Trying to start a band with Chris Adams and Jeff Smith (1981).
Glenda Faye Warren

Backstage with Bo Diddley and the Road Kings (1992).
John Huff

Recording with Doug Sahm (1994).

With Johnny Cash in Nashville, Tennessee (1997).

With Johnny Cash in Nashville, Tennessee (1997).

With Waylon Jennings in Nashville, Tennessee (1997).

At the Hootenanny Festival in Orange County, California, with Ron Heathman and Eddie Spaghetti from the Supersuckers (1997).

With Kris Kristofferson in Nashville, Tennessee (1997).
Laura Robles-Huff

In Jim Jard's garage with Ryan Bingham (2005).
Emily Kaye

With John Lee Hooker and his old Stella guitar (1998).
Charlie Sanders

On the set of Rob
Zombie's *Halloween II*
(2008).
Jesse Dayton

Anyone but my mama:
With my mother,
Glenda Faye Warren
(2009).
Emily Kaye

With Shooter Jennings (2012).
Jesse Dayton

With my son, Samuel, who's making a goofy skateboarder face (2015).
Emily Kaye

ie Nelson wearing a Jesse Dayton
irt on his tour bus, the *Honeysuckle Rose*
5).
Nelson

A new gold tooth at LAX with Billy Joe Shaver
(2015).
Jesse Dayton

On tour with X (2016).

With Emily Kaye at a photo shoot for our film titled *Zombex* (2011). *Linda Hughes*

With Beto O'Rourke (2017). *Emily Kaye*

With Duff McKagan at the Scoot Inn in Austin, Texas (2020). *Emily Kaye*

Rob Zombie. He was like "Hey man, this is Rob, got your number from Lew. We're making the ultimate white trash horror movie called *The Devil's Rejects* and we think your music would be perfect." I didn't really understand the whole concept yet about finding the lost tapes of a '70s country band, but I got on a plane, went out to L.A., and holed up for a few days at the Chateau Marmont with Lew drinking copious amounts of bourbon, smoking lots of weed, and writing hillbilly horror songs. We had songs like "I'm at Home Getting Hammered (While She's Out Getting Nailed)," "Dick Soup," "Tried to Quit (But I Just Quit Tryin')," and even a sadomasochist tune called "Honeymoon Song" about a guy who marries an unassuming farm girl who turns out to be a freak in bed and pulls out a red ball, sticks it in his mouth, then covers him in black shiny latex and begins to beat the living shit out of him on their wedding night in the back of a Good Times van. Who knew there were so many S&M music fans who would come out of the woodwork and love this song?

A few days into my trip to L.A. we drive over to the movie studio with an acoustic guitar, and I sit down and sing the songs for Rob. This was the first time I met him, and I was very impressed by what a cool and laid-back guy he was. At first, walking into this office in L.A. it felt like I was going to have to do the whole "dance, monkey, dance" audition thing, but Rob made me feel comfortable by cracking some funny jokes.

Just for the record, people in the entertainment business who go out of their way to make you feel comfortable, and don't make you feel like just another hack they have to see because some manager or agent sent you over, well, these people are usually the most talented ones. Nothing to prove, total confidence.

Anyway, I started singing, and he immediately started cracking up. And after three songs he said, "Great, let's do a whole soundtrack like this!" So now we've got the keys to the kingdom.

A real record budget from Universal's soundtrack division, a Hollywood studio film release, and an executive producer/director/rock star behind us who happens to have sold millions of records. What could possibly go wrong?

Actually, not much did go wrong. It all kind of came together without a hitch. I went to the Directors Guild in L.A. with Lew to watch an early screening of the film, and while I don't think Lionsgate executives really understood how cool the movie was (they didn't get the whole '70s B-movie vibe, but Quentin Tarantino did and said it was his favorite film of the year on several big talk shows), the film went on to incredible reviews and a massive cult following that's still going strong today. The horror world and all of its crazy horror fan conventions that happen weekly all over the planet gave the highest praise to *The Devil's Rejects*—both the film and the soundtrack. The original songs I worked on with Lew and Rob, recorded in the front room of my friend Steve Chadie's house in Austin, also became cult favorites. There might have been some comedic elements to the lyrics, but the players on the "Devil's Rejects presents Banjo & Sullivan" record are world-class monster bluegrass and country pickers. I actually did an interview with David Fricke from *Rolling Stone* as someone who had found the "lost" Banjo & Sullivan tapes from the '70s and helped Rob get the music into the film! The whole thing was one big con, but in a crazy, fun, unpredictable way. It was so weird, but it helped me gain a whole new following of folks that would never have been into my music in a million years.

Right around this time SiriusXM radio started a new station called Outlaw Country. Jeremy Tepper, the program director, and head DJ Mojo Nixon were crazy for the record and played it every single day. Listeners were contacting the station directly asking to hear that "duo from the *Devil's Rejects* soundtrack," but no one knew it was me, Jesse Dayton. "Hey brother, could y'all play that Home Getting Hammered song again?" Or "So what's the song y'all played yesterday about she's getting nailed?" Like, 99 percent of the people couldn't remember the actual title of that song, but they still remembered enough of it to call and request it.

The trick to "I'm at Home Getting Hammered (While She's Out Getting Nailed)" is it sounds like there's a curse word in it, but there isn't. So of course terrestrial radio was too scared to play it. Also, when the song popped up on the radio in people's cars it had the name of the band from the Rob Zombie movie on it, "Banjo & Sullivan," so no one knew it was me. I would go out and play the songs at my shows and someone would always come up to me and say, "Hey man, that's a pretty good rendition of that song from that Rob Zombie movie!" having no idea I wrote it or sang it in the first place. This is still going on till this day! But I did make some mailbox money off of it, and it's become a part of the show that fans demand. There are loads of local small-town redneck bands doing songs from this soundtrack on YouTube, and it's one of the funniest internet rabbit holes you'll ever go down. Punk bands, classic-rock bands, country-and-western bands, singer-songwriters . . . all doing these bawdy Banjo & Sullivan songs from *The Devil's Rejects*. We played in North Carolina one night and the opening band came out and played a couple of my songs from the soundtrack and introduced them by saying, "These are our two biggest songs on YouTube!" I told them after that I was the guy who wrote them, and they were embarrassed because they were clearly trying to pass the songs off as their own. Oh well, didn't Oscar Wilde say "Imitation is the sincerest form of flattery that mediocrity can pay to greatness"? OK, I'm not saying those songs are "greatness," but they're pretty damn catchy and stuck in enough folks' heads to help me pay a few bills.

Little did I know that this was just the beginning. Rob had made his own version of the *Halloween* film, with the not-yet-publicly-accused sex offender Harvey Weinstein producing. And yes, this was part of the franchise of John Carpenter's famous 1978 horror masterpiece *Halloween*. Even though Weinstein was a total asshole, Rob's first *Halloween* movie did gangbuster numbers at the box office, so they asked him to do another. Rob called me to work on the soundtrack for *Halloween II* and to be a character in the movie known as Captain Clegg, who was a psychobilly-singing bandleader during the film's infamous Halloween costume murder party. I had absolutely no idea what to expect when I flew out to rural Georgia and made my way to the middle of nowhere. Rob had basically taken over an entire small farming community.

There was a lot of press interested in the film, so CNN did a full segment on me while I was in Atlanta. By the way, Ted Turner designed the CNN home offices in Atlanta like a government building, with an insane security clearance you have to pass to get in. CNN is like Fort Knox. Anyway, the film starred Malcolm McDowell (an amazing talent, and I'll talk more about him in another chapter); Rob's wife, Sheri Moon Zombie; character actor legend Brad Dourif; and young scream-queen horror actress Scout Taylor Compton. My buddy Lew Temple was in the first *Halloween* film Rob did, but his character was killed off, so we didn't work together in this one. Rob and his team had hired hundreds of misfit/crazed extras to drive in from Atlanta dressed to the nines in Halloween costume and then I got into the most authentic-looking gory makeup you've ever seen. Rob's hair and makeup department spared no expense and made those extras in the party scene look totally real and terrifying. We shot the scenes for Captain Clegg with two naked strippers onstage on either side of me dancing with go-go boots during this raging costume party while the legendary Jason character, played by Tyler Mane, was slitting throats outside of the party in the parking lot. We shot it all in this big barn, and these local country folks who lived in the area were literally pulling over on the side of the road and just standing there in total disbelief with their mouths open watching all the freaks. Rural residents, who looked like every redneck cliché person I grew up with, would just hang out on the tailgates of their pickup trucks, staring at us all day long. It was like they were having a tailgate party with coolers of beer, but instead of a football game it was a horror-film set loaded with hundreds of decked-out ghouls. They would point and slap one another on the back. The circus had definitely come to town, and Rob, who doesn't just create movie sets but creates entire gore-filled, shocking worlds, had brought a circus to these folks that they would never forget.

The set directors Rob had on his team were so talented, and they turned this barn into something way beyond what you would normally see in one of those "fright-night" Halloween haunted houses that pop up every year across America in October. This barn we were filming the party scene in had been completely transformed. After you walked through the barn doors, you had no idea you were in a barn out in the boonies. Every single extra (background actor) in that barn had their shit together and was focused and into it. Sometimes, extras who aren't taking things seriously can completely ruin a whole shot just by goofing off, laughing, or not being in the moment. But these extras were serious horror nerds. If you're not familiar, true monster makeup is an art. We're not talking about the Day of the Dead kits you order online for Halloween, we're talking professional-level scary-as-fuck makeup that takes a long time to put on. I can't stress just how freaked out the locals were while this was going on. It was like the most quiet, rural, conservative place on Earth had been invaded by Charles Manson and his gang, but it was a gang of hundreds of freaks instead of twelve dirty hippies! Rob Zombie really created the feeling that this party was actually happening, with everyone dancing. The music that I had wrote and recorded was playing at eardrum-shattering levels. Rob brought this big PA system into the barn and just cranked it up so the actors would feel like it was a real party. Like I did for

Devil's Rejects, I had recorded the original songs for *Halloween 2* in Austin at my friend Steve Chadie's front room, but this time it was a new vibe, a hybrid of '60s surf and '80s psychobilly. This soundtrack ended up doing even better than the one for *The Devil's Rejects*, and we ended up filming a documentary about Captain Clegg and the Night Creatures and getting it into Hot Topics in malls all across America. This was an Emily Kaye manager move, because she called an old friend she used to know in the L.A. music business scene who was now an executive. They put a deal together with Hot Topic to place these Captain Clegg DVDs on the front counter. Yep, she's a pretty smart gal.

So, this is where it really gets crazy. Lo and behold, Rob calls me to open up for him on his *Hellbilly Deluxe 2* tour across North America. We were playing forty cities, in big venues every night, and we were billed as Captain Clegg and the Night Creatures, and we were supposed to play all the music from the *Halloween II* soundtrack and a couple of the songs from *The Devil's Rejects*. So the really cool thing about this was that all of Rob's fans had already seen the movie, so most of them knew who we were. My wife, Emily Kaye, was our onstage go-go dancer, Mistress Clegg. Emily would come out in a short, tight black miniskirt with these '60s go-go boots on and dance for two or three songs in the middle of the show, and people went nuts for it.

The *Hellbilly Deluxe 2* tour was pure insanity. Not in a debauched drugs-and-alcohol way (although our camp had some whiskey and weed, but nothing like the early years), but as in the actual shows, and the Zombie fans who are second to none in terms of pure fanaticism. Every night there were topless girls showing off their boobs while sitting on the shoulders of their dates in the first ten rows. Rob would grab a handheld spotlight and say, "Captain Clegg told me backstage that Salt Lake City was the craziest town

so far. Well, show me Salt Lake!" Then he would point the spotlight out in the crowd and girls' shirts would start flying off! Every night our merch booth was flooded with chicks trying to get
backstage, dudes trying to give us drugs, and just overall insanity.
While this was not quite as wild as the Supersuckers tours, it was
a hell of a lot bigger in terms of ticket buyers and venues. We were
playing big theaters, amphitheater sheds, rock halls, hockey arenas,
convention centers—basically anyplace that held between 5,000 to
15,000 screaming Zombie fans. It was also some of the craziest sex
for my wife and me, because we usually had the dressing room all
to ourselves, and the band would go to the bus. She'd walk offstage
in those knee-high go-go boots, that leather miniskirt, a tiny top
with her boobs pushed up, and a '60s bouffant hairdo à la Priscilla
Presley meets Elvira, and we'd be going at it like animals in the
showers backstage at some sports arena in God knows what state.
This happened almost every night on tour, and I have to say it was
hands down the wildest sex I've ever had. As you can imagine, as a
young musician I had some crazy escapades over the years on tour,
but nothing beats crazy sex with someone you're actually in love
with. And let's face it, keeping the "crazy" in a married sex life ain't
easy. But being in a big empty sports-arena dressing room, with a
running shower, covered in sweat from the show, still hearing the
roar of the crowd outside, well, it was raw, animal workout sex, and
I gotta say, we still think about it all the time.

I met some incredible people on that tour as well. On the first
night of the tour in Las Vegas we met the king of the freak film directors, John Waters. He didn't say hello or introduce himself. He
just said, "Welcome to the freak show," and gave me a wink and a
smile. Later we said hello to the Aerosmith guys while in Boston
and they were super cool. We met Joe Walsh and Anita Thompson (Hunter S. Thompson's widow) while in Colorado; Gene Sim-
mons in L.A. (Gene was like a sweet ol' Jewish grandfather once

I told him my wife was Jewish, and told me, "You need to save at least 20 percent of every dollar you make, kid!"); and Danzig on Halloween night. He was standing on the side of the stage staring at me while we did a version of the Misfits song "Hollywood Babylon" in Hollywood at the Hollywood Palladium. I don't know if Danzig liked it or not, but he watched the whole song, and the crowd was going crazy. Maybe he just permanently has that scowl on his face 24/7. A really unexpected person I met was Pulitzer Prize–winning playwright Edward Albee. I was a big fan of his from Lew's theatre days. He started following me on Facebook and wrote on my Michael Jackson eulogy, "Very moving piece . . . thx for writing! Best, Edward." I said to myself, *This can't be the same guy!* For the record, I wrote this thing about Michael Jackson on my Facebook that went viral, saying that if Jerry Falwell and the pope had that many pills in their systems, they'd be hanging babies off of balconies and having a doctor put them under with anesthesia to go to sleep every night too. Addiction is still so misunderstood. Anyway, back to Edward Albee. I messaged him and found out he was teaching at the University of Houston, so I invited him to our big show with Zombie, and surprisingly enough, he came out. Edward seemed nervous, like he didn't like crowds, so before the show we talked for a few minutes about my hero, Sam Shepard (who put the first song I ever got into a film in his movie version of *Curse of the Starving Class*), and writer Horton Foote, who took Harper Lee's *To Kill a Mockingbird* and turned it into an award-winning movie script and who was from right down the road from where I grew up, in Wharton, Texas. Edward was a fascinating man but completely out of his element. He has now sadly passed away, but I feel honored that I got to spend time with one of the great American playwrights at a noisy rock show that I'm sure he couldn't stand.

Every day on the Rob Zombie tour I wrote two or three pages of a script I'd been working on. It was a Roger Corman–inspired political horror movie set in New Orleans after Hurricane Katrina. I would jump on our RV and handwrite those two or three pages no matter what, and the dialogue was just flowing out of me. After forty shows I got home with a 110-page script that I would rewrite five more times. No, this script wasn't going to set the world on fire, but looking back now and considering the apocalyptic tone of it, and how I'm writing this on quarantine lockdown because of the Covid-19 plague, it all feels very surreal. The film was called *Zombex*, and little did I know I would go on to direct this little indie B creature feature and it would star Malcolm McDowell, Sid Haig, Lew Temple, John Doe from X, and include lots of other cameos from folks like Corey Feldman, Tom Araya from Slayer, and Kinky Friedman. More on that later! I remember at one point I told Rob I was writing a script, and he said, "That's the easy part. Getting it made is a whole other set of problems." Not that encouraging, but at the time I was just thinking that I'd try to license the script and be done with it. Directing it was not something I had even thought of. I had already written a play with Lew before this called *Balmorhea*, and we had had some stuff going with it for a minute through a friend in L.A. Lew had just beat cancer, and we were on a long road trip driving on Interstate 10 all the way from Los Angeles to New Orleans. We switched off drivers, took turns writing, and would stop in little towns along the way and just hole up in a shitty, cheap motel and write. It was Cormac McCarthy–influenced but with more action, about a dysfunctional Texas ranch family. It's a damn good script, if I do say so. Maybe one day it'll see the light of day.

None of this would've happened if my old friend Lew Temple hadn't introduced me to Rob Zombie. I was just a guitar slinger from Texas before I met Rob, but all that changed after he so graciously invited me to work with him. Well, let me rephrase that: in my mind I'll always just be a guitar-pickin' Beaumonster, but meeting Rob did lead to some doors opening for me that I never thought about before. Dumb luck? Probably. But I was ready and willing to work my ass off. I remember way back when Lew showed up to sleep on my couch in Los Angeles and literally left every morning before we got up to go "find an agent." Well, after a few weeks Lew found a fucking agent! Looking back, the whole thing seems so weird.

I remember when we were shooting music videos on the set of *Halloween II* so Rob could release the videos as extra content for the DVD, and it was so bizarre. There I was with my band, dressed as Captain Clegg and the Night Creatures, and we were set up in a real-life Civil War cemetery in bumfuck Georgia, with our music cranked super loud through a PA, and Rob said to me with a sly grin, "What are you going to do if this Clegg thing blows up?" I told him, "Well, I know one thing for sure, I'll have a Halloween-night show to play for the rest of my life." And I do. Since the film's release and the massive tour, I've had offers from all over the world for Captain Clegg and the Night Creatures to play some of the biggest, baddest Halloween parties you could imagine.

I knew in the back of my mind that I was going to have to eventually get off of this merry-go-round and get back to being Jesse Dayton, but it was a blast while it lasted. It's almost like we worked so hard for that one year doing the movie, then the Clegg soundtrack, then the big tour with Rob, that everyone in that world knew about us. And then, *poof*: we just disappeared. We didn't put out any more Clegg records or play any Clegg tours, which just somehow magically added to the demand, and the cult following keeps growing.

Every Halloween, radio stations play the hell out of Captain Clegg. I remember Rob telling me to write a song for Halloween, and I think we're one of the only, if not the only, country Halloween records. The record has all kinds of influences besides country, so the different styles of songs pop up on different radio formats. SiriusXM plays Clegg every October, and the sales go up. Little Steven's Underground Garage will play one of the more garagey-sounding songs, and Outlaw Country will play the more country-type songs like "Honky Tonk Halloween." And the songs on the Clegg record have been licensed to other film and TV shows as well. The Clegg thing just won't die! It's like a ghost record/movie that keeps haunting me and reappearing in my life over and over every October. And the horror nerds are like no others when it comes to being fanatics. At least once a week, somewhere, some middle-aged hillbilly guy at a gas station in Tennessee, or some tattooed housewife at a Sprint store in Indiana, or some awkward teenage goth kid dressed in all black who sees me walking down the street somewhere in California will say, "Hey, wait, are you Captain Clegg?"

ZOMBEX WITH MALCOLM MCDOWELL, SID HAIG, AND COREY FELDMAN

So we were on location at five thirty a.m. in a big abandoned hospital in the middle of the deep East Texas Piney Woods. In just one hour, I was about to start directing my first feature film, and the first scene I'm directing stars British thespian Malcolm Mc-Dowell, best known as the lead actor from Stanley Kubrick's film *A Clockwork Orange*, but who has been in lots of big films and TV shows since then. I was as nervous as a pregnant hooker in a Pentecostal church but was tuning out the Shitty Committee and doing my usual impression of someone carefree who belonged there and was not overwhelmed and had done this before. This "fake it till ya make it" act has actually gotten me through quite a few of these situations and served me well.

Just so we put the time frame in order for y'all, when you direct a film you have to be there an hour before the crew and two hours before the talent arrives. At least, that was my schedule. A lot of times on independent films this usually means the director is working fourteen to sixteen hours a day, sometimes more, and gets very little sleep at night, which is a bitch, but that's why they call it work. Any truly talented person who works in film will tell you, it doesn't matter if they're the lead actor, the producer, the director of photography, wardrobe, hair and makeup, or the transport driver, any day that you get to be on a movie set, you're incredibly lucky to be there. It's amazing how much a sleep-deprived human being can accomplish doing just about anything if they psych their minds into saying, *You're so lucky to be here.*

The abandoned hospital was a location that my friend-producer Karma Montagne scouted outside a small town in the middle of the "Pine Curtain," which is slang for East Texas because of the region's ultra-thick pine forest. It seems every outsider from Civil War deserters to escaped prisoners and slaves to overzealous Bigfoot hunters have gone there to get permanently lost. I grew up hunting in the Big Thicket area, and from time to time we'd stumble upon a burned-out biker crank lab (that's speed, as in methamphetamine, as in illegal narcotics), or sometimes it would be a rusted old, forgotten moonshine still and deserted shacks with a wood-burning stove and maybe a little cot to sleep on, where it looked like someone had been hiding out from the law.

So there I was, walking through this spooky abandoned hospital hallway with flickering fluorescent lights and it already felt like a horror movie. I was running on about three hours' sleep because I'd just wrapped a three-month stage play in Houston called *Becoming Kinky,* where I played the part of Texas songwriter/author Kinky Friedman.

OK, I can't just skip over that, so here's the CliffsNotes version: Three months before I'd passed the *Zombex* script off to movie producer and close friend Karma Montagne, who helped get the film green-lit. I also got a call from a playwright in NYC named Ted Swindley to audition for his new play. Ted had written the very successful musical *Always . . . Patsy Cline* about the legendary singer's life, and he sounded like Tennessee Williams when he talked, like that rare Southern playwright/effeminate dandy who was an established character in the New York theatre scene but still hadn't lost his Southernness. I walked into an audition with about fifty actors, all in cowboy hats with cigars in their mouths, trying to look like Kinky Friedman, and I guess because I was a musician with a guitar who could act and who had grown up on Kinky's music, well, I got the part.

In short, the play was a success and ran for a while, and there was solid business talk about taking the play to New York City. Houston is a great theatre town where a lot of stage producers take their shows to work out the kinks (no pun intended) before they bring them to New York City. But I was extremely relieved when it was over, because it's really stressful and petrifying to do that six nights a week and have these intensely long solo monologues with the constant fear of forgetting your lines always hanging over your head. The play got good reviews, and I learned a lot about acting doing that project, but I had absolutely no intention of going to New York to work as a stage actor.

So where were we? Right. So it was the ass crack of dawn, I was exhausted from traveling from the closing night of my play in Houston and then driving with my guitar tech Brandon for four hours out to the middle of nowhere to start directing the first scene that morning. I was running on adrenaline and coffee, and my assistant director and I were walking around this creepy old hospital to go meet Malcolm McDowell. He'd called me over to the hair and makeup department to meet and talk about my script before we shot the first scene. My AD said on the walk over, "So you've never really directed any films before, have you?" I said, "No, only music videos and a short music documentary." She said, "You're about to direct your first feature film scene and your first scene is with Malcolm McDowell. Aren't you nervous?" *Of course I'm nervous, you idiot*, I thought but didn't say. *Are you trying to make me* more *nervous?* But I played the ol' Beaumonster hand and told the East Coaster AD in a calm voice, "Well, how bad can it be, darlin'? Nothing can scare me worse than walking into a recording studio with Johnny Cash." Now, either she wasn't a Johnny Cash fan (there's one or two out there, believe it or not) or she didn't know my history of playing music, but she cocked her head and looked at me as if to say, *That was a very weird response*, and we kept up our fast clip down the hallway into the hair and makeup room.

Note to self: Don't suffer petty small talk; it drags you and your ideas down. Stay focused so the Shitty Committee doesn't take over and start talking you out of thinking big. Contrary to popular belief, it's OK to think as big as you fuckin' want to. Also, there will be other folks, not many, just a few along the way, who have completely convinced themselves that they should be doing what you're doing and somehow you personally robbed them of the opportunity. Protect your sincerity and vision by not letting yourself get involved in those passive-aggressive head games. I know, it's hard, but blocking out and compartmentalizing certain situations can protect your mental health and overall mood. Setting boundaries with people who have weird energy has been a big life lesson for me. And it works. People come and go, especially on movie sets, and you should still be nice to everyone, but save your sentimentality for your family and inner circle when the work is done.

So I walked in and Malcolm McDowell was in his character's costume. He was playing a scientist with a long white lab coat and was looking very official and intellectual (though he already is intellectual and official regardless of costume). Malcolm shook my hand and said, "I think we worked on the same Rob Zombie film together, right?" And before I could answer, he said, "I hope this goes as easy as that did. Now, let's get all the Kubrick questions out of the way, darling, so we can discuss the work at hand."

Malcolm, being the consummate professional, immediately cut to the chase with his commanding British accent (I mean, the guy went to the London Academy of Music and Dramatic Art and studied at the Royal Shakespeare Company) but somehow still put me at ease. But it's OK, because by this time I'd gotten semi-good at being who I am, and besides, as the old saying goes, everyone else is already taken, right? So I said to Malcolm, "Well, since you put it out there, amigo . . ." He smiled at my accent.

Side note: people who aren't from where I'm from have been smiling at my accent my entire life, and I pick up on it instantly. If you don't take offense to the fact that their first thought is *Hmmm, that's quite a hillbilly accent* and remind yourself that you've read *Wuthering Heights* three times and they probably haven't, then it's no big deal. After touring so much, though, I can usually read people and tell if there's a high propensity that someone in their family tree is probably from some factory town like Birmingham, England, or some lower-income working-class section of Newark, New Jersey, which are both their own kind of version of where I'm from. We Texans need to remind ourselves that we didn't actually poke our heads out of our mother's vagina months before we officially came out to say, "Uh, can y'all cross the border into Texas when the contractions start, so I can be born in God's country?" It's great to be proud of where you're from, but it's also important to remember that you had absolutely nothing to do with it.

It's similar to this false nationalism that people have these days, where they act like they had a hand in where they were born. Am I proud to be a Texan? Damn straight, ol' son, but it's also my responsibility as a Texan to be a good world citizen who's not full of some faux macho bullshit because of somewhere my parents birthed me. You won't hear many Texans say this, but you should.

As soon as Malcolm mentioned "getting the Kubrick questions out of the way," about ten or twelve Kubrickian conspiracy theories ran through my mind like: "I know *Clockwork Orange* was made first, but did you ever talk to Stanley about the movie *The Shining* being about the demise of the gold standard?" Or "Was Kubrick trying to use *2001: A Space Odyssey* to really prove that we didn't go to the moon?" Or "When you were on the set of *A Clockwork Orange*, did Stanley ever confess that the film was about government mind-control experiments?" Yes, those questions did go through my mind, but there was no way in hell I was gonna bore Malcolm McDowell with that before six a.m. And let's face it, he probably didn't care about those things whatsoever. So I just asked him, "Look, I'm sure this discussion warrants a few hours in a dark pub with a Tullamore Dew on the rocks, but before we move on can I simply ask what it was like working with Stanley Kubrick?" Malcolm said very politely, "Kubrick was incredibly methodical and seemed to have very specific answers to every question that anyone on the set asked him. He had more of a New York accent than I thought he would, kind of the way you have more of a Texas accent than I thought you would." Malcolm was an old pro at putting everyone at ease and getting on with the business at hand. Then he said one more thing: "I once saw Stanley do one hundred takes with an actor, just to exhaust them, so they would stop acting and just say the lines on the page. I don't think we'll need to do a lot of takes today." Pretty smart guy, huh?

Then we briefly both professed our love for the brilliant and twisted mind of one Rob Zombie, went through the plots and moods of the scenes that Malcolm would be in for my little Roger Corman–esque creature feature movie, and got to work. I brought our sound guy into the hair and makeup room to make sure I could get Malcolm reading the narration parts of the film while he relaxed between scenes.

Malcolm McDowell's voice is pure gold, and I didn't want to waste any of the limited time I had with him on my set. In the scenes where Malcolm was not present, I wanted him to do narration voice-overs so it would feel like he was in the movie more than he actually was, which worked. Watching Malcolm work was like a crash course in the tonality of acting. He could do everything, from going super big to some tiny, minuscule actions that only the camera would pick up. I remember watching the dailies at the end of the day/night, and his range on camera was staggering. Most working utilitarian actors have one switch and that's what you hire them for. Malcolm has about five switches, so the trick is to get him to explore all of that so you get a dynamic performance. I didn't really "direct" him so much as made sure I got what I needed for the scene. Malcolm would always give me two, sometimes three different versions of whatever scene we shot, and later, as we were editing the film in Burbank, long after we wrapped, I realized how lucky I was to have worked with such a brilliant actor. Our producers definitely paid Malcolm well, but in the long run he was doing us all a huge favor by being in our little schmaltzy indie horror film. That first day set the tone, at least for me, for the rest of the shoot. And I gotta say, watching Malcolm work puts me in the same kind of awe I get watching anyone else I've ever witnessed do their magic, be they guitar players, baseball players, entrepreneurs, writers, you name it.

Later that morning the great character actor Sid Haig arrived, along with one of my childhood acting heroes, Corey Feldman. The first time I saw Sid Haig was in a James Bond movie called *Diamonds Are Forever*, which I saw for the first time with my daddy at a cinema in Beaumont. My pops took me to see all the James Bond movies. I'll always be grateful for those memories, and I passed it on by also taking my son, Sam, to see the Bond films.

Sig is a part of the fabric of American film and TV from the late '60s on. Besides being in all those great Blaxploitation films that

Jack Hill made, like *Coffy* and *Foxy Brown* (which, I must admit, I only initially watched because of the voluptuous African American actress Pam Grier, whom I had a major boyhood crush on), Sid was in all the great TV stuff that was either still on the air when I was a kid or was in constant rerun rotation, like *Star Trek*, *Get Smart*, *Charlie's Angels*, *Fantasy Island*, and even an episode of *The Dukes of Hazzard*! Sid and I had both worked on Rob Zombie's film *The Devil's Rejects*, so again, we broke the ice with a few minutes chatting about that brilliantly twisted mind of one Rob Zombie. Like Malcolm, Sid came in and nailed his scenes quickly just by being Sid. I could tell that he knew which lines would be important by the way he said them in that classic Sid way. (Well, as "important" as the lines in a small budget creature feature can be!) Sid would slow his dialogue down when he knew a big line was coming, take a beat, and then deliver the line like it contained the most important words to ever come out of his mouth.

At the end of the shoot with Sid, I remember him coming over to me and being so nice, saying, "Good day today. I think we got a lot of good stuff." A lot of times, an artist just won't make that kind of effort because either they're too shy, too inside their own head with the character, or they've got some kind of personal turmoil going on. Having Sid walk over to video village, where I was looking at playbacks, and say that one little thing meant the world to me, considering it was my first film. See how much the small stuff matters? I'm thinking about it enough to put in my book. Love is an action.

Sid Haig passed away on September 21, 2019, and the outpouring from his fans around the world was unbelievable. In the last couple of years, Sid had started an Instagram account that became incredibly popular with horror-film freaks and movie nerds all over the world. One of the great things about Instagram is that you get the version of someone's life that they themselves have curated.

While we're on the subject, we live in incredible times right now. When I was a kid, I used to have to really beat the streets to find out how to get my hands on what I needed, be it a punk-rock record, an old foreign film, or whatever. Now it's all at our fingertips. If I want to watch Clarence White play a B-Bender Fender Telecaster with Lester Flatt and the Byrds on Bob Dylan's song "You Ain't Goin' Nowhere" live in somebody's backyard, I just jump on YouTube and type in "Clarence White and Lester Flatt." I would've killed to have access to all of this when I was a kid. But looking back, there was something romantic about ordering a new record by the Damned out of the back of *Maximumrocknroll* magazine because our local record stores wouldn't carry it. So yeah, to circle back, the pictures Sid Haig put up on his Instagram probably blew all of his old fans' minds who remember the limited access of the pre-iPhone years.

Corey Feldman was a whole other ball of wax. Corey showed up with dyed bright-orange hair in a faux-hawk cut. I had to tell him we had to dye his hair normal for the film, which didn't go over very well. But after we got through that tiny misstep, things went fairly smooth with Corey. He did disappear for a few hours in the middle of the day and was supposedly driving a friend's Italian sports car through the back roads of the Sam Houston National Forest, which weaves through that area of East Texas. The producers freaked out about that (but then again producers freak out about everything), but I thought it was punk rock as hell and loved the guy for it. Corey had a reputation for being a total wild man, but me being a musician and used to dealing with subversive creative types, I actually thought this grown-up child actor, who had survived being friends with Michael Jackson during his *Thriller* heyday, been shot out of a cannon into stardom, chewed up and then spit out again by Hollywood, and had also lived through the overdose of his good friend Corey Haim, well, I thought Corey Feldman was cooler than a motherfucker.

That's the thing about the public that bums me out when they trash-talk whoever the star of the day is during their water-cooler conversation or at the bar for a cheap laugh. Again, I'll revert back to my theory that if you have a big vision for your future and want to take risks, unless you come from a lot of money or your parents were already famous (which by the way, comes with its own problems), we all face similar challenges of moving beyond our limitations. So maybe you don't have a big plan? Maybe you just fall into a pretty safe existence of going four years to college, starting your career, buying a house, getting married, and having some kids. That's great! You'll get no blowback and nothing but support from me on that. But if your dream is to be an actor and you leave Bumfuck, Indiana, or Small Town, Arkansas, and get into your little banged-up twenty-year-old Toyota, drive a million miles to New York City, rent a dirt-cheap apartment in a sketchy hood, get a job waiting tables and do about 253 auditions for the next two years, only eight of which are callbacks, and only one of which is a real acting job, maybe on a TV show if you're lucky, but most likely on a Crest toothpaste commercial, well, to me you deserve an extra set of wings to get into heaven. The risk of doing that is astronomical and the odds of doing that and making it work are next to zilch/zero/nada.

So the next time you call someone "washed up" or a "hack" or "too old," just remember, you're probably calling them that from a pretty safe situation, where, sure, there might've been a lot of hard work, but let's be honest, very little risk involved. Not to mention, anyone can come back at any time with the right part, the right song, the right show, the right vehicle to do it with. Ya never know, so never count anyone out. I've seen music and film businesspeople do this over and over where they say, "Aw, so and so is washed up," and these same business folks end up with egg all over their face for talking shit when the artist bounces back. John Travolta was making fuckin' baby-talking movies before *Pulp Fiction*, so yeah, these careers go up and down and up and down and sideways and all over the place.

Anyway, Corey nailed his scenes with ease. The guy had literally grown up on movie sets, so there was a lot to learn from watching him work. He did some real subtle things in his performance that we didn't pick up on until we got in the editing room. The camera loved Corey, and he knew how to work it for everything it was worth. This is the trait of a solid film actor, not so much a stage actor, but someone who grew up in front of a camera like Corey did in films like *Stand by Me*, *The Goonies*, and *The Lost Boys*. These films are why I fought the producers to cast him even after they told me he was "washed up."

I later learned that the reason why I was able to get these three actors, who would help us sell the film with their pictures on the movie poster, was that they all wanted to act together. Pure luck? Probably. But at this point I stopped second-guessing and asking myself, "How did I get here?" At some point you have to realize that an artist just wants to do good work, get paid, and go home, which was where my head was at as well. There was no time for preshow jitters or indecisive nervousness. To quote that Waylon Jennings sticker on his road case, "This ain't no dress rehearsal. We are professionals and this is the big time!"

I got to bed that night after my first day on the set at four a.m. and had to be back at six, but I didn't care. There was literally no time for any of that "Be careful what you wish for" reflective-thinking bullshit. This was one of a thousand situations that would help me to adopt my mantra: "Embrace the Struggle, Son!" I didn't really have any time to worry about things going wrong. In the music business things are more laid-back, and face it, when you're on tour you're only playing for a mere two hours—sometimes more, but usually not much. Directing a film was so much plate spinning and juggling, I was always so afraid I was forgetting something on my never-ending shot list that I wasn't listening to the Shitty Committee in my head trying to tell me, *You're not good enough to be here!*

One thing I learned about all this film-versus-music stuff is this: when people say "musicians always want to be actors, and actors always want to be musicians," well, let me tell ya firsthand, it's a hell of a lot cooler being a musician than it is being an actor. No offense to my thespian buddies, but it doesn't matter if you're Robert De Niro or George Clooney, you're still waiting around in a fuckin' trailer all day, on a set in the middle of God-knows-where, to do a scene that usually lasts only a few minutes, and you have absolutely zero control over it because it's a director's medium and the director is going to film you, light you, and edit your part the way they see fit. Not exactly instant gratification, right?

Meanwhile, musicians go onstage to be greeted by a whole room full of people, could be 20,000, could be 200, and they have paid money to see a performance and they clap, scream, and whistle, and it's straight-up instant gratification. If this weren't true, Johnny Depp, who is arguably one of the biggest movie stars on the planet, wouldn't be on tour nonstop for the last three years playing guitar with Alice Cooper and Joe Perry.

I didn't enjoy directing that much, as it turns out. It was the grind of all grinds to me. It's much easier as an actor: show up and do your thing, get paid, and go home. I actually like screen acting and have been in several films. Directing was a two-year babysitting project that involves lots of businesspeople who, frankly, just don't have a cool bone in their bodies. The difference between the music business and the movie business is that in the music business they'll just stab you in the back and you kind of expect them to. Hell, you might even do business with them again one day, who knows? But in the movie business, some of the producers, agents, and distributors will stab you right in the *face* and you won't even see it coming and then they'll completely disappear from your life forever. Now, this is not the case in every situation, and some of these music and film businesspeople become lifelong collaborators and friends.

I've written about five scripts so far. One was licensed but never made, and one was made into a film. I still love movies and watch them almost every single night of my life. As much of a grind as it was doing *Zombex*, I'm grateful I got to work with that cast and grateful I was able to write and direct that film. It's on Amazon Prime, where most B movies go to die, but *Zombex* turned into one of those cult films that folks either just love or love to hate. At least they're talking, right?

I think the worst thing would be if people didn't care enough to say anything. My recordings and my shows usually get the same response. I've been doing this radio show on a new station called Gimme Country. We've done dozens of episodes, and I've had all kinds of special interview guests on the show, like Raul Malo from the Mavericks, Kinky Friedman, Lew Temple, John Doe from X, Kathy Valentine from the Go-Go's, Rhett Miller from the Old 97's, Ray Wylie Hubbard, Billy Gibbons from ZZ Top . . . the list goes on and on. The reason I bring my radio show up is I've found it's good to have opinions, to stand for something, to bring an editorial narrative to the party. Even though it's a radio music show that plays all kinds of music (not just country), I approach it like a podcast and spend ten to twelve minutes talking about what's happening in my life, what's happening in the world with films, politics, music, popular culture, you name it. Sometimes, it riles people up and sometimes people love it. Either way, it's OK. We don't all have to agree on everything. We don't all have to demonize one another when we don't agree on things. That's why you hire certain actors like Malcolm, Corey, and Sid. They're going to give you their specific take and tone on what you give them. They're going to bring something to the table that is innately something only they could bring, like it or not. This is one of the reasons why art has become so watered down. The art of giving zero fucks has been traded in for the non-art of being accessible to everyone. Good news is, audiences, mainly through technology like iPhones and computers, have become a lot more sophisticated and they can see through the corporations who are trying desperately to stamp out individualism and opinions in order to appeal to the greatest number of people. In fact, I think audiences are dying to see actors like Malcolm McDowell live and breathe in those impossible-to-pin-down characters he portrayed in *Caligula* or *A Clockwork Orange*. And sometimes, rarely, the subversive hand of art and the conservative hand of commerce actually shake and make a little money together. That's not so bad, right? It's called risk, and Malcolm McDowell has been taking risks his entire career.

One last thing. When Sig Haig arrived on set, Malcolm had just finished doing a couple scenes and greeted him with a warm embrace and said, "You're going to enjoy it, Sid." Seeing these two old actors I grew up watching, both of whom have been to hell and back in terms of their careers, shaking and hugging and saying "you're going to enjoy it" meant more to me than anything. Creating an environment for artists to play in is the greatest thing you can do. Looking back, my parents did it for me, and that's how I ended up where I'm at. Going into my room as a little kid and drawing for hours and having my folks just leave me the hell alone until it was suppertime, well, that's pretty much the same damn thing I'm doing now. In fact, this chapter's over because I'm being summoned for supper right now. Onward, amigos.

SET BREAK: ALEX CHILTON'S COUCH

When I was nineteen I made a trek to Memphis with my little trio to play one show for $100. There were no shows booked on the way there or on the way back, and the $100 would pay for gas, which was about $0.97 a gallon at the time. We had no manager, no agent, no record deal, and only forty copies left of a five-song cassette to sell. The gig was a Saturday night opening first of three on a bill at the Antenna Club with Panther Burns and Wanda Jackson. I would've done it for free.

Like for most of the gigs back then, we drove ten hours straight from Texas to Memphis, loaded in like amateurs in front of the crowd, who were not there to see us, and played forty-five minutes of obscure rockabilly B-side cover songs by Johnny Carroll, Warren Smith, Joe Clay, and Glen Glenn. As usual back then, people liked it but they weren't there to see us. But also as usual, there were cool girls at our merch booth who kept us alive, buying our tapes, giving us a place to crash, feeding us, and so on. My rhythm section disappeared with the girls and left me another illegible phone number to call later. Like clockwork. Poof. Gone. Tav Falco, leader of Panther Burns, was incredibly bizarre, but he liked me and said I could drink his beer. Wanda Jackson showed up two minutes before she played and kissed me on the cheek. I thought I'd died and gone to Memphis, because I had.

This cool guitar-player guy who was playing with Panther Burns that night asked me where I was staying. I said, "I think we're crashing on this chick's floor." He said, "You can come stay at my pad. I've got a big wrap-around couch." I had no idea it was Alex Chilton. I had never even heard of Big Star. But the next morning he brought me a cup of coffee and a cigarette while doing an exaggerated rockabilly impression of me singing the song "One Cup of Coffee and a Cigarette" (look it up, it's by Glen Glenn and it's cool), and he mentioned something about his song "The Letter" to someone on the phone calling from NYC. He was cool to me without caring too much. He was animated and talked about how he "couldn't quit Memphis" but really wanted to because he was "tired of going back and forth from NYC." I never saw Alex again after that. But he had that hobo code that most of us musician types have, which is we look out for the ones we like. Well, some of us do. Alex did that night. Some of us are miserable self-serving bastards. But Alex must've seen something in me, and I think he was surprised that I was talking about other music—punk, soul, country—than what he heard me playing. Wish I would've known who he was then.

PUNK FROM THE COUNTRY: ON TOUR WITH MIKE NESS

Most of the punk bands from 1977 and 1978 have either hung it up or they're playing throwback package shows with similar bands to help fill up seats at medium-size venues. That's not a dig. I actually still go see these bands. If I'm a fan I would see them wherever and however they present themselves. My first punk show was the Ramones at the Lamar University Student Hall outside of Beaumont, with Jason and the Scorchers opening up, and not only were not that many people there, the rednecks in the crowd who did show up, I guess because there was nothing else to do, absolutely hated it. But my point is that most of these acts are just no longer around. Social Distortion, who started in Fullerton, California, in 1978 are bigger now than they've ever been. They sell out big venues multiple nights in the same town, months in advance, and don't rely on any massive hit songs from national radio to sell those tickets. It's a lot of word of mouth and talk on the street through the lifestyle brand Mike Ness unintentionally created. Their iconic skeleton logo can be seen on shirts just as much as the DK logo from Dead Kennedys or the Ramones circle logo or the Misfits skull logo. Becoming successful by word of mouth, whether in 1978 or now, is still about as punk rock as it gets, and this success has allowed Social Distortion front man Mike Ness to live out his own version of the '40s/'50s punk/rockabilly/country dream that's full of the best vintage hot rods, guitars, motorcycles, clothes, furniture, you name it.

I did two lengthy tours opening for him, and being on tour with Mike Ness was like being on tour with one of the characters Marlon Brando portrayed in his films. The black-leather-jacket-wearing, tough, quiet motorcycle guy Johnny from *The Wild One* was the one I saw the most. The Irish boxer, Terry, from *On the Waterfront,* who was always working on rebuilding himself and staying out of the streets, was another one. At this point when we toured together, Ness had been walking the walk and living clean and sober for years after his insane past life of much-documented alcohol abuse, drug overdoses, and run-ins with the police. During our days on tour, before the evening concerts, the Ness I saw was working out, doing heavy bag work at boxing gyms and staying fit. Every once in a while he'd pop his head in and discuss some daily events from the news. "Those fuckin' asshole politicians don't care about the working class!" he'd say. He's right, most politicians don't care about the working class, and Ness would probably be wrenching on cars as a mechanic at some shop or gas station like his working-class fan base does if he wasn't a rock star. If you were lucky and Ness was in the mood to actually hang out and tell stories (which was very rare), you got Brando's Don Corleone, where he would tell tales about the early days of Social Distortion and how they were more like a street gang defending their punk politics against the injustices of racist skinheads and how he and the original Social Distortion guitar player, Dennis Danell, were punk rock when it was still called "hey faggot!" (By the way, I'm a thousand percent pro gay rights, but this is what these idiots used to call anyone who looked different.)

Listen, whether you're a fan of Social D's or not (and trust me when I say this, Mike Ness gives zero fucks if you are not a fan), I'm not even slightly painting a rosy picture here. I'm sure there are some haters out there reading this who think I've been corrupted or compromised by Ness's charm, but they've never been on tour with him. No musician I've met lives their truth as hard and as rigorous as Ness, and I'm not fuckin' throwing in hyperbole to make this pop on the page. Here's why.

In 1998, I'm hanging out with the love of my life and future business manager Emily Kaye in Laguna Beach, California. A song by a not-yet-famous band called Sublime, "Santeria," is starting to get on the radio there in Orange County (where the band is from), and the DJs are playing it like every third song and the local punks and skaters are already starting to turn away from the song because of its commercial success. Weird how that happens, huh? The beaches are full of local surfers of all ages, and the weather, considering where I'm from where the humidity is so thick you could cut it with a knife 'cause it's so hot and rainy, well, Laguna Beach weather is absolutely postcard perfect. So Emily is working as an A&R person signing bands at Time Bomb Records, which is run by her boss and Social Distortion manager Jim Guerinot. My band at the time was the Road Kings. You may remember from earlier chapters that we were a highly dysfunctional three-piece rockabilly band with a strong punk influence and a high-energy, take-no-prisoners-style stage show. Our managers were Dave Kaplan and Niels Schroeter, who also managed Brian Setzer. (Let me just say that I still work with Niels today, not as a manager, but in lots of different capacities, and he is a big reason why I have the career I do have today.) Our managers got the Road Kings a great time slot at the Hootenanny Festival in Orange County, and we absolutely crushed it. This is where we met Mike Ness for the first time and saw the West Coast phenomenon known as Social Distortion fans, who might be the most loyal fans of any act I've witnessed outside of the Dead, Willie Nelson, and Bruce Springsteen. But loyal in a different way from, say, Deadheads or Jimmy Buffett's Parrotheads (hey don't laugh, those two acts had the biggest-grossing tours for decades). Seeing Social D outside of California is not the same as seeing them on their home turf. Social D could play every night for a whole month (that's thirty shows in a row, folks) if they wanted to at the old House of Blues on the Sunset Strip and sell out every single show in advance in record time. That's how hungry their old-school California base is.

So that day at the Hootenanny Festival, which also featured Reverend Horton Heat, Little Richard, and Supersuckers, we got to say hello to Mike Ness, who had evidently seen some of our show. "Nice show, gentlemen!" Ness said as he was shaking our hands when we came offstage. We had all listened to *Mommy's Little Monster* a thousand times, and my girl Emily had the bright idea of rereleasing remastered versions of all the early Social Distortion records on CD and vinyl on Time Bomb, which gave the label a big shot in the arm with quick sales and cash infusion. I had heard through the Time Bomb Records grapevine that Ness had been working on writing songs for a solo country record that he was keeping quiet about until its release. My first solo country record, *Raisin' Cain*, had already come out in 1995, and there was a strange sea change happening at that point in American music, with country and punk genres finally starting to shake hands. And I do mean the genres, not the fans of the genres, who were completely against one another, so yeah, it was a weird time to say the least. This was before Hank Williams III or Mike Ness had done national country tours, and I had been out playing in front of punk-rock audiences with a pedal-steel guitar and fiddle behind me and they just had no idea what to think about it. In fact, later when I played with the L.A. punk band X, filling in for Billy Zoom, Dwight Yoakam told me that he had only done shows around L.A. opening for X, not touring nationally with them. He had toured with the Blasters, who definitely had punk energy but were not a punk band. They were an American roots-rockabilly based band (and probably the best in the world, song-wise). Playing hardcore honky-tonk in front of punk audiences on national tours was a brand-new thing in the '90s. All you could hope for was that a few die-hard people in the crowd who had one of those Johnny Cash shirts that featured Jim Marshall's iconic image where he's shooting the finger would raise enough hell to inspire the other punks to get into it. Sure, X had been singing some country-style duets as far back as 1978, and Social D had been covering "Ring of Fire" in '79, but these were punk versions of those songs. When I went out opening for the Supersuckers, X, and Social D playing real outlaw country music, the audience just stood there stunned for the first few songs, then started getting into it, eventually loving it by the end of our show. Anyway, after my first solo record started getting international attention, I was getting offers to work with other producers, and the owner of my label wanted to produce the follow-up record, which was a big conflict of interest for me. Three different highly respected producers had told me they thought we could make a great record together, and I wanted to try something different, but the label wouldn't budge. So I ended up in a lawsuit with the label I was on. My friend Danny Bland actually helped me navigate my way through all of this emotionally, so I didn't get too depressed about the fact that I was losing career momentum by getting held up in a lawsuit. I was young and just wanted out of the deal, but it wasn't that easy. So the Road Kings got offered another record deal through Hollywood Records and my rock-star lawyer in L.A., Peter Paterno, said, "There's no clause saying you can't go make a record with your old band, so while you're tied up, why not go have fun with your old buddies?"

Typical insanity ensued. We were so fucked-up all the time, either missing or barely making it to shows, getting busted for everything and anything by the cops, fighting with one another constantly . . . just total dysfunction while simultaneously having the world handed to our punk asses on a silver platter. I look back on it and laugh, but sometimes, well, it bums me out. We were like brothers, and if we could've been just a country hair more mature, there's no telling what would've happened with that band. Wait, you've heard this story before, right? Insert young, talented, immature rock 'n' roll band! What got us that far, besides the songs I was writing, was that upright-bass player Jason Burns (who looked like he could be my brother) and I were 100 percent nuclear onstage together. So, we made a record in L.A. that we didn't like with a producer who was dying to please our manager and a record label who wanted to get us on KROQ radio. We, on the other hand, didn't give a shit about radio. We wanted to make a cool record. That's it. So somehow or another Ness heard the record and invited us to open up for him on a six-week national tour. It was a big deal for us.

First night of the tour me and my bass player Jason were at each other's throats during sound check over what songs were going in the set list. He and I were yelling over the microphones. Jason: "These songs suck, where's the fast stuff?" Me: "I'm the one who has to sing this shit, and I'm tired of trying to spit the lyrics out 'cause we're playing everything too fast." The whole time we never noticed that Mike Ness was watching us through his dressing-room window howling with laughter at us. So embarrassing.

But we weren't just fighting each other on this tour; we ended up getting into brawls with way bigger knuckleheads than us after the shows. At a bar after our show in St. Louis, it got very ugly. We walked into this small punk-rock bar and immediately started getting shit from some skinheads, and these weren't the amazing Oi skinheads who were born out of the Jamaican/British scene that love ska music and wear cool clothes, they were the idiot, racist skinheads. Before I go any further, let the record show that Mike Ness has been plagued by racist skinheads since he first started out back in the late '70s and told the audience that there's "no place in punk rock for Nazis!" I mean, till this day he has those nationalist skinheads buying tickets to his shows just to go there and fuck with him while he's onstage. What kind of dipshit pays to go to a show, gets wasted, and proceeds to heckle and even try to physically assault the singer? That's the level of pure stupidity we're talking about. So the long and short of it is, we walked by these skinheads, which was the only way to get close enough to the bartender and order a drink, and one said to me, "Did you have to suck Mike Ness's dick to get that jacket?" Earlier that night backstage, Mike Ness had personally given me one of the official tour jackets. (I still have it!) So Jason immediately charged toward the guy and said, "Fuck off before you get beat up!"

Now, this is what a small handful of musicians and friends from Louisiana to Houston and all the way to Austin know as a "Jason Situation." Jason Burns was crazy. He would fight anyone. I've seen him get destroyed by huge drunk assholes, covered in blood, but never stop fighting. I've also seen him beat the shit out of people. Lots of crazy pent-up anger in Jason. So even though the guy was talking to me, I'm saying to myself, *JD, you don't want to get in a fight while you're on tour with Mike Ness,* so I broke up the semi beef that was about to start and got Jason to the other side of the bar. I ordered us drinks—always a shot of whiskey and a beer, always. We toasted and threw the shots back and I saw this evil look in Jason's eye. I looked across the bar, and this one skinhead was shooting the rod with both hands and his fingers out at us. Jason slammed the whiskey down and took his empty shot glass, threw it, and beaned the guy right in the forehead from across the bar. And it was like the whole bar saw only what Jason did, nothing that happened leading up to it. I'm not exaggerating when I say the entire bar beat me and Jason up. There was this colossal number of people just shoving us out the front door and into the middle of the street. We took a brutal ass whipping from about six or seven big bruisers who had us on the ground in the middle of the street and they were just punching and kicking us mercilessly. By then we're just doodle-bugging, trying to roll up into a ball and protect ourselves because we were being kicked in the sides, in the head, and in the legs from every direction. Blood was everywhere. I could feel it gushing out of my mouth and my nose and there was a pool of it right under my face. Thankfully, two of Social Distortion's roadies showed up (who were class-A dirtbag punk-rock badasses), pushed them all back and got us into a friend's standard white touring van. We could hear the police sirens arriving before the van drove us away. In fact, while we were lying down in the back of the van with broken bones and bloody faces, we passed three siren-blasting, light-flashing cop cars arriving on the scene and looking for us. We found out later Ness's other road crew guy stayed behind and told the cops we were in a red four-door Toyota Camry.

The next day we both had broken ribs, black eyes, busted lips, and broken noses with big bruises. I'd like to romanticize it and say we looked like every old prizefighter who stays in the game too long, but we really looked like a couple of young idiots who got the living shit beat out of them 'cause that's what we were. We were trying not to laugh about it 'cause our ribs were broken and it hurt to even take a deep breath. We were nervous about what Mike Ness was gonna say too. Causing drama on any tour is never cool, and now that I'm older I stay as far away from that bullshit as humanly possible.

The next show I think Mike knew that we had been avoiding him, so finally he came up to us after his sound check and said, "I heard ya did a little bobbin' and weavin' last night boys?" We couldn't even look him in the eye. Then he said, "I wish I would've been there, I would've helped you beat the fuck out of those guys!" Sure, this is some macho knuckle-dragging BS for those of you who may never have gotten your ass severely kicked in a real street fight, but at that moment, when we thought we might get reprimanded or even kicked off the tour, Mike Ness treated us like heroes for taking our lumps and still making it to the next town on time.

For the next two weeks it hurt to sing because my ribs, and Jason's too, were broken. I wrapped my ribs up every night and drank a bunch of whiskey to try to blunt the pain during the shows when I was singing, but it didn't really help. After that we kept our shit together. We stopped going out after the shows and neither of us partied backstage. We just went to friends' houses or drank at the hotel bar. By the way, if you've ever wanted to throw a television set out of your hotel window like Keith Moon from the Who used to, don't. All hotels charge you twice, sometimes three times, as much as the retail price for the busted TV, because they know they can call the police and get you on damaged property charges, so you'll pay whatever. Plus it wouldn't be near as much fun watching them explode on the ground these days with these skinny flat-screen TVs.

Years later Ness would ask me to do an entire national tour, opening for him with my solo country band. Compared to the nonstop drama of the Road Kings, my solo country band was considerably more laid-back after the shows, but there was one thing that happened that will live in infamy in Texas. We had just played the Dallas House of Blues and we were on our way to play in Houston when my old MCI tour bus got pulled over by the Texas Highway Patrol. We were in Centerville, which is pretty much just a barbecue pit of a tiny town off Interstate 45. In fact, they have a BBQ joint there called Country Cousins that's awesome, but the name says everything about the little speed-trap town. The cop was your classic redneck cliché highway patrol officer. Ya know, that kind of thing where his daddy probably whipped his ass too much growing up and berated him for being a shitty wide receiver on the high school football team. The guy was just a simple-minded, angry country hick with a gun. "Who owns this bus?" the state trooper asked. I said, "I do, sir." He said, "Something's off about your plates and I want everyone out of the bus!" We were all standing on the side of the highway as semis and vacationing families passed by, staring at us. He got on the bus without even asking us permission and grabbed my backpack and said, "Who owns this backpack?" Again I said, "I do." He walked over to me and showed me two joints he'd found in my bag, and I noticed there was a little piece of paper that the joints were rolled up in and a note that said, "Here's a couple for the road!" Someone had obviously stuck a couple of joints in my backpack as a surprise and didn't tell me. I told the state trooper, "There's no way in hell I would've not flushed those two joints down the toilet before you got on my bus had I known they were in there, just look at the note!" He dropped my backpack at the entrance to the bus, turned me around, put handcuffs on me, and said, "Son, you're not gonna make your concert performance tonight because you're going to jail!" Once I realized this asshole was actually going to take me to jail, impound my bus, and leave my band stranded on the side of the highway, I threw my phone to our drummer and told him to call the guy in my phone under "EMERGENCY LAWYER!" and tell him what happened and that I need him to get me out of jail! The state trooper immediately responded by saying, "Boy, there's no way you'll get out of jail until tomorrow afternoon." Now, I can't tell you which lawyer I called. It just wouldn't be cool for me to name him in this book. But he's a big-time lawyer in Houston who, thankfully, loves me and my music.

On the way to jail, this dickhead state trooper and I really got into it. He kept egging me on, saying, "Do you get busted for drugs and not show up to your performances all the time, son?" I said, "Actually no, you're the first asshole who's ever done this to me" (which was true, I'd never been arrested while on tour). So before the state trooper handed me over to the processing office, before I put the orange jumpsuit and the flip-flops on, just when the state trooper was taking my handcuffs off, I tell him, "I'll bet you your badge I'll be out of your jail today." He laughed and said, "I don't bet my badge with potheads, boy."

About four hours later, these three Mexican guys I'm in the jail cell with all got up and went to the cell door window to watch this little old cowboy man walk by. He had a big cowboy hat on and muddy cowboy boots with his jeans stuck in them and a big suit coat on. The Mexican guys turned around to me and said, "Who are you, homeboy?" I said, "Why?" One of the Mexican guys said, "The judge just walked in, and he's not letting us out until Monday morning, so he must be letting you out. He doesn't come in on Saturdays. He works on his ranch on Saturdays." The jailer came over and pulled me out of the cell. The state trooper walked over in front of the judge, and he was so angry it looked like his red face was about to blow off of his neck. "Mr. Dayton, apparently there's a very important lawyer in the city of Houston who called in a big enough favor to get me off my ranch and up here to let you out of jail." He slammed a little gavel down and said, "Twelve hundred dollars, and you can get your bus on Monday. I've got things to do!" Even though we'd have to borrow equipment for the next two nights, and get friends to drive us the rest of the way to the show in Houston, I said, "Thank you, Judge." And just to rub salt in that asshole cop's wound, I said to the judge, "I told your arresting officer that you, sir, would probably let me out today, but that I would always check my bags before driving through Centerville again." I could feel the rage of hate-filled energy coming off that state trooper as he stood there next to me. I looked at him and smiled and walked past him and out the front doors.

We made it to the show that night by, like, ten minutes, and we had some friends help us throw our gear onstage. And with no sound check, we just started playing. After the first song I told the crowd the story and that I had just got released from jail on marijuana charges, and of course they went crazy. This eventually made the Texas news, which was good and bad. This was before the internet, and all it said was "Singer Jesse Dayton Arrested for Drugs." So immediately everyone thought it was heroin or cocaine, not just two joints. I told Ness what happened before our show started that night, and he went out onstage and berated the state of Texas for putting me in jail for something as stupid as two joints, which would've only been a small fine in California.

Let me also say, even though this incident gained me some street cred, I was pretty embarrassed by the whole thing. I had this great new bass player named Kevin Smith on tour with me, and I felt like I had dragged him into a bunch of unnecessary drama, and I had. Kevin left right after this tour to join Dwight Yoakam's band and is the guy who replaced Bee Spears (RIP) in Willie Nelson's band and still plays with Willie. It's all water under the bridge now, but just for the record, Kevin is one of the best of the best bass players in the world and even though he laughs about it now, I still feel a little bad that he and the band and the crew had to see me get busted and wait around for me to get out of jail.

Anyway, I'll always be indebted to all the fans I made while touring with Mike Ness and Social Distortion. His guitar player, Jonny Two Bags, and bass player, Brent Harding, have also become friends of mine over the years. I still have rockabilly friends who show up to my shows outside of Texas and ask me, "Who are all these people?" Playing country music in front of punk-rock audiences, while it was not by my own design, turned out to give me a bigger and more loyal following than I could ever have had by just sticking to my scene. Or at least it gave me more than the sixty or seventy retro butterheads in every town whom I love, but let's face it, it's damn near impossible to make a living with that tiny of a following. More punk-rock shows would be in my future, when no other mainstream acts would take us on tour. But eventually we started playing with everyone from Americana to Southern rock to country to rockabilly to blues to pop, and even big heavy bands.

You name it and we could somehow win them over. Well, most of the time. But the thing that helps me sleep at night is embracing the idea that I'm not for everybody. It's OK if some people aren't into what I do. I definitely don't lose sleep over it. With the rise of social media, I think it's pretty apparent that we'd all be a hell of a lot better off admitting that there's no enjoyment in trying to impress people you don't even like. On the flip side of that, nothing makes me happier than when a new fan comes up to me and says, "You know, I don't really listen to this kind of music, but I love what you do." That makes me feel like a million bucks.

I learned early that going out with bands like the Supersuckers and X and Social Distortion, then taking my acoustic guitar and being able to go out by myself and play listening rooms was my ticket to cherry-picking fans from all genres. My longtime booking agent, Todd "Aggie" Gardner, and I have been doing this nonstop for years, and because of it we have a pretty eclectic fan base. Most musical touring acts are pretty easy to label. I'm not. I know that if I just stuck to one specific genre, like straight country music, I'd probably have a bigger audience, but that just sounds so boring. Maybe it's because I'm a Beaumonster and grew up listening to a whole gumbo of different musical styles? Maybe it's because I'm a Gemini and I get bored quickly after I've successfully done something or have done all 10,000 hours of homework and there's nothing left to find out? Maybe all of it. Happiness seems to get put on the back burner with folks who are grinding their way toward success. Hey, I get it, and I'll be the first to admit it can't always be all fun and games.

In 2020, the entire working world had the proverbial rug pulled out from under their businesses; it's forced me to reevaluate what I've been doing with my life. Have I been using work and my career as a way to escape my life? Sometimes. Have I put too much emphasis on chasing dollars instead of just living and trying to experience new things? Probably.

Last night I was with two of my good friends, Sean and Nick. It's the first time that I've seen people in months because of the isolating we've all had to do in order to not get sick with Covid-19. Sean had been isolated with his two young kids, so I trusted him. And Nick just had a Coronavirus test a few days earlier that came back negative. So Sean made this amazing dinner for us and we were sitting out on the back deck, the stars were out, there was some vino flowing, and we were eating this high-culinary-style dinner, with Nick Lowe playing on low volume in the background. Sean said to us, "We'd better enjoy this, 'cause it ain't gonna get any better than this." And he was right.

So now when I think about all the work that went into the tours I used to do, like the ones I'm so grateful to have done with Mike Ness, I think about them differently. I think, Yep, that was important to me, but not as important to me as some things. It's called checking yourself. I try to do it as much as possible. And by the way, Mike Ness is a master at checking himself on what's truly important. I learned a lot about it while watching him work, seeing how he ate and took care of himself and his family. It should be noted that Mike is very open about his long-term recovery and has inspired countless people to live the clean and sober life. Words are overrated. Action, that's where it's at.

BEYOND AND BACK
WITH JOHN DOE, PUNK
QUEEN EXENE, AND X

As I mentioned earlier, during the Rob Zombie *Hellbilly Deluxe 2* tour I was writing three or four pages a day of the apocalyptic zombie horror film script called *Zombex,* which was set in NOLA and had a post–Katrina/Big Pharma political component to it. When it was done I handed the script off to some people I had met or worked with, and it made the rounds of producers, agents, managers, and actors. As usual, I had zero expectations after decades of hearing the word "no," so I was stunned when my meager attempt at a campy B-movie script got picked up by a small production company who gave me the green light to make the film. Yet another situation where the Shitty Committee in my head was saying *When they find out you're just a hillbilly from Beaumont, it'll* *all be over!* This is how I met John Doe from the legendary punk band X.

I had written this character into the script named Seamus O'Connor, who was a burlesque club owner in the French Quarter in New Orleans. Initially, I wrote the part for Mike Ness, but it turned out that Mike was going to be on tour while we were filming. But Mike got word back to me that I "should get a real actor like John Doe who knows what he's doing." Hmmm, who do I know who knows John Doe? I wondered. My friend Nick Tangborn was good friends with John, so I called Nick and said, "Hey brother, think John Doe would be interested in being in my zombie movie?" Now, Nick Tangborn is a film geek on a whole other level. Nick's seen every obscure horror/sci-fi/western/B-movie/foreign film on the planet and can tell you everything from the script notes to the budget to casting to production to what they did in post and why the film flopped or was a cash cow. I'm a huge film buff myself (I've watched on average three to five films a week since video stores were invented), and I have several friends in the Austin film scene, like director Alex Johnson and even the great Mike Judge, who are way bigger film geeks than I'll ever be. By the way, this is something I do from time to time in my life: spend lots of time with expert nerds who live, eat, drink, and sleep their passions, whether it be guitars, films, different genres of records, songwriters, motorcycles, baseball, food, you name it. OK, back to first meeting Doe. So Nick said, "I don't know. But I'll call Doe and give him your number." It was like a cartoon how fast the phone rang again after I hung up. Guy on the other end said, "Hey this is John Doe. I'll do your film under one condition: That our friend Nick Tangborn can be a zombie in the film and get killed on camera. He has to make final edit." Bam! Done! And that's how I met John Doe.

Sure, I had an old copy of the classic punk record *Los Angeles* by his band X, but I had been out of touch with that music for a while. Yep, I had seen X in the '80s in Houston and I thought they were great. But did I think that Doe and I would meet making a zombie movie? Hell no.

So the long and short of it is, John Doe came in and nailed all his lines and was in and out in no time. The guy was a pro on set. Didn't need anything special, said what's written on the page with total conviction, just no bullshit whatsoever. John Doe had been in a lot of films that I loved like *Road House*, *Great Balls of Fire!*, *Roadside Prophets*, and *Boogie Nights*, so I knew the guy could play the part even though it was written for a more macho badass type like Mike Ness. Later in the shoot our mutual buddy Nick got to portray a zombie and was fatally gunned down on a boat dock in slow motion. So I got what I needed. Doe got what he needed. And Nick Tangborn ended up in the film too. It was a win-win-win for everybody.

Then, out of nowhere John called me up one day. "Hey, I'm do-ing an acoustic show at SXSW, come play some guitar with me." This is when the real fun started. John got me up onstage at the Hole in the Wall in Austin to play "The Call of the Wreckin' Ball" from the Knitters record, and right after the song started he went over to my amplifier and cranked the volume all the way to eleven! The crowd saw what he did and went buck wild. This was the first time I made music with my new movie pal, John Doe, and it would be just one of many unpredictable stunts John would pull onstage.

Doe and I stayed in touch. But I had been focusing on film stuff because that was what was happening for me. I'd done the Rob Zombie films, acted in a few films playing the white-trash biker from the South (check out Alex Johnson's Texas crime film *Two Step*), and then was writing and directing *Zombex*. I'd been off tour for a while, hadn't made a record in four years, and was just doing the occasional weekend concert here and there or flying to Europe for a festival, but not doing whole tours. I had this weekly show at the most legendary honky-tonk in the world called the Broken Spoke in Austin. Willie Nelson, Ernest Tubb, George Strait, all kinds of people played there regularly at one time or another. We played Thursday nights, and the place was just packed every week. It was a big place, so for a good stretch of time our Thursday had become the biggest weekly residency show in Austin and the place that newer Austin "country" clubs would base their whole business on: cheap Lone Star beer, two-step lessons to teach the tourists how to country dance, and a band that played classic country. These bars would never have the history that the Broken Spoke had, but some of the places like the White Horse, where I used to hang out when I was younger when it was an old-school Mexican Tejano bar, went on to become incredibly successful. Every month when we played at the Spoke it seemed like some star was at our gig, like Vince Vaughn, the Black Crowes, Sean Penn, the Foo Fighters, the late, great Fred Willard, Robert Plant, Robert Duvall, you name it. Condos were built up on each side because of the massive growth that Austin experienced, but the Broken Spoke has been the same inside since 1962, when the king of all Texas dance hall owners, James White, built it with his own two hands. Low ceilings, uneven floors, an old bandstand in the back, a big dance floor with a sign on it that says NO LINE DANCING! People just wanted to experience the place, and my crackerjack band that was playing old-school country shuffles, polkas, waltzes, and every other kind of country song known to man was a perfect fit. After touring, writing, and recording nonstop seemingly forever, it was nice to get off the hamster wheel and work on film projects with actual budgets and then stroll into the Broken Spoke and do a low-pressure country show that made money.

Finally one Thursday John Doe comes in and sits in with my band and brings the house down with a version of Merle Haggard's hit "Silver Wings." After the show, Doe asked me if my band and I wanted to go on tour with him. I was pulling killer money out of the Spoke every Thursday, and it was only one and a half miles from my house, but at this point it was starting to become a *Groundhog Day* grind. I knew I needed to go back on tour, and my agent, Todd "Aggie" Gardner, was wanting me to grow my fan base more. I didn't have anything going on, no record deal, nothing. So of course I said yes. This was the beginning of the end for our days at the Broken Spoke, because we couldn't miss more than two weeks in a row or some other band would take it over. My old manager, Gary Moore, had got me about as far as he could take me, and I'll always be grateful to him. But it was time to change things up and hit the road again.

The tour with John Doe was a blast. John had just released a new solo record and there was some heat around him, so the shows were really great. My band would open, then we'd back John Doe, and the beautiful and talented Cindy Wasserman would come out and sing harmonies with us for the rest of John's set. When we made it to NYC to do the *Late Show with David Letterman*, I remember what a huge deal it was for me meeting Paul Shaffer backstage. I had been a fan of Paul's since I was a kid watching him as a cast member on the early *Saturday Night Live*. Paul is one of those cats who has continually popped up on America's music radar throughout my life, and not just on Letterman. "Oh look, Paul's on TV jamming with the Who" or "Paul's on this awards show backing up Aretha Franklin" or "Oh wow, Paul's on another show backing B.B. King" or "Oh man, Paul and Bill Murray are doing the lounge-singer/piano-player bit!"

So my bass player, Chris Rhoades, and I ended up in an elevator with Paul Shaffer and Paul said in that great little voice of his, "So you guys are from Austin, Texas, huh? Do you know Ray Benson from Asleep at the Wheel?" I immediately said, "Uncle Ray? He's our man!" Now, for anybody who's ever been around the Austin music scene, they know that Ray Benson is as much of a pot smoker as Willie Nelson himself, maybe more. And I had heard that the reason Paul Shaffer wore sunglasses every night on *Letterman* had nothing to do with the bright lights, if you get my drift. So I thought for sure we might be able to burn one with Paul. Unfortunately it didn't happen. But if another musician brings up Ray Benson to you, there's a high probability that the next thing to happen is they will pull out a joint. It's a way for them to find out if you're cool or not. Paul couldn't have been more charming and cool, though, and he watched us rehearse and play our song. When I think about all the old, jaded TV guys who have seen everyone under the sun come and go, and then this guy still sat there and watched our whole performance like a true music fan, it just made me love Paul that much more. By the way, the great Brady Blade was sitting in on drums for us that night and had probably played *Letterman* more than anyone because the guy plays with tons of musicians. So it was great seeing all the local NYC union crew members treating Brady like he was a regular. I mean, come on, admit it, the drummer never gets enough love!

Soon it's showtime and all my friends back in Texas are watching and we go out onstage to do John's song "The Golden State." After we finish, David Letterman commented twice, "What a nice guitar you have" (it was something he said so often to musicians on his show that there are compilation videos of it on YouTube), shook my hand, and exited stage left. I have to admit that even the Shitty Committee was agreeing with me and saying, *Not bad for a Beaumonster.* By the way, the black hollow-body double-cutaway guitar I played on *Letterman* and in the Rob Zombie film *Halloween II* was built by Road Kings bass player Jason Burns. He's now been a luthier for custom guitars and upright basses for years with his company, Blast Cult, and has locations in London, England, and Orange, California. And yep, you can buy a guitar exactly like mine from him online at Blast Cult.

Not long after this, John and the band and I were broken down on the side of the road in the middle of the night outside of New York City with sixteen-wheeler diesel trucks whipping by. While we were waiting to figure out how to get a tow truck on the case,

John Doe, who's standing on the side of the highway as it started misting rain, looked at me with a big grin and said, "Ever hear the story about the two old friends that get back together after not seeing each other for years?" I said I hadn't. Doe said, "The one guy says, 'I'm an accountant. I've been married for twenty-three years and have four kids; how about you?' The other guy says, 'I work for the circus. I stick my forearm up the asses of the elephants and give them an enema, then clean the shit off of me and them and then put them on the train to go to the next town.' The accountant guy, horrified, says, 'Well you must make good money, right?' Circus guy says, 'Not really.' The accountant says, 'You must get weekends and vacation off, right?' Circus guy says flatly, 'Nope.' The accountant says, 'Well then, why don't you find a better job?' Circus guy says, 'What, and leave show business?!'"

No greater joke could've been told on the side of the highway in the middle of the night in a scenario that's been happening to traveling minstrels since the beginning of time. These were just some of the pearls of wisdom that John Doe gave to me along the way. If anything went wrong on the road, like the sound was feeding back onstage or we were running late or the money was short or whatever was going wrong, Doe would remind me, "Hey, we don't have to do this, we *get* to do this!" Sure, I had played with some heavy cats before I met Doe, but we had a different dynamic from touring together so much. All I can say is, you might think you know people really well because you've known them for years, and you might have even lived with them for years, but when you tour with someone day in and day out, seeing how they solve an array of insane problems that are being thrown at them on tour, well, that's when you really know someone. Living with someone in the same house is *Groundhog Day* (why does that movie keep coming up?) compared to the constant bobbing and weaving that is necessary for months of indie touring, changing hotels, cities, food, culture, you name it, night after night.

Not long after that tour was over, I was sitting in my friend Sean O'Connor's backyard when John Doe called and said, "Are you sitting down?" I said, "Why yes, Dr. Doe, I am sitting down." And he said, "Do you wanna play guitar for X on our next tour?" Glad I was sitting down. I ended up filling in for Billy Zoom on a whole American tour with X. It was like running away with the circus. Sitting here writing this right now and looking back on it, none of it seems real. X was the one gig in my life that I may have just chunked my solo career out the window for because the sheer excitement onstage was like no other experience I've ever had. Not that it was ever a possibility for me to really join the band. I was 100 percent temporary because Billy, who was undergoing treatment for cancer, was eventually coming back. But musically, I could hear all the different influences that appealed to me, so the music never got boring.

We had just walked offstage for our very last X show of the tour, and Exene Cervenka is lying down on a plush, long-haired rug backstage. She looked like a little girl to whom someone just said, "OK, the circus is closing, kid, time to go home." But it's the little kid inside of any artist who is the true key to unlock who they really are. The folks who lose touch with that little kid inside of themselves aren't very much fun anymore, are they? All business, no dreams. I can spot the ones who still have it from two hundred yards away. They are the parents at the restaurant who are not only letting their four-year-old turn the salt and pepper shakers into rocket ships, they're making the sounds of the rocket ship while the child looks on, smiling in total amazement. But mostly we see the folks who look like they're just not having much fun. I had so much fun hanging out with Exene, and I'm pretty sure she has about twenty of these little dreamers living inside her, which is why you'll have more fun with her than you will a one-kid dreamer.

I started out this story talkin' bout the Exene who is the sensitive artist, the seeker of all things off the beaten artistic path, but this is not who I met when I first rehearsed with X in a little gymnasium in upstate New York. The Exene I met was worried about her friend/guitarist Billy Zoom, who had just been diagnosed with cancer. The whole band, lead singer/bassist John Doe and original drummer DJ Bonebrake and Exene, were worried about Billy. It was all over their faces, as if to say, *What are we doing here without Billy?* Sure, X had played with a couple of other great guitar players who had jumped in while Billy was going through whatever, including Dave Alvin, who was a legend in his own right. He and his brother Phil were a big influence on me. Dave wrote the song "Fourth of July," which would become an X fan favorite. The great Los Angeles guitar player Tony Gilkyson also joined them, but neither Tony nor Dave joined under these circumstances. Not over a scary cancer diagnosis that could possibly, God forbid, lead to death.

When I jumped in the van with X, you could the cut the air with a knife. I had to convince myself pretty early on that it had nothing to do with whether I was a good enough player or whether I fit in. This was bigger than me and something I couldn't personalize, something I needed to be very sensitive to. After all, this was one of the most important punk bands in history, who had made legendary records while I was still in junior high, embarking on a big tour without their brother, who was an original member and who was back in a California hospital too sick to tour.

Every great band has a strange chemistry among its members, and X is no different. DJ Bonebrake, the great drummer on all those songs on the record *Los Angeles* (and every other X album), helped break the ice with a big smile and said, "Ready to play some punk-rock music?" On the surface DJ looks like the normal one, but he's not normal at all. No one in X is "normal." That's why they're X, and that's how they changed the rock 'n' roll landscape. DJ's mother and father passed away when he was young and still in school, and his older brother helped raise him, so DJ grew up with little to no supervision, doing things like skateboarding from the

Valley into Hollywood and going to rock shows by himself when he was an underage kid. Just for the record, heading out alone into the country in the middle of nowhere, like I did when I was a kid, might have had its own set of horrible things that could go wrong, but hanging out in Hollywood as a unsupervised kid in the '70s was probably a wee bit more dangerous. He's kind of that same kid to this day, because he still takes off after sound check on tour and goes for a two-hour walk in whatever city he's in and explores. No pun intended, but the guy really does march to the beat of his own drummer.

DJ and I talked about the songs in the backseat until the van pulled up to the rehearsal space. We'd been in the van for a couple of hours now, and still no peep out of Exene, sitting in the front. I'm ready to break the ice and start playing. I had about nine days before the tour started to rehearse all of Billy Zoom's weird guitar parts. Luckily, because I was not just a punk-rock guitar player and I had done lots of sessions, I wrote charts for every song and brought them with me to rehearsal. Billy Zoom's guitar parts were definitely strange and required a lot of attention, but by this time I had played with Glen Campbell, and Glen's songs had constant modulation, frequent key changes, and parts within parts of songs that sounded like completely different songs than the song you started out playing. Don't get me wrong, Billy Zoom's lead guitar parts were strange for sure, but I could still see where he was playing Chuck Berry licks in weird keys that would throw the untrained ear way off track.

Billy also did harmony guitar parts over what John Doe was playing on his bass that were really ingenious. It sounded like there were more guitars than just one. He also wrote some super-catchy melody parts that would stick in my head. I walked around for days humming the little hooks that Billy wrote. They were so tiny yet so powerful, and if you didn't play all those small bits, it wouldn't sound right. Billy's playing had lots of subtle details and lots of jazz-oriented double-stop licks, and if you didn't pay attention to all that, you'd sound just like any other power-chord punk rocker doing Chuck Berry licks. It's the little things that are sometimes the most important part of nailing a guitar part.

Just for the record, X's tour manager helped me put out those charts for the first few shows, duct-taping them on the floor by my side of the stage. Punk rockers know that everything can be fixed with duct tape, or as my people call it, "Arkansas Chrome."

Anyway, we were set up to rehearse for the tour in this small dance studio/gym in upstate New York and the place had these huge mirrors covering the walls. I thought, This could not be a worse place for acoustics. I had seen X several times before and Billy was one of the loudest guitar players I had ever heard. I didn't want to give Exene any excuse to tell me to turn down, so I played with my volume at about two and a half. The first song we played was "Los Angeles," and it sounded good. Exene looked at me after with a sly, catlike grin, but definitely not a full smile of acknowledgment. I said to myself, *You're not out of the woods yet, JD. Let's get through a few more songs, ol' son.* Then we played "The New World," "Burning House of Love," and "Soul Kitchen," and Exene looked at me again but this time with a teensy bit bigger of a grin. OK, I wasn't a shoo-in at this point, but the ice was broken. Sure, I had the gig, but I wanted to make sure Exene was happy. That's what it was all about for me. I had played with John Doe before, and DJ had been very cool to me in the van on the way over, so it was Exene who was my big test.

We took a quick break and I went across the street to say hello to my friend Chris Masterson and his wife, Eleanor, who were playing guitar and fiddle with Steve Earle. I figured I would give DJ, Exene, and John a minute to talk about everything without me being there. I knew the whole time I could never fill Billy Zoom's shoes, but it's always been my intent as a guitar player to make the hang as comfortable as possible and to have as much fun as I can during the two hours that we are onstage. You have to give people their space during the other twenty-two hours and let them have time to get used to you. I came back and John, DJ, and Exene were all ready to pack up and split. I said, "Is that all the practice we're having?" Doe said, "Yep, you know the songs, right?" I said, "Well, yeah . . ." Doe said, "Well, then let's go grab some dinner and save our energy for the show tomorrow." We had run through the set, and tightened a few things down, and besides, John Doe had already played with me extensively and knew we didn't need to beat a dead horse. When it comes to being the new person in an established group, the professional can't practice enough, but at some point you gotta just jump in and go for it. I will say the difference between a professional and an amateur is a pro will rehearse something a thousand times and an amateur will be lazy, blow it off, and end up clamming. Clams are musician-speak for bum notes during a show or a recording. I try to not play with these people and instead surround myself with people who don't make clams. Hey, you folks clamming, you know who you are, so stop fucking around and learn all the little shit! So I went back to my hotel room and practiced the living hell out of the songs till I crashed, then woke up and started practicing again. Exene, John, and DJ had played these songs a million times. I was the one who needed to internalize Billy's parts.

That night I played my first show with X to a big crowd at a cool old theater in New York. At one point, Exene stopped a song and told John Doe, "Johnny, that's not the right song!" Doe answered back, "OK, cool!" Then he smiled real big at us and yelled out the next song on the list, which was "Blue Spark" and we went right into it. We finished the last song, the crowd was going nuts, all standing up, and as soon as we walked off, Exene said, "What do you like to do when you get offstage?" This was the first time she'd really asked me anything, so I said, "Oh, well sometimes I like to take a couple of hits off a joint and decompress a little bit." Exene said, "You got a joint?" I said, "Yeah, I got this one-hitter in my pocket." She said, "Cool, let's go out in the alley and smoke some." I said, "Well, aren't we doing an encore?" She said, "Yep, right after you and me smoke some pot!" We laughed, took a few hits apiece, and went back onstage and did "The New World."

For the record, I never smoke pot before I play, and definitely not before I sing 'cause it kills my high end and falsetto, but I wasn't singing, and smoking with Exene was too much of a rite of passage to pass up. By the way, I guess that whole straight-edge thing started with some punk rockers saying, "Real punks don't smoke that hippie shit," but I just wanna go on the record and say that's total bullshit. Every punk in England was obsessed with Jamaican culture, records, music, and they pretty much all smoked weed in the '70s. And almost all the Detroit and New York punks smoked weed except for Johnny Ramone.

Anyway, right when we walked offstage, with the crowd going nuts, a photographer snapped this shot of all four of us. Exene and I had so much fun every night after that. We would go out after the shows and have drinks pretty much every night, or hang out at the hotel bar with Dead Rock West, the opening act featuring Frank Drennen and Cindy Wasserman, and have the best conversations about music, art, where we grew up, how the world was changing, books, poetry, and films. One of the things that makes Exene so sexy is that she's smart. Maybe I'm just getting older, but brains are way sexier than just a physically hot person with nothing to talk about. Between Exene and Cindy Wasserman (who, like Exene, is the whole smart/talented/cool package too), I got to hang out with two of the coolest gals on the planet who had seen and done a lot of crazy stuff in their lives. I knew this tour was temporary, but it seemed like we just kept getting better and better as the tour went on. I even got Exene to sing "L.A. Woman" by the Doors in Atlanta, and people went totally nuts hearing an empowered punk-rock woman singing Jim Morrison's macho lyrics. Good Lord, it was so fuckin' great!

At one show in Los Angeles we played a double bill with Dwight Yoakam, and I'm a huge fan of his. At one point I thought I was going to play guitar for Dwight after guitarist Keith Gattis left the band, but it didn't work out. As much as I love Dwight's music and I know I could play the living shit out of Pete Anderson's hillbilly Telecaster guitar parts, I needed to go find my own way and make my own records. Anyway, Dwight had this sofa onstage that he used to sit on during his show and do this kind of intimate acoustic-type segment of his show. There was a note on the couch that said DO NOT SIT ON THIS COUCH! So between songs during our set, while Dwight was standing on my side of the stage watching us, John Doe said over the microphone, "Hey, Jesse Dayton, I'll give you a hundred bucks if you sit on Dwight's couch and start off 'White Girl.'" Oh man, I looked back at Dwight, and he was mouthing, *Don't do it!* So I said to myself, *Fuck it, there's 7,000 people here, you're playing with X, and it's not gonna be very punk rock if you cower to Dwight.* So I sat down on the couch and started the opening riff to "White Girl," and out of nowhere Dwight came out onstage. The crowd goes nuts! We're already into the song by now. Dwight came over, sat down by me on the couch laughing (thank God he was laughing!), and started literally kicking me off his couch with his cowboy boots! By the way, this is all on YouTube, 'cause there were thousands of cell phones filming it. Exene, Doe, and DJ are cracking up laughing, but somehow I still managed to get through "White Girl" without totally fucking up Billy Zoom's parts.

After the show Dwight came to our backstage with actor/comedian Jack Black in tow. We all signed a poster for Jack Black, who was a super cool guy like I thought he would be. Then Exene and I got pictures for some press folks with Dwight. I think John Doe and DJ were talking to the other three hundred friends who showed up for the hometown reunion show with Dwight. Dwight told me that night, "I'm glad you're doing this gig with X . . .

sounded great out there." Dwight's not a big compliment guy, so it made me feel special. Plus, I knew that if shit would've gotten crazy with the whole couch situation, Exene would've been the first one to jump on that couch with me. After fronting X for forty years and seeing all that she's seen, she's fucking fearless.

After one of the last shows at Kaboom Fest in San Diego (with my longtime friends Old 97's from Dallas on the bill, the biggest X fans of any band on the planet), Exene and I were the only ones left that the transport van had to take back to Los Angeles. Exene invited me to hang out at her house that night in Orange County, so we had the van drop us off. I walked into her house, and the place was packed with art. Art everywhere. Paintings and sculptures and records and anything else that she could create. I gotta say, the sheer output blew my mind. All these pieces of art explained why she was so uncompromising with businesspeople when it came to her art or music. Sure, she's had some rough spots, been knocked down a few times, but how many of us got to turn all that into art? She's a survivor of the highest order.

That night she turned me on to this early L.A. punk band called the Plugz, and the record blew my mind. I had known Charlie Quintana, the drummer, God rest his soul, from when I toured with Mike Ness and from his earlier band, Cruzados, but for whatever reason the Plugz had escaped me. That night Exene and I smoked a little weed, listened to the Plugz record on repeat, and talked for hours about everything from Bukowski to God. We didn't talk about her personal life or her marriages to John Doe and Viggo Mortensen or any gossip whatsoever. Just art, art, art, and I was totally fascinated. Being around anyone from that early original punk scene is always a treat, but this was next level. If it sounds like I fell in love with Exene that night, you're right, I did. But it wasn't sexual; we were just friends who genuinely loved each other. Hell, everyone I met on that tour was in love with Exene. She's the queen of punk rock. What's not to love?

A few months ago I saw Exene when X came to Austin to play at the Austin City Limits Live theater with the Violent Femmes. It was John Doe's girlfriend's birthday party, and all band members were there. Billy was a bit nicer than his usual gruff/contrarian self, and he actually talked to me for a while, which was completely out of the norm. The first time I'd met Billy was at the first X reunion shows in Hollywood at the House of Blues when my first band, the Road Kings, were opening. Billy came into our dressing room and just stood in the middle of the room with a devilish grin on his face, and yeah, it was pretty weird, but we loved it. That night, I told him how happy I was that his cancer was in remission and how excited I was to see my favorite punk-rock guitar player on the planet rip it up that night, and he just smiled that evil grin at me, like he does onstage, that reaffirms none of us have any earthly idea what's going through that man's mind.

DJ was his usual upbeat self, playing his drumsticks on a book and talking about how many songs he had to learn for some gig he was doing when he got back to Los Angeles. DJ is an in-demand player and happens to be one of those guys who can play jazz, blues, rockabilly, country, you name it. A band is only as strong as their drummer, and if you listen to all those great X records that Ray Manzarek of the Doors produced, a strength of those recordings is DJ Bonebrake's drum parts. John Doe lives in Austin now, too, and put me on the spot to make a toast backstage to a room full of folks that I think went over fairly well. And after the toast we all went out into the venue. Exene came up to me as I stood there with my wife, Emily, and said, "Hey man, thanks so much again for filling in for Billy . . . you did such a great job." These are the tiny moments in my life that mean the most to me.

Then Exene walked out onstage to a big roaring crowd and proceeded to put on the best show I've ever seen her do since I first saw the band at Cardi's nightclub in Houston in the late '80s. She was not shut down, or hiding behind her hair and standing in one place. She was on fire, dancing across the stage, inciting the audience, just going for it in a big way, and the fans were going absolutely nuts. But like I said before . . . she's the queen of punk rock, and this is why we're all in love with her.

All this touring had put me back on the map as a national act, which led to another record deal where I went out on tour for three years straight with all kinds of acts, like Reverend Horton Heat, Scott H. Biram, Supersuckers, Ryan Bingham, and Reverend Peyton's Big Damn Band. Also, another thing that really helped me was this new satellite radio station called SiriusXM Outlaw Country that had started playing my music all the time. Radio programmer Jeremy Tepper hired DJs Mojo Nixon, Shooter Jennings, Elizabeth Cook, and Dallas Wayne, and they all had very popular radio shows on the station that were feeding America's hunger for real country and roots music that the mainstream terrestrial radio stations simply did not play. Again, Jeremy Tepper has been one of my biggest cheerleaders and helped put me back on the map.

Touring with Doe and X was the ultimate in micro- and macro-level show business. Most of the time, when folks asked me who I had been playing with and I told them John Doe and X, they couldn't believe it. The country picker and singer from Beaumont had been touring with X? Only a few months back I saw Mike Ness at the Bouldin Creek Cafe in South Austin while Social Distortion was on tour and he said, "What ya been up to?" I told him I had just got off tour and was meeting John Doe for lunch later. Ness proceeded to tell me what so many other musicians say when John Doe's name comes up. "Oh, John Doe, that guy can sing his ass off!" If you know Mike Ness, he's definitely not one to give compliments freely. Everyone from Eddie Vedder to Bob Dylan is a John Doe fan. I don't know if John knows what an amazing singer he is, because John doesn't spend much time thinking about stuff like that, but his voice is one of the purest out there. I don't spend a lot of time talking shop with John Doe. He's still punk rock to his core and is very suspicious of music-business talk and of ambition in general. Out of all the older road warriors I know, John is probably the least interested in talking about the past. He's always writing new songs and is still flying in and out of Austin to act in movies and television shows, so he's busy doing new stuff. The last thing he wants to talk about is what he used to be doing, but there were things I really wanted to know about the old days, so I had to pull them out of him. He's a new-idea guy. That's what gets him out of bed in the morning. But his history in the emerging Los Angeles punk scene is so important that in 2016, he and friend Tom DeSavia wrote an award-nominated book called *Under the Big Black Sun: A Personal History of L.A. Punk* that became a hit with music fans worldwide. The book did so well, they followed it up with the 2019 release of the book *More Fun in the New World: The Unmaking and Legacy of L.A. Punk*. Both of these books have chapters about all the legendary folks from that scene, including Dave Alvin, Henry Rollins, Keith Morris, Peter Case, Jane Wiedlin, Chris Morris, Jack Grisham, and others. One night I saw John at our friend Jack McFadden's house. John told me that X were about to go into the studio and record their first new record of all original material in, like, twenty-two years, which became the excellent *Alphabetland*. The entire X experience was a wild gift.

SHOOTER AND MISTY

It was around 1996–1997, and I'd been "the kid" on quite a few recording sessions full of old-timers. At the time it didn't really feel that odd to me, being twenty, thirty, even forty years younger than everyone else in the room, because unlike most of the musicians who were my age then, I was the young weirdo who was into older music. A lot of it had to do with the microcosm of the retro classic country/blues/rockabilly world I was living in, in Austin, but truthfully, my love affair with older musicians from the 1950s onward had been going on since I was a kid. I just felt comfortable around older people, and I was used to being "the kid." But looking back on it now, my level of comfort with older folks instead of hanging out with younger people who were closer to my own age seems pretty strange. I can ask myself all day long, *How did you end up recording with Rockin' Dopsie at nineteen?* And the only thing that springs to mind is it was a perfect storm of preparation meeting a shit-ton of luck.

But it's more than that. There I was in a recording studio where everyone else is a lot older than me, and well, I'm not pretending: I actually felt like I belonged there. And it wasn't because I thought I was some great guitar player. There's a lot of great guitar players in the world. Looking back, I think it was because I could hang out. Like I said before, an important part of all this is the hang. Money and adulation will come and go, but the hang, or the time, is something you can never get back. Was I sometimes an over-zealous kid who put his foot in his mouth? Absolutely. But for the most part, I kept my mouth shut and tried to have plenty of ideas, plenty of hooky parts, to throw out to whoever I was working for, be it the bandleader or producer or label guy, if and only if they called on me. Sometimes I didn't get to prepare. Sometimes I was at the right place at the right time and I just had to pull a guitar part out of my ass and pray that everyone in the room dug it. But most of the time, I had time to prepare and I used every single second of that time sitting on hotel-room beds, or in lounges of studios, or in my living room at home writing charts for the session, writing simple little hooks that I thought might stick in a listener's head, writing three separate lead guitar parts in case after I played my favorite one, the one I personally dug the most, the producer said, "Meh, what else you got?"

A lot of this tendency toward obsessive preparation came from being raised by a military man. My pops left absolutely nothing to chance. He was so prepared for anything you threw at him it was ri-diculous, and that rubbed off big-time on me, as well as my brother and sister. Learning to have options ready for people I would be working for was a huge lesson learned early, one that would serve me well later when I would go in and try to pitch a script to a bunch of suits in Hollywood or New York and they would eventually re-spond with a flip, "Yeah, that's OK. What else you got?" It was the same in the recording studio. After having some of my favorite ideas shut down hard and fast, ones that I thought everyone was going to love, well, I wasn't married to anything idea-wise after that. Whatever approach they wanted, I was game. Now, if it was my own music, that's a completely different situation. If something doesn't feel right on your own music, unless you're working with a bona fide legend of a producer who wants you to get outside your comfort zone, you gotta stick to your guns. But when you're a studio player, you can't get emotionally attached to things when you're working for someone else. Sometimes the person you're working with will say, "Sorry, I'm not that crazy about what you're doing here," and they'll really mean it and want another idea on the spot. And sometimes they're not sure if they like it and they're trying to see how much you'll fight for it. You gotta be able to read these folks and read them quickly. You don't try to sell the people who hired you on an idea that they're not into. That's a quick way to never get asked back. It's a slippery slope, and being able to read the room is almost as important as what they're asking you to play or write.

This is team-player shit I'm talking about. If you've never had to do it because you're independently wealthy or you got extremely lucky early on in your chosen career, well, good for you! But if you're rolling your eyes right now, you'll probably be shit out of luck if and when you have to walk into a room full of tenured experts one day and perform to their, not your, standards. Again, looking back on it now at my age, it was weird being in a room full of legends, trying to navigate my way through playing with some personality while not stepping on anyone else's parts. So it was great when I would finally meet someone my own age on these sessions. It almost never happened. But when I did, we usually became fast friends. Sure, I would go outside the studio in the parking lot and smoke cigarettes with the rhythm section on breaks, and yep, they were usually cool to me as the kid on the session (it was rare, but sometimes there were those cranky old farts who thought I was "out of my depth," but whatever), but most of the time these old session cats would tell me amazing stories about who they played with and how it all went down. In fact, that was one of the reasons I wanted to write this book, because the session players and the band members saw things from a totally different angle than the stars they were playing for. But yeah, whenever I did meet someone at these sessions who was closer to my age, it was usually like "Oh man, we found each other!" And that was what happened when I met this kid who was about ten years younger than me.

When I met Shooter at the legendary Woodland Studios in Nashville back when I was playing guitar on his father's, Waylon's, record *Right for the Time,* he was a young high school kid wearing a Nine Inch Nails T-shirt. Fast-forward to now, that same kid has won a Grammy for producing Brandi Carlile's blockbuster record *By the Way, I Forgive You* and Tanya Tucker's comeback album, *While I'm Livin'.* Although I've always been a student of the older musicians I've run around with, I was so young compared to all the other older players in Waylon's band and I felt like I had more in common with Shooter than I did them. Shooter actually turned me on to Nine Inch Nails, whom I'd never heard before. (I know, I was living in a bubble.) At that time Trent Reznor really wasn't my cup of tea, but I do appreciate how NIN came into the music business and turned everything on its ass, the way punk rock did. Plus I could hear the David Bowie influence, and I'm a big Bowie fan. There's always common ground in musical genres if you look for it.

Being Shooter Jennings ain't easy, and I have several friends who are children of iconic musicians and legendary actors and athletes, and I can tell you, it's no walk in the park. Sure, nepotism might get you into the game, but the world is twice as hard on you when you're trying to make it off the bench and onto the playing field. If I had a dollar for every time somebody said, "Shooter, he ain't no Waylon," I'd have more money than a show dog could jump over. But I always respond by saying, "Comparison is the thief of joy. I played with Waylon, and I'm here to tell you, *no one* will ever be Waylon Jennings." Shooter never wanted to be his father, the same way Hank Williams Jr. never wanted to be Hank Williams Sr. And by the way, Waylon told me one time, "Hank Jr. sang so good, he made his father sound like a sharecropper." If you were born and raised on country music, you will understand this statement. But if you came to country music later, with all the other cultural and social influences that were projected onto the later careers of folks like Hank Jr., odds are you won't understand. One last thing about Bocephus: I may not agree with his politics or his infatuation with Kid Rock, but he is and will always be one of the greatest country singers and songwriters to ever live. In my opinion, "Whiskey Bent and Hell Bound" is as good of a song as anything his daddy every wrote. It's OK if some of y'all are screaming "Blasphemy!" right now.

Anyway, Shooter was the only child that Waylon Jennings and Jessi Colter had together, and they were a very tight-knit family. Waylon, like so many other superstars who didn't have a "how to be a country superstar" guide book, was very mindful of his relationship with Shooter and made sure that he wasn't making the same mistakes he made with his older kids. In fact, in the studio he talked about Shooter a lot. I think when he saw how young I was, me being this kid guitar player from Texas, bringing up Shooter was his way of relating to me. He would say, "Shooter just played this for me" or "Shooter told me about this the other day." I can say that out of all of the older guys I played guitar with, Waylon talked more about his son than any of them. Willie talked about Micah and Lukas, too, and he used to bring them into the studio a lot in the mid-'90s when they were small, but Willie had a bunch of kids, and we didn't become good friends with Paula and Amy Nelson till later. But Waylon's face would light up when Shooter and Jessi would walk into the control room.

OK, so if you look pass the sentimental side of this story and look at how old Shooter was when I met him, it shows you just how long Shooter Jennings had been hanging out in recording studios. He was born hanging around recording studios. Although he's certainly put in his 10,000 hours plus (probably more like 100,000 hours), it's not that big of a shock that Shooter has become an award-winning record producer and a whiz in the recording studio.

Shooter and I have worked on some really cool recordings together that have led to some amazing friendships for me. I was out on the East Coast, touring in Vermont, when I got a text from Shooter saying he was putting together a band to record a soundtrack for a movie about Jack Daniel called *Chasing Whiskey*. So my agent set up a break in the next leg of the tour so I could fly out to Los Angeles, do the recording session, then fly back and meet the band to resume our tour. If Shooter calls about a session, gigs or no gigs, I make it a priority to get my ass there. So we ended up at this funky recording studio over in Silver Lake in L.A., and when I walk in I find out the band was Shooter on vocals, guitar, and keyboards, me on vocals/guitar, Matt Sorum from Guns N' Roses and the Cult on drums, and Michael Devin from Whitesnake on vocals/bass/harmonica. Crazy, huh? I'm here to tell ya that the Old Number 7 Band (that's what the filmmaker, Greg Olliver, kept calling us in the studio) was absolutely killer! Shooter put four musicians in a room that you wouldn't normally think would be in a room together and just let us try all kinds of different things. Ideas were flying around faster than we could get them on tape. There was blues, there was classic heavy rock, there was classic country, there was prog-keyboard stuff, and all of it was melting into one sound. I was amazed at drummer Matt Sorum's arrangement skills. Most drummers don't hear the entire arrangement of a song like Matt does. They might be great drummers with technical ability or even great feel, but they're usually not thinking about expanding the last chorus of a song, or making sure we're not throwing away a cool part that needs to be highlighted or working on a needless part that needs to be thrown out. He was writing little hooky drum parts, and even wrote this whole bridge part that just kept building and building that was, well, fucking amazing. After that session I looked at Matt in a different way, 'cause you get a whole lot more than just a drummer when you're working with him. We've stayed in touch since then, and after that session Matt went on to play with Billy Gibbons from ZZ Top's solo band (Billy is one of my greatest influences on my guitar playing in terms of feel), so we reconnected when he came down to Texas for those shows with Rev. Billy G.

Michael Devin is another one who's more than just a bass player. The guy sings so fuckin' great he could've joined the Beach Boys in their prime—crazy high and low harmony singer or lead vocals. And besides being one of those riffing '70s-style bass players who never misses a note, he also played the shit out of the harmonica to boot. Michael and I have kept in touch, and Emily and I came out to see him in Austin when he was on tour with Cheap Trick playing with Jason Bonham's band. What a fucking band.

Another session that Shooter called me to play guitar on was the Duff McKagan solo record he was producing. Duff and Shooter were recording it between both of their crazy schedules while Duff was on a world tour with Guns N' Roses and Shooter was producing Marilyn Manson's record. Anyway, Shooter sent me the tracks via email, and I laid all my guitar stuff down in Austin at a friend's studio, and that was that. Later, when the record came out, Duff emailed me to say thanks and that he loved my playing on his record and gave me his number. So I shot him my number back and we kept talking online and lo and behold when Duff came through Austin on tour with Shooter's whole solo band backing him up, I ended up getting onstage and playing with Duff on a solo song, "Breaking Rocks," the Bowie song "Cracked Actor," and another song called "River of Deceit" by Duff's friends from Seattle called Mad Season. Anyway, Duff was just on my radio show the other day, and even though it seems like we're from two different worlds, we both have a lot in common. And I'd be remiss if I didn't mention that Duff's book *How to Be a Man (and Other Illusions)* has been an inspiration for me for how I live my life. Besides Duff being a martial-arts combat warrior who's six-four and looks like an Irish Viking, he's a pretty normal dude who puts his family first and works harder on himself than anyone I've met outside of my wife, Emily. Right now I'm almost five months into hard-core alcohol abstinence, eating only clean food, and training, and I was inspired to do it in large part by Duff. Luckily, I never had the addiction gene, but I did have a big awakening that with so much good stuff happening in my life, the best way I could show my gratitude for it was to stop fucking around and get in the best shape of my life. 2020 was a designated time to get my health together. But yeah, I'll probably have some Paddy whiskey every once in a while and with my big brother on New Year's Eve. And by the way, I saw Shooter on the Outlaw Country Cruise, and we have had a tradition of pulling an all-nighter at least one night on the five annual cruises so far. Those nights always end predictably, where Shooter and I smoke way too much reefer, kill all the bourbon, and are the only ones left standing after the other partygoers have gone to bed and we're still deep in a discussion at five a.m. concerning the machinations of how Hank Jr. made *The Pressure Is On* in 1981. It would always come to a close with his wife, Misty, poking her head in at almost daybreak and saying, "Good lord, you knuckleheads need to go to bed!" But in 2020 I had to break the news that I was going the year without drinking so I could really concentrate on getting in shape, and Shooter couldn't have been more supportive. That's a real friend. God bless 'em, but some of my other drinking buddies were definitely not as supportive.

Waylon passed away in 2002, and it was a soul-crushing gut punch to me and I'm sure to millions around the world. It had been a few years since I had seen Shooter and had heard he was playing in a band in Los Angeles. The music business is really a small world. People who are actually out there consistently making records year in and year out and touring the world are not a very big group of folks. Shooter and I have connected around the world, once even in Holland, where we raged with his bass player, Ted Russell Kamp, in a hotel room till four in the morning listening to Hank Williams Jr., drinking some god-awful Dutch booze, and smoking that good old legal Amsterdam lettuce. When we reconnected in Los Angeles, Shooter had just divorced *Sopranos* star Drea de Matteo. Their divorce was amicable, and they both got two great kids out of it, Alabama and Waylon. I knew the drill too—remember I was married before and got a great son out of it named Sam, whom I named after my friend the playwright Sam Shepard. These things happen, and it's nice when everyone is civil and actually puts the kids first.

So Shooter and I ended up going out one night, and he brought up an old friend of mine named Misty Swain. Misty was the hilarious and gorgeous blonde who ran the outdoor bar patio at the Rainbow Bar and Grill on Sunset Boulevard in Hollywood. I always treated her like a little sister because there were so many damn wolves licking their fangs around her, I kind of felt protective of her. I met Lemmy from Motörhead through Misty, and he seemed to have the same kind of relationship with her. When I found out that Shooter was interested in her, it all made such perfect sense. They were cut from the same mold, Shooter and Misty. Two incredibly wild spirits who somehow magically kept their shit together through it all, and let me tell you, those kind of people are few and far between. In my experience, most of the wild ones do not have their shit together. I know this firsthand from my own shortcomings. So we went for drinks in Hollywood that night where Misty was bartending, and I got drunker than Cooter Brown, then had to take off in a cab because I had a meeting the next morning at a production company that was interested in one of my film scripts. It seemed like not that much time had passed after that when Shooter and Misty called to tell me they were on their way out to the desert in Joshua Tree to get married. Hey when you know, you know, right? One of the most goddamn romantic situations I've ever seen. Now they've built an empire together and it's an "us against the world" story. I think they've been married almost ten years now and I couldn't be happier for them.

RYAN BINGHAM'S RODEO

Growing up in Texas you see cowboy hats, cowboy boots, and big rodeo belt buckles pretty much everywhere on the almost thousand-mile drive from Beaumont to El Paso. My band can tour through three, four, sometimes five countries in Europe in the time it takes us to drive just from Lubbock to San Antonio. It's hard for folks who grew up outside of Texas to truly realize how massive our state is and how big the ranches are that put the state on the world map.

The King Ranch is a whopping million acres, and there are several others, like the O'Connor Ranch or the Waggoner Ranch, that come in at around a half a million acres. With over 7,000 square miles of ranch land, which is a little over 4 million acres, about 95 percent of the land in Texas is privately owned. And by the way, the U.S. government will use immigration or any other "crisis" they can to come in and steal that land. Our government is dying to get their hands on that much land, and all my friends, both Republicans and Democrats, Americans and Mexicans, who own land on or close to the Texas–Mexico border have all known about eminent domain for a long time.

I know what you're thinking: *OK, we get it, Texas is big, now move on with this BS, JD.* Where I'm going with all this is most of the people you see wearing cowboy boots, cowboy hats, or big rodeo buckles might be descendants of tried-and-true real Texas cowboys, but most of them do not even own a dang horse. How do I know? Because I'm one of them. Yes, I had the classic Texas childhood picture taken on a Shetland pony with the fringed Roy Rogers cowboy outfit on and the big hat, but I did not grow up on a ranch. Luckily, I did get introduced to horses the right way, as a kid, and while I'm far from a cowboy or a natural on horses I'm definitely not scared of them like some folks are and I love riding them. But no one put me on a fresh, cantankerous young mare and slapped it on the backside to watch me get dragged under trees and bucked off.

My first ride was on an old, docile Paint Horse so I could get used to riding. I cannot tell you how many folks I've met in Texas who are absolutely scared to death of horses because one of their jackass relatives threw them up in the saddle of a wild horse when they were kids. That's a very common traumatic story I hear a lot. But even though I personally had a nice time trotting around an open field at my cousin's farm, I've never owned a horse or lived on a working ranch and don't really know anything about horses except how to keep my reins low and the basics of how to get one to go where you want it to. Sometimes. But I'd wager most Texans you see in these cowboy outfits can't ride a horse or have never even been on a horse. So next time you go to a big country music concert in Texas, just know that, for most folks sporting their cowboy gear, it's a cultural thing more than an actual working lifestyle. I

wouldn't call these Texans poseurs—after all, some of them probably did grow up around ranches and a lot of them do listen to
country music 24/7. But an expression does come to mind that my
grandfather used to say about these folks: "All hat and no cattle."
And just for the record, I do own a few cowboy hats I wear from
time to time when I wake up with bedhead, and I've been collect-
ing vintage cowboy boots since I was a kid and even have my own
line of vintage-style cowboy boots called "JDs" through Heritage
Boot in Austin. And of course I own a veritable shit-ton of western
clothes that I've collected over the years, but although I've been
thrown on a few fresh horses in my day, truth be told, I, too, am
one of the "all hat, no cattle" Texans. Well, certainly in comparison
to this guy I'm going to tell you about.

Ryan Bingham is a lot of different things to a lot of different
folks. He's a master songwriter, a surfer, an underrated guitar
player, a working character actor, a fence builder/mender, a hell of
a front man onstage, owner of his cattle dog, Boo, and one of the
most committed fathers you'll ever meet. But to his core, in terms
of the blood that's running through his veins, he is an honest-to-
God bona fide cowboy. I didn't say he was the best competition
rodeo rider, but unlike me and the folks that I described earlier, he
was born to ride horses.

I met Bingham at a hot-rod garage in Houston that was owned
by our mutual friend Jim Jard. Jim is one of these rare soulful characters who has done very well for himself and uses his resources
to bring talented people together, whether it's musicians, businesspeople, artists, car and motorcycle collectors, politicians, or what
have you. Jim's a self-made guy I've heard is a take-no-prisoners
lawyer who ended up investing in everything from real estate de-
velopment to restaurants. To be perfectly honest, as good of friends
as we are, I've never really asked Jim what he does "for a living,"
because we never talk about anything but music, hot rods, and
motorcycles. Sometimes, when things are heated, we talk about

politics. There is literally nothing Jim loves more than to bring an incredibly eclectic group of talented people together in his "garage" around the coolest vintage hot rods and classic motorcycles you've ever seen and just hang out, exchange ideas, and play music. At any given get-together at Jim's hot-rod garage, you might see Billy Gibbons from ZZ Top, or Texas legend Joe Ely, or three or four of the hottest guitar pickers and songwriters in the state. There's no telling who you'll see, and it's not unusual to see a congressman talking to a painter and a songwriter along with a restaurant or bar owner and a bestselling author.

So one night Jim came up to me and said, "You gotta get this cowboy kid Ryan up onstage with you and sing one for us." Hey, what the hell? It's not like it was a packed club, it was just Jim's garage and a few of us hanging out drinking tequila. Jim had put in a full-blown honky-tonk inside his garage, which included an old juke-joint stage with chicken wire wrapped around it, a PA system that I think he got from Steve Wertheimer from the Continental Club in Austin, some of the most beautiful vintage guitars and amps and drums you've ever seen, and a long saloon bar, where we would usually end up getting extremely hammered on world-class Mexican mezcal.

So Jim introduced me to "the cowboy," who turned out to be Ryan Bingham, and Ryan looked like he just got off the ranch. Dirty cowboy boots and a weathered old cowboy hat that was still bent and shaped to fight off the wind and other elements. By the way, that's an important detail. People who just put on any old cowboy hat, well, that's a big red flag to us Texans. We can tell by the bend of your hat if you're from Fort Worth, the Panhandle, Coastal Texas, or down by Mexico. So as a warning, if you show up to one of our honky-tonks with one of those goofy-ass gas station cowboy hats and expect to get any real respect, you're shit out of luck. Anyway, another thing I noticed was that Ryan was wearing a real rodeo buckle. That's another dead giveaway. Most of those big shiny gold and silver buckles you see are not earned at actual rodeos, they are purchased at the local western clothing/boot store. I forgot which one Bingham was wearing, but it was an honest-to-goodness, rodeo-issued belt buckle. The first thing Ryan said to me was very unassuming and easy-going and came with a big smile: "Hey man, I'm Ryan, wanna do a Townes Van Zandt song or something easy?" This was years before the legendary songwriter-poet Townes Van Zandt started appearing on hipster T-shirts in Brooklyn, Silver Lake, or even Austin for that matter. I knew things were changing with Townes when I played in Williamsburg, Brooklyn, recently and saw a hipster with a waxed mustache wearing a reproduction Townes shirt from one of the many new online stores that I hope are not ripping off the Van Zandt family. For the record, for a very long time, Townes was a god that only a select group of inside songwriters were praying to. But after a good number of years (and thank God it happened), after a great documentary called *Be Here to Love Me* spread like wildfire and the rerelease of documentary *Heartworn Highways* resurfaced, pretty much everyone, musicians and fans alike, would kneel and pray at the altar of Townes.

So Ryan and I went onstage and did the Townes song "White Freight Liner Blues" and switched off singing the verses. Our buddies at the shop went wild, and after the show (if you want to call it a show), it was just us, and we were playing acoustic guitars, smoking some Mexican lettuce, and talking about what we had coming up. Bingham sang a few of his own songs that night, and I was impressed, not only by the poetry in the lyrics but also by his no-nonsense delivery of the songs that said to me "I couldn't sing any other way if my life depended on it." After a couple more songs, Ryan said in his thick accent, "Hey Jesse, I'll be at the Continental Club next week playing happy hour if you're in town." I said, "Oh yeah? Y'all come by the house before the show, and I'll put some food on the grill and we'll eat and drink a beer." Sure as shit, a few days later, Bingham showed up in his beat-up old van that he was literally living in at the time. I could tell he had gotten pretty good at living lean. Some folks can do it, some folks can't. The folks who are good at it, you'll notice their situation or lack of money never seems to affect their mood. The others who are upset about missing their creature comforts, well, they look depressed. This is a real poker tell to know whether someone is born to be a gypsy road musician or not. Musicians can survive dangerous weather, lack of food, lack of money, and still sing till their throats bleed or do the old soft-shoe till their feet hurt, all with a smile on their face because that's how much they love it.

Bingham jumped out of this old van with a big smile and said, "Well, here we are again!" So we ended up on the patio in the back-yard, sipping on Lone Star beer while I grilled some apple-juice pork chops, which are the most succulent things you'll ever put in your mouth. This was a recipe I got from an old Black man who cooked at a country club in Arkansas. And just for the record, this was before I made big dietary health changes that basically saved my life, but more on that later. So I started asking Bingham about his life. By this point we'd only met each other once, and to be honest, I didn't really know anything about him except I thought he had killer songs. So Bingham told me these crazy stories about growing up, but he can tell you those stories if he wants to some-day. That being said, for a kid to grow up in that kind of environ-ment explained a lot about the deep poetry I heard in his songs. But that's not really what this chapter is about. What this chapter is about is him being a hard-charging young buckaroo who finally lit out and thumbed his way out of his crazy situation and down to Mexico and started riding bulls in the Mexican rodeos, which, let's face it, you gotta be crazier than hell to do. When I heard this, my ears perked up. Felt like a Larry McMurtry story come to life. One songwriter I know said, "Riding bulls is like driving a high-performance race car at 200 miles an hour, and then just chucking the steering wheel out the car window." I am Texan enough to know that the Mexican rodeos are nothing like the ones here in America, or even in Texas, for that matter. They're full of scrappy characters with nothing to lose. Only thing I've ever seen that's come close to those little Mexican village rodeos I saw once or twice in Nuevo Laredo, and that's the prison rodeos at the Huntsville Penitentiary. When I was a kid we used to go to the Huntsville prison rodeo, and those inmate cowboys really and truly were some of the most desperate folks I'd ever seen. But those rodeos still seemed more organized and nicer than the Mexican rodeos I went to in Nuevo Laredo back in the day when we'd drive down there and over the border to party all night. I went to a few Mexican rodeos and a few Mexican bullfights on the Texas–Mexico border towns of Boquillas, Acuña, and Juárez as well, and sure there are a lot of normal, nice, working-class Mexican families, but there were also some extremely dangerous characters at these events who wouldn't hesitate to take full advantage of a white boy gringo who didn't speak the language.

Bingham had a darker, tanned look about him, wore a big cowboy hat pulled over his eyes most of the time, and spoke Spanish and was familiar with the Mexican traditions, so he must've blended in a hell of a lot better than our car full of young white boys with bull's-eye targets on our backs that pretty much screamed, *Take our money!* After we talked and he told me a few crazy stories about Mexico that involved the federales and the U.S. Border Patrol, he then proceeded to say, "And then I moved to Paris, France, and became a trick rider at Buffalo Bill's Wild West Show." This is when my inner WTF alarm started sounding off. "Really? No bullshit?" is what I think I said. Let's just go on the record and say right now that Ryan Bingham is not the kind of guy to sit around and talk about himself, nor his accomplishments. I'd say out of all the "famous" musicians I've ever been around who've really been skyrocketed to another stratosphere of popularity, Bingham is probably the least affected by it. If I call him while he's at home, there's a big chance he's mending a fence by his corral where he keeps his horses. That's the same damn thing he was doing twenty years ago. I've been on tour buses with him all over the United States, and the last thing he wants to talk about is himself. He really doesn't seem to feel comfortable with fame or any of its trappings and seems to go out of his way to make sure things stay as normal as possible. And I gotta say, this is a very refreshing character trait from someone in show business, because most show business folks cannot shut up about what they've done or what they're "working on." I mean, look at me, I'm writing a book about it right now! But in all seriousness, we musicians talk about this stuff for two reasons:

1. All the great musicians I've ever met, we're way bigger fans of music than anyone will ever know. For example, when the Faces released a new record, Mick Jagger would hibernate in his hotel room playing the album over and over, obsessing on it. Art inspires more art.
2. No one is more surprised by a musician's success than they are. They might try to play it cool in interviews and even say things like "I knew I'd be this big!" But just know that when they're alone looking in the mirror they're thinking, Holy mother of Pearl, I can't believe I got to write a song with Terry Allen today! (Look up songwriter/artist Terry Allen. He plays a big part in Ryan's story.)

So anyway, back to Paris, France, and Buffalo Bill's Wild West Show. Ryan tells me about how this guy who saw him doing tricks with a rope on a horse asked him if he wanted to go to Paris. He said by this time he had learned a Mexican flamenco-type song, "Malagueña," and was really getting into listening to everything from classic country like Waylon and Willie to the Rolling Stones to songwriters like Guy Clark and Townes Van Zandt. So knowingly or unknowingly, he was already doing his homework for what would happen in the next act of his life. He then told me about living in Paris, and it's just an unbelievable story. Picture some Wild West Cormac McCarthy character stumbling into a Mark Twain/Huckleberry Finn sort of thing.

After dinner we headed up to the Continental Club and I watched him play to about thirteen people and he acted like he was playing to 13,000, and those folks who worked at Steve Wertheimer's legendary Austin venue loved him. That's always a big indication that you must be on the right track: when people who work at a venue where it's not easy for just any musician to get a gig—folks like club manager Celeste Martin, who's seen everything on that stage—like you.

Fast-forward to one week later and I was playing the biggest outdoor country music festival in Europe right outside of Nice, France. We were late getting onstage because the traffic to get onto the ferry to cross the English Channel was backed up coming over from England. As I walked off the stage I told this hippie-looking French soundman, "Thanks for making everything sound so good without a line check, the ferry getting here was late." And in a very French voice he said, "Are you from Texas?" I said yes. Then he said, "Do you know Ryan Bingham?" I said, "Yeah, he was just at my house for supper last week, why? How do you know him?" The Frenchman said, "I ran sound in Paris at the Buffalo Bill Wild West Show when he was a trick-riding cowboy there." I broke into a big grin and thought to myself, OK, that's the kind of stuff they caught Dylan lying about. Bob Dylan at one point in his early career had told some journalist that he had run off from Minnesota with the circus. Then he changed the story and said he ran off with the rodeo. Neither of which he did. But Ryan Bingham had in fact run off with the rodeo and made it all the way down south into central Mexico, and then over to Paris as a working cowboy. It's not that I ever thought Ryan wasn't being honest, it just never dawned on me how crazy it actually was till some French guy relayed the exact same story back to me two weeks later halfway around the world. Later, Ryan would go on to massive success, winning an Oscar for his song featured in the movie *Crazy Heart*, not to mention a Grammy Award and a Golden Globe.

Bingham called me not long ago when I was between record cycles and asked if I wanted to come play guitar on a show with him and Willie Nelson for two nights in Austin for New Year's Eve. I said, "Absolutely, I'll be there." When I got to the gig at the Moody Theater I saw Billy Gibbons from ZZ Top, a huge hero of mine, and he said that he was going to be playing guitar for Willie Nelson both nights. These were two really amazing shows to be a part of. Eventually I started doing tours with Ryan and it seemed like almost every time he called me to play shows I just magically happened to have those dates open. I do a lot of touring with my solo band all over the world, and it was just pure coincidence that I had all these dates available. The last thing I did with him was playing guitar for his 2019 *American Love Song* record tour. The tour was amazing and Bingham took first-class care of me and the killer band he had put together. Trading licks onstage every night with Lubbock, Texas, fiddle legend Richard Bowden was nothing short of a genre-bending musical journey that only the most fearless, outside-the-box musicians could survive. Richard is a special musician and is one of the most Zen and wise old cats I've ever traveled with. Every night there would be some actor or some pro sports player or some other famous musician who would come out to Ryan's show and come backstage to say hello, but the biggest thrill was seeing the love these card-carrying rodeo cowboys and real-life working ranch families had for Bingham.

On that tour we played a run of sold-out shows at the histori-
cal venue Billy Bob's in Fort Worth, and the crowd was screaming
so loud that we had to stop playing in the middle of a song and
just stand there onstage with our fingers in our ears, smiling and
mouthing the words *What the fuck?* and *This is crazy* to one another. Bingham mania is a hell of a thing. Traveling all over the
United States on two tour buses playing sold-out venues was a big
reminder to me of how far Bingham had come in such a short time
from living in his van and playing to empty beer joints. But I'm
here to tell you, in my opinion, while there may have been a little
luck involved, the 100,000 hours of road work and constant songwriting is what did it. The guy went out there and slugged it out,
living in his van and really paying some hard dues, and when his
opportunity came, he not only had the talent to back it up, but
he seized the opportunity. Creating your own luck is a big part of
this whole thing. Making records that you don't have the money
to make, doing tours that you can't afford and that will not be
profitable, writing songs that you're not really sure anyone is going
to ever hear . . . It's a leap of faith, but one that pretty much everybody I've ever met who's in love with music, or whatever their
business is, has tried. I know this is a recurring theme in this book,
but when people say "He got lucky," to me it feels like it's people's
way of rationalizing why it didn't happen to them. To flippantly
throw someone's success entirely under the "luck" umbrella feels
disingenuous. Sour grapes.

One night before we played one of those sold-out shows in Fort
Worth at Billy Bob's, a couple of the guys from the band and I
followed Bingham over to the rodeo that was going on. Before we
knew it, Ryan was on a horse with a number pinned on the back
of his shirt and the old cowboy rodeo announcer was saying, "Out
of the chute and into the arena, it's Ryan Bingham." Bingham had
gone out and rode in the rodeo just for the hell of it, about thirty

minutes before we were set to walk onstage to a sold-out crowd. No agents or businesspeople telling him "Don't do it! You might get hurt!" Just Bingham roping calves at the rodeo like he used to do. I'm just glad that I showed up that night at Jim Jard's hot-rod garage. If Bingham and I never do any work together again, we will have already had a hell of a run.

WHISKEY AT THE WHITE HOUSE

Politics. **Religion. Money.** Three conversations people used to run away from like their hair was on fire. Now? Not only are these subjects a ginormous ratings boost for right- and left-leaning multinational media corporations to profit off of, they seem to be on the tips of the tongues of almost everyone on the planet. In the intro of this book I talked about not neutering your content and about my "rants" that some folks like to soften and call "commentaries." As a radical centrist, I spent a lot of time in the last four-plus years in particular making points on my social media that I thought were relevant and thought-provoking, so I'm not gonna rehash all of that insanity here. We all lived it. I've always paid attention to politics and policies, which we'll get into a bit later, but just in case y'all decide to skip this chapter (don't, there's some funny stuff in here if you stay with it), I'll put the most important part right up front. VOTE. Not just in high-stakes or lesser-than-two-evils presidential elections but in primary and local elections all the way down the ballot.

I'm all for taking it to the streets and protesting, too, but if you want real change, you have to vote. Voting is the most patriotic thing you can do, and regardless of what the cynics or the apathetic folks tell you, our founding fathers did a hell of a job setting the whole voting system up. And despite gerrymandering and obvious voter suppression in lower-income areas, it happens to work if enough folks do it. But sadly, about only 60 percent of Americans actually vote. If more folks turned out, this place would look a hell of a lot different. Make your voice heard.

I can extend the olive branch till my arm is sore to my fellow Americans who support the right-wing GOP but, at the end of the day, to them I'm just another "pinko commie musician from Austin." In reality, I'm a centrist Beaumonster from Beaumont, Texas, who's nowhere near the "radical" they make me out to be. The goalpost has been moved so far from the middle (which is pretty much where I consider myself to live politically, policy-wise) that by today's standards, a true conservative and icon of the Republican Party like Barry Goldwater would be considered a "liberal." I've always leaned way more to the left on social issues, but as a Texan I do in fact believe in some of the libertarian ethos. Libertarian concepts, not like the actual political Libertarian Party, which I think is bonkers, because it's totally OK with me that my government provides Americans with nice highways, post offices, public schools, fire departments, and hospitals so we don't turn into a Third World country. That being said, if your political belief system is keeping any other human beings from having equal justice, opportunities, a decent way of life, or worse, is killing them or hurting them, we have a big fucking problem. We can't have a "civil discourse" when folks are being treated inhumanely or are given less than what they need to survive. Ever read *To Kill a Mockingbird*? That's where all this outrage and equal-rights stuff started for me as a young kid. Fairness has always been big with me. Every fight I've ever been in (and I've had my ass kicked way more than I won, probably a solid 70/30 split on that) was because of a bully. It amazes me how many bullies came out of the woodwork in the last five years. Lots of people still walking around with resentment because maybe their parents didn't have time for them or maybe they were emotionally abused? Maybe they got dealt a shitty hand? But good Lord, y'all, go talk to a professional, work it out, and quit carrying that shit around with ya! I see it year after year, people I personally know, just getting more and more cynical and eventually dying off from all the anxiety and depression they walk around with in their hearts.

Anyway, I have about four things I lean more to the right about, and this is what they are:

1. The IRS: I pay my taxes in full every year like clockwork, and unlike some Republicans who believe that they shouldn't have to pay taxes at all or corporations that rely on massive tax breaks and end up not paying a cent, I do believe that paying my fair share of taxes is an essential part of being an American. But I do not like the IRS, and I think the power that they possess to destroy average, hardworking American lives is unacceptable. If they were a smaller branch of government that specialized and focused more on not the working class but on investigating tax evasion for Wall Street, the banks, and all the other greed-driven multinational corporations that don't pay their fair share, and in some cases pay no taxes whatsoever, I'd be OK with that. In fact, I think the IRS is a borderline criminal entity that strong-arms and extorts money from working-class Americans. I should know: They came after me for $40,000 years later out of thin air for a record-deal advance that my manager at the time filed the

wrong way and that I signed when I was twenty-three years old. They were extremely aggressive and so hard-core they put a lien on my house and immediately started taking money out of my personal savings account without notifying me. I went to the bank one morning and my account was low and the teller dropped quite a big bomb on me when she said, "Looks like the IRS has taken over your bank account." No, I wasn't mean to the teller, but yes, I did freak out big-time with anger once I got to my car out in the parking lot. That day I hired Mickey Mann, a superaccountant in Austin, and she cut a deal with them and I paid it all off. Was it my fault? Within the lines drawn by the IRS, you'd have thought I was a cartel drug lord cleaning millions of cocaine dollars through the Bank of America, but no, it was just "filed wrong." Although Mickey helped me get all my business affairs airtight, going to the mailbox now will never be the same for me. It could be a large or small check to me for songwriting/acting/writing, or it could be the U.S. government leaning on me for something that some manager I had did twenty years ago. So yeah, I don't like the IRS and I think they're gangsters. If that philosophy leans more right, then so be it.

2. The Federal Reserve: Just because the Federal Reserve Bank came about by an act of a bunch of wealthy congressmen, that does not make it a legitimate government entity. It does not have working-class America's best interests in mind. I'm a capitalist in the highest sense of the word. I think people should be able to make as much money as their hard work and talent can bring, but they gotta play by the rules. For the sake of blah, blah, blah explanations, just Google "Who owns the Federal Reserve?" You'll see some solid, factual investigative journalism come up that has nothing to do with ridiculous right-wing conspiracy theories that cloud the issue and turn this all into the nutty subject it gets dismissed as.

3. Private Land Rights: I think the government should stay the hell out of my business concerning anything to do with my land. No, I'm not talking about commercial zoning. I'm talking about how the federal government abuses its power—the last administration was trying to steal private land, and in some instances succeeding, under the guise of building a border wall. The government has been stealing land from Texans since the very beginning of our massive state's existence using "eminent domain" before they even started using "immigration problems" as their bogeyman. Oil and water rights, along with geographical placement, are highly desirable to the government.

All of my friends in the Terlingua area (hippies and rednecks alike), who've coexisted with our neighbors in Mexico for generations, know that the hundreds of land-rights lawyers put on retainer by the last administration were trying to use "The Wall" as an excuse to steal their land. Most of America has no idea what the real truth is behind what's really happening with eminent domain. But again, none of this seems to matter to the current extremist voting base, who continue to make excuses for government's real-estate grab under the guise of "bad hombres" or other bogeymen. The truth has been hijacked by the age-old divide-and-conquer tactics.

While we're on the subject of private land, did you know Texas ranchers were some of the first in North America to understand how to protect wildlife and ecology, and their lands are being gutted by hundreds of thousands of wild pigs that have overtaken their ranches. And sadly, like most great things in America, most of these old ranch families have been exploited by the corporations who own the politicians and now have eventually bought off the deeds to their livelihood. Privately owned ranches and lands in Texas have dwindled away so much that Texas lost 1 million acres of open-space land between 1997 and 2012, and it's still decreasing.

I'm working on buying a ranch myself and I don't care if you're a liberal or conservative politician, I don't want you involved in my land.

4. Gun-Ownership Rights: I grew up in a town in Texas that was next to a massive rural forest area called the Big Thicket, where wartime soldiers who had gone AWOL and criminals on the run would hide from the world. I was also right down the road from the Gulf of Mexico by Bolivar Peninsula and Galveston Island, which was a haven for all the legendary pirates, but even more for less legendary criminals. I can tell you firsthand, growing up hunting, fishing, boating, camping, and being around lots and lots of livestock, that if Mother Nature sends in wolves to kill your chickens, that's a big problem. With thousands of wild hogs on your land that can give birth and procreate two or three times a year and may carry disease and rut and destroy the land you farm and ranch, not to mention usually being two hundred to four hundred pounds big with tusks, well, you might need a Winchester 30-30. When deer overpopulate and get sick and spread disease, and not to mention if you're fifteen minutes from your nearest neighbor or the police and fire departments, you might wanna have a gun. Now, I'm not saying you need to own a military-grade weapon that can wipe out a class full of elementary schoolkids—that's faux macho BS. My family is full of military folks and I know those weapons were made to hunt human beings. I'm talking about a .20-gauge shotgun, a 30-06 hunting rifle, a Beretta, or Colt pistol. My point? I grew up with guns. We never took them to baseball games or political rallies, or to school, church, or the tavern for drinks. We might've had a .12-gauge pump on our gun rack in the back window of our pickup truck, but

we never walked into places with military-grade weapons on our hips. In case you don't know this, the United States government has the weapons technology now to implode your house by satellite or drone with such precision that zero debris will fall into your neighbor's lawn. So folks who misinterpret the "right to bear arms" in the Constitution to make themselves feel like a comic-book superhero are not gonna need that M16, 'cause they're not coming in through the front door of our house, my friend.

I still have a shotgun and pistol for the rare instance that a home invasion occurs. I don't want to wait on the cops to make it over from the Dunkin' Donuts while my family is tortured. If I'm out in Terlingua, Texas, and it's either me or a diseased, crazy, two-hundred-pound mountain lion that's got me cornered, yep, I'll need a gun.

This might sound crazy to some of my fellow progressives, but it's a lot more common than lifelong urbanites might think for country-based folks to own guns if they live far away from their nearest neighbor, be they conservative or liberal. Even though I grew up hunting and fishing almost every weekend as a kid in southeast Texas on the Texas–Louisiana border, and even though it's been a very long time since I've gone hunting and I don't really enjoy killing animals anymore (can't say I truly ever did), I'm still not going to wait eight and a half minutes for the Austin Police Department to get to my house and let someone not in their right mind torture me and my family if I can help it. Are the odds of this happening slim? Yes. Can it happen? Definitely.

Am I being paranoid? My question to you is: Have you ever had a personal friend or family member killed during a break-in? A friend of mine in high school back in Beaumont was shot and killed by a meth head who broke into his house. It was a sad day for our little circle of buddies.

My seventy-eight-year-old, barely five-foot-tall, salty old aunt Bert, who used to take a Greyhound bus from out in the country to come see us in Beaumont in the summers, always carried a Smith & Wesson snub-nose .32 caliber handgun in her purse with her everywhere. In fact, she lived out in the middle of nowhere in the woods, and two escaped prison convicts broke into her house one night. She heard her hunting dogs, three beagles, start going crazy when the front door was breached, so she grabbed her pistol off her nightstand and walked out into the hallway in her nightgown. Two big men were standing there, telling her, "Just go back to your bedroom, old woman, and this will all be over soon," so she shot both of them where they stood, called the sheriff, smoked a Kool cigarette till he got there, made a statement, and went back to sleep. I never pressed her to find out if she killed them, but for me that's a little more than just another propaganda piece of anecdotal evidence.

As a kid, I remember riding home from school with my older sister in her old 1965 Rambler car, listening to the news on the radio, when we heard that John Lennon from the Beatles had been shot outside his apartment, and both of us quietly shed a tear over it. John was the true rockabilly singer in the Beatles, and I was a loyal fan throughout his musical journey. Still am.

I'm sure all these stories of random violence have had some impact on why I feel the way I do about guns. While I never carry a weapon on me, please don't break into my house, or you'll be the one calling 911. It's absolutely fine with me if you don't want to own guns. I'm all for you not owning guns. Most of my friends don't own guns, and to be honest, I'm really disappointed by all the faux macho horseshit that people who do own guns spew out of their mouths. But that being said, if you're my neighbor and something happens to you and you don't have a gun, I will help defend you, if you so desire, while you're waiting on the police to get there as the second hand on your wristwatch slowly tick-tocks.

I'm old enough to remember when the NRA was a small foundation that primarily existed to teach kids about gun safety. This was decades before they morphed into a multinational weapons-lobbyist corporation that pays off politicians and makes zillions of dollars off of fearful voters. None of this is about "freedom," and all of it is about money.

It doesn't matter if I tell the Second Amendment hardliners that I am in fact a longtime gun owner. They don't care, because as soon as they hear that I don't believe in civilians owning military-grade weapons with magazine clips that can murder twenty-six first graders in less than three minutes in a public schoolroom, they glaze over and tune out. This is a deeper cynicism my charm can't penetrate, and Lord knows I've tried. Also, if I have to get a license to ride my Harley-Davidson or drive my '78 Vette, it's not that unreasonable for me to have to get a license for a weapon that's sole use is to kill or maim humans and critters. I'm a common sense gun owner who understands common sense gun laws.

So yeah, that's about it. Besides those four points, I'm pretty dang progressive. While my accent can set off alarms in a more liberal-minded brain that I'm a card-carrying KKK member, it takes only a small amount of time with me to stumble onto the fact that I've read a few books and traveled to a few places, and have an open mind when it comes to really dissecting politics. I'm not going around quoting James Joyce left and right, but I know how lucky I am to have had a mother who forced me to read. Books helped me become who I am today. Books are how I learned about the institutionalized racism our country needs to do a better job of fighting against and that our school history books are not admitting to.

This is in stark contrast to the Germans, who've done a great job of owning the dark aspects of their country's history by teaching mandatory classes on the extermination of Jews and outlawing certain behavior. We need to look at all of our missteps, faults, and crimes against humanity. Whether it's the extermination of Native Americans, chattel slavery of Africans, Japanese internment camps, or more recently, ripping screaming babies out of their mothers' arms and putting them in cages on the Texas–Mexico border, we can do better.

Believing in universal healthcare makes me a target for those who think I'm "trying to give lazy people a free ride." I just don't get how out of thirty-three industrialized nations, we're the *only* one that doesn't have universal healthcare. When it comes to music, motorcycles, and baseball, I'm good when I'm back home, but I take shit constantly about my political beliefs, mainly from rednecks who have no interest whatsoever in learning about economics, the military-industrial complex, or how they sold their right to unionize away and gave up their economic infrastructure to a bunch of ruthless politicians who are puppets for traitorous multinational corporations. Yeah, that's what I believe and it's too late to turn back now. I do believe that America's well-traveled, educated forefathers framed our Constitution to eventually weed out corporate fat cats and religious zealots. I really believe that. Where the rub comes is how it won't happen on our time schedule, and the wheels of justice move slower than most impatient Americans can deal with.

The climate was incredibly different in the mid-to-late '90s from how it is now. The software boom and Silicon Valley was in full swing and raining money on the economy, so the national budget was balanced and in the black. Seattle grunge had just highjacked rock radio from corporate power ballads by the second wave awful hair metal bands. People were still scared to death of AIDS, but there were rumors even then that scientists were on their way to having a cocktail of pills that might keep it in check like they do now. I lost some amazing friends to AIDS, so I keep up with the science updates and always try to contribute where I can. But politically back then, compared to now, all they could get on Bill Clinton, after all of his scandals (some definitely real, some definitely conspiracy theories), was, well, a blow job. Sure, they impeached him, but it was for *lying* . . . about getting a blow job. Crazy, huh? I remember when the media didn't know how to say it on air and just started saying "blow job" on the news! Grandparents were saying "blow job" at the dinner table all over the world! How liberating was that? Hard to believe we were still that uptight that late in our country's history, isn't it? Shows you just how long puritanical religious zealots have had America under their thumb.

Well, here's how I met that complicated guy from Hope, Arkansas. It's January 1997 and my manager gets a call from a White House staff member in charge of the entertainment for Clinton's second inaugural ball. "Uh, yes, we'd like to have Jesse Dayton play the president's inauguration party, would he be available?" I'd just had some success with my first solo record, and things were cooking, but this was way out of left field because I was still considered pretty edgy after touring and playing hard-core honky-tonk music for punk-rock audiences. It's not that I wasn't popular with mainstream audiences, I just was not on their radar. So my manager called me on tour and said, "You and the band are flying to Washington, DC, to play the presidential inaugural ball." All I said was, "Hell yeah, we are!" If it would've been another president, I don't know if I would've said yes. George W. would later call on all those preppy college kids in Texas who dominated the scene with their "how to play the Eagles on guitar" songbook, but that was not for a few years yet. But as slick as Bill was, and as right-leaning as his politics were, I still voted for him. Why? Well, lots of folks who come from old-money, blue-blood families graduate with law degrees from Harvard and Yale. Lots of those same blue-blood

families know all the right people to get their kids into politics. Lots
of them can buy their way into whatever they want. Bill became a
Rhodes Scholar and went on to graduate from Yale with a law de-
gree, and he was from a lower-income single-parent household that
had absolutely no strings to pull to get him there. That ain't easy.
And after I found out his backstory, it didn't matter if I only agreed
with him on half of his platform, there was no way I was gonna vote
for a Texas governor who was born and raised next to the Kennedy
compound in New Haven, Connecticut, who they had to teach to
"talk Texan" for his campaign speeches.

I was around twenty-six years old then, not as political as I would
later become but still definitely not trusting of any politician. But
when I heard Lucinda Williams (whom I loved) and Billy Ray
Cyrus (not so much) were going to be on the same stage, I knew
it would be a big deal. Even though I was young, didn't know shit
from bean dip, and I thought with my little head way more than I
thought with my big head, I did have my principles. I walked away
from a big payday that same year when the Houston-based Halli-
burton war-contractor corporation asked to use one of my songs
for a new hiring campaign they were gearing up for, and at a time
when I could've really used the money. And when I say I could've
really used the money, I mean I was broke as hell. I was living out of
a suitcase on tour with absolutely nothing in my bank account and
a newborn son back home. Look, I'm not trying to pretend to be
Mr. Virtuous here, but I imagined how awkward the conversation
would be between me and some of my heroes, who wouldn't take
that blood money in a million years, if they found out I did. That's
how you curate your art once you make it. You keep it out of the
hands of folks who will rewrite its original intent and use it for their
crooked narrative. Anyway, it just didn't feel right, so, much to my
manager's surprise, I passed on it. But hell, I was young, dumb, and
bulletproof, and America's economy was swimming in money back
then. Between Silicon Valley's brand-new computer/tech world,

Wall Street's Wild West trading, and a construction boom that had cranes on every damn block in every major city in America that we toured through, the country was ready for a party. A very big party.

We arrived at the Omni Shoreham Hotel, and the Secret Service was crawling all over the place. It seemed like there were about a hundred black suits everywhere you looked, talking into their wristwatches. I'd experienced the Secret Service before at a party at lawyer tycoon Joe Jamail's house when George H. W. Bush and Barbara Bush were there, but that's another story. We were staying in and performing at this hotel at that night's inaugural ball. We went through a makeshift security checkpoint in the hotel lobby (similar to what would become the norm at airports post-9/11, with dogs, body frisks, and a walk-through metal detector), and we all swore the German shepherds could smell our weed. Then we checked into our rooms without a hitch and headed back down to this huge ballroom for the sound check.

After we sound-checked, Lucinda Williams came up and gave me a hug and said in her sexy, twangy Southern voice, "Hey man, think I'm gonna use your pedal-steel guitar player for a few songs during my show, cool?" I worshipped Lu's songwriting and all her early records with Jim Lauderdale singing harmonies. This was right before her groundbreaking record *Car Wheels on a Gravel Road*. Lu's father, Miller Williams, who was a genius in his own right and a tenured college professor of English, had been chosen to be the inaugural poet. What a special thing for Lu and her father to experience together.

Billy Ray Cyrus had just finished sound-checking the national anthem. He actually turned out to be a really nice guy and offered me a bottle of beer, but right then the Secret Service, like, ten of them, came backstage and said, "Everyone has to leave the room, we're bringing in dogs to do a bomb sweep." Lucinda Williams, whom I'm sitting across from, kind of sighed and then, as if the Secret Service were the waitstaff, said, "Hey, that's cool, but can

y'all get me a drink?" And these Men in Black with earplugs in
and armed to the teeth returned immediately with a glass of red
wine! Reason #836 why Lucinda, who gives zero fucks about au-
thority, has balls of steel, and, frankly, is why she's Lucinda Fucking Williams. So with a little time to kill before we went onstage
and all the tuxedos and ball gowns just waiting outside to flood in,
my bass player, Chuck; his gal, Catherine; Lucinda's guitar player,
Charlie Sexton; and I went back to the hotel room to smoke a joint.
As I remember, Chuck and I were the only ones who really smoked
it. I don't think Charlie and Catherine smoked any. But Chuck
always had killer weed and we were both young and just trying to
kill time and stay sane. Remember, it's not the two hours you're
onstage that's the problem, it's the other twenty-two hours that'll
drive you crazy when you haven't been home in a long time.

An hour later we're onstage killing the place, still baked from
the Mexican lettuce we smoked and playing to a pretty damn wild
bunch of folks for what we thought would be a stuffy political party.
I had played a Republican event in Texas for Kay Bailey Hutchison
once. She was a fan of my music and, although I didn't agree with
her politics, was an incredibly nice lady. But let me state the obvious
by saying her event was about as uptight as you could possibly imagine, with everyone on their best behavior. Kay Bailey Hutchison's
party made Clinton's inaugural ball seem like *Animal House*. These
Democrats were throwing down hard on both the booze and the
dance floor. It felt like we were playing a wild party that just happened to be for the president of the United States of America.

Afterward, I went backstage to a small room, and *bam*: there are
the Clintons and the Gores in the hallway surrounded by security.
I'll be honest, Al Gore, Tipper Gore, and Hillary Clinton came off
super uptight to me, but Bill walked in with a Jack and Coke and
said in that classic weary Southern accent, "Great show! Me and
my brother, Roger, played in some bands back in Arkansas!" This
guy, leader of the free world or not, was having a blast. I mean,
like, the time of his life. He had his whiskey in one hand and was

singing along to a Stevie Wonder song that was pumping through the PA at stun-level volume. Secret Service must've been freaking out, because they were walking in and out of that room constantly, while Bill's entourage just stood in the hallway looking put out and talking to their assistants. "Nice to meet you, Mr. President, I'm Jesse Dayton from Texas," I said. "Glad to meet you, Jesse," he said. "Hey, I play saxophone, wish I could've sat in!" Then he danced out the door with his drink in the air, singing, *"Ooh baby, here I am . . . signed, sealed, delivered, I'm yours!"* The entire encounter lasted a whopping thirty seconds but will remain in my memory till the end of time.

Later that night I walked by myself to a small bar down the street because everyone else was either too exhausted from touring or too wasted from the party. This is just how it went on some nights, when I'd end up alone and wanted a nightcap because I'd had to be on my best behavior earlier and not be buzzed onstage. And yes, I've been 80 percent straight, 15 percent buzzed, and about 5 percent sloppy fuckin' hammered onstage, and I'm not proud of that last bit, but oh well, live and learn. After playing thousands and thousands of shows, some nights, well, shit just gets completely out of hand. But on this particular night, after playing at an event that I'd probably never experience again in my life, I rambled down K Street alone and walked into this small bar that was crowded with DC folks in suits and work dresses who were all the last raging drunks left in the place. I sat down at the bar and ordered a double Maker's Mark on the rocks, and the bartender, who was probably tired of the party animals, asked me, "So what have you been up to tonight?" I wanted to say, *Well, I met and played for the president of the United States while baked out of my mind,* but I didn't, because I still couldn't believe it myself and I didn't want to sound like I was bragging. But looking back on it now, I'm pretty sure POTUS was feeling no pain himself.

It has been no easy political journey getting to the place I am now and owning up to my beliefs, especially in my predominantly

Red home state. Trust me, my life would be so much easier if my brain wasn't wired like it is and I just went along with everything. As I said before, one of my first childhood memories was my African American nanny, who helped to raise us kids, listening to a gospel station on the radio while she was cooking sweet potatoes and collard greens for our Sunday dinner, ever so quietly breaking down and crying over the kitchen sink during Martin Luther King's famous speech. I can still picture that transistor AM radio propped against a sugar bowl on my grandmama's old white gas stove. I was probably all of four or five years old, sitting at the kitchen table at my grandparents' house, trying not to embarrass Ms. Victoria by staring, so I just sat there and listened to the man on the radio. Hearing this powerful orator's voice, well, it affected me in ways that I had no idea of at the time, and it would stay with me for the rest of my life. Hearing Dr. King's commanding voice say he dreamed of a day when "little Black boys and Black girls will be able to join hands with little white boys and white girls as sisters and brothers" . . . I knew *exactly* what that was all about.

Ms. Victoria looked at me and said with all the love in her heart, "Don't worry, sweet boy, I'm all right. This is a good thing . . . Dr. King was a sweet man." Christ, I'm holding back a tear right now, thinking about it. This sweet old Creole woman who took care of me in her midseventies while my parents were working and my brother and sister were at school would have an amazing effect on who I would become. She taught me how to cook buttermilk fried chicken and how to make a dark-penny roux for a gumbo, where you put an old penny on a white stove and stir that flour into the vegetable oil till it turns the color of that old dark penny and then add the "Holy Trinity," which was onions, celery, and bell peppers. Real exotic "swamp food" to the rest of Texas, but still French as hell. A bunch of those Gulf Coast recipes I look back at now and realize they were pretty advanced French-based layered seasonings, sauces, and flavors that some people actually pay to go to culinary school to learn. (All the men in my family have been great cooks. Guess it's a Gulf Coast thing.)

She also turned me on to music that I would've never heard otherwise. East Texas blues legend Lightnin' Hopkins and Clifton Chenier Zydeco records from Louisiana that made her dance in the kitchen. On Sundays on her gospel radio station they would play Mahalia Jackson and Aretha Franklin and she would always say, "We don't play no secular music on Sundays, baby." To say she had a profound effect on me and my music would be an understatement. I always gravitated toward Black music, and because of her I could even hear the Black influence in the country records that would pop up throughout my childhood.

Later I would become more radicalized, finally getting turned on to punk-rock music at my buddy John Cook's house, listening to the Clash and some reggae/ska records, and later protesting KKK rallies in downtown Beaumont, and because of all this I became more acutely politically aware of my surroundings at all times. Most of the time I never spoke about politics to any of my friends because I knew that they didn't have a political consciousness and it would've been totally awkward. If I did say something like "Governor Clements is an asshole for letting the Klan march in downtown Beaumont," I would usually get a weird look and a reply like "What the fuck are you talkin' 'bout, JD? What do you care? Why are you even saying shit like that?"

I could not wait to move to Austin with all the other freethinkers who hung out in a forever Blue county in the center of the state. My redneck uncle used to say, "You know why Austin, Texas, is in the middle of the state, son? So the rest of us can keep an eye on you!" And he was dead serious. When I first got to Austin I couldn't believe how many protests there were every week out in front of the Capitol Building smack-dab in the middle of town off of Congress Avenue. Austin was like the Berkeley, California, of the South. Sure, there were some other college towns throughout the South that definitely leaned left, but Austin was and still is the mecca of Southern liberalism.

Being from Beaumont, I still have a tough time with some of the silly reactionary PC stuff that liberals whine about and that makes them lose sight of big-picture issues like civil rights and justice for all, but after a while I learned that most folks on the left were scattered into so many subgroups that the infighting was undermining the basic tenets they all shared. The left has a big tent, and everyone's trying to be heard at the same time. My grandfather had a union job, and while he definitely could say some racist things every once in a while, he was way more suspicious of anybody who made over $100,000 a year than he was of any poor/working-class Black people or Mexicans.

I remember when the big media spin happened in America. Even in Beaumont, where we had a decades-long middle-class economic infrastructure in place, the corporate money that backed Reagan started sending men, outsiders, down to bust up all the union jobs. Eventually when Fox News came on the scene, selling "patriotism" and using bogeymen to promote xenophobia, they locked that whole area of the country down and sealed the deal via the terrorist event of September 11. But before all that happened, most of the working class were all union, and not all, but most of them had nice houses that were paid for, a new pickup truck, a nice bass boat, healthcare for the entire family, free or cheap college, worker's comp in case someone got hurt on the job, and a full pension and retirement plan. Sure, there were still problems with housing and feeding poor people, but most people in the working class back then pretty much laid their heads on their pillows each night before going to sleep knowing that if someone had a medical problem—a broken hip, a heart attack, or cancer—they would not have to sell their houses to pay some insurance corporation to get out of debt. So up until the mid-1980s most of these working-class union people had a hell of a lot fewer financial worries than folks do today.

I lived to see this great transformation of wealth that was orchestrated by the corporations and Wall Street taking place all over America, and for those of us who were paying attention, it was shocking to see folks who used to have some control over their lives voting away all their rights and just giving away their entire economic infrastructure. It was all started by greedy multinational corporations who had no allegiance to America whatsoever but had the money and the power to get the politicians elected who would help them stay unregulated and destroy the American labor movement by stripping workers of all their rights and eventually sending all those jobs overseas for pennies on the dollar.

This, in my mind, has been the true downfall of America, and it is currently still destroying what's left of the American middle class. The *Nationalist* can whine about immigrant fruit pickers trying to take their accounting and business jobs all they want, but you gotta admit, the GOP has done a phenomenal job of convincing their people that the bad guy is not in fact a billionaire globalist corporation owner but a penniless, kindhearted, hardworking, God-fearing small brown man who's sneaking across the Rio Grande to escape violence and corruption and make a better life for his family in America. That's a hell of a spin.

My early political days in Austin were spent reading Molly Ivins pieces that ran in everything from the *Houston Chronicle* to the *Texas Tribune* to even the *New York Times*. Her writing was so witty, so irreverently funny, that it was hard for even her political enemies to withhold credit where credit was due. Going to Governor Ann Richards's rallies was a reminder to me not to lose my Texan-ness while incorporating worldly ideas into who I was becoming politically. Ann Richards was as Texas as Texas gets, and meeting her briefly and shaking her hand, then years later attending her memorial service at the Erwin Center in Austin might've been the highlights of my political experiences in Texas, along with listening to Barbara Jordan, the first African American woman elected to the Senate in Texas. Her civil rights speeches resonated all around the world. Barbara Jordan was so smart and intellectually astute that she made the majority of the old white Republicans in Texas look like the superstitious, uneducated knuckle-draggers they truly were. Barbara Jordan was all about science and facts, which was incredibly cutting-edge back when good-ol'-boy Texas politicians who drank copious amounts of whiskey, chain-smoked cigarettes, and always had several women on the side would hypocritically use religion at every turn to scare their constituents into voting for the bills they needed passed for their corporate masters, who were paying for their elections.

By the way, if sometimes I use the term "Black people" and sometimes I use the term "African American," it's all coming from a place of love, and I mean no ill intent. My Black friends have told me repeatedly, "While our ancestors might all be from Africa, not all of us migrated here from Africa. Some of us are from places besides Africa, so if we call you white it's OK for you to call us Black." Don't be scared to discuss this. Not creating a dialogue with folks of other colors, and more important, not listening to folks of other races, is why all this BS is happening right now. So all you virtue signalers, quit pointing fingers and open up the dialogue so we can learn how folks want to be referred to. I'm all about treating folks the way I'd like to be treated. It's very simple. No one's asking for "special treatment"; they just want equal treatment. Sometimes equality feels like oppression to those who've never had to worry about it. If "all lives matter" was really a thing, white people are sure doing a horrible job by putting immigrant Latino kids in cages on the border, treating mainstream tax-paying Muslims like terrorists, and carrying out nonstop attacks on Jewish synagogues.

I just don't see how white folks can listen to rock 'n' roll, blues, or jazz music in good conscience and not support Black folks. I know one thing's for sure, seeing footage of a white cop choking a Black man to death for nine minutes broadcast on global television means America still has a long way to go with its race problem. If I'd been shit-faced and passed out in a Wendy's parking lot, been woken up by the cops, given them my license, been frisked for weapons, and then whipped both of the cops' asses and took off with their Taser laughing, they definitely wouldn't have shot me in the back in front of all the cameras. They probably would've given me a DWI or even called me a cab and laughed about it. This is not just about a few bad cops; it's about a larger systemic problem.

Anyway, I wanna tell y'all about the first time I heard about Beto O'Rourke. I was working on Chris Bell's campaign, a Democrat who was running for governor of Texas against Republican Rick Perry, Independent Carole Keeton Strayhorn, and another man, who later would become a close friend, Independent Kinky Friedman. This was 2006, and I still had friends on the right who were sane people. I had met George Sr. and Barbara Bush at mega-lawyer Joe Jamail's house in River Oaks in Houston, and they were the nicest people you could imagine. No, I did not agree with them politically, nor did I vote for them, but they were self-deprecating, good-natured folks who had lots of friends on the left. Yes, of course I know their history. But in comparison to what's happening now? Come on, y'all. I met George W. Bush at a Kay Bailey Hutchison fundraiser, and he just seemed like a nice, rich frat boy. Little did we all know that we'd give our left nut for George W. Bush instead of the narcissistic con-man monster we had in the White House in 2020. I had hung out with Republican James Baker III and Chris Bell in Washington after a fundraiser I played for Chris, so I had been exposed early to partisan politics, reaching across the aisle with an olive branch, and the concept of having an eclectic group of political friends in order to pass bills and get deals done. This was before Washington, DC, changed into the toxic, poisonous environment it is now, where no one can be seen with each other.

Robert Francis O'Rourke, a nice Irish Catholic kid who was raised in a predominantly Latino town, had just become the youngest person to ever win a city council seat in El Paso, Texas, then become the mayor pro tem by unanimous vote. The way I heard about Beto was at a local El Paso punk-rock dive bar called Wild-hare's Booze & Adventure. Yep, I know, hell of a name for a night-club, huh? A local Mexican dude at our show with a mohawk and plaid creeper shoes said, "Yeah, Beto used to be in a punk-rock band that I used to go see called Foss." Although I was touring through El Paso at the same time Beto's band was playing there, we never crossed paths. But that was the first and probably the only time in my life I'd ever heard of a punk-rock musician transitioning into running for office and winning, outside of Jello Biafra from Dead Kennedys running for mayor of San Francisco. By the way, when Jello Biafra came backstage to say hi to me at my last show at Slim's in San Francisco, it reminded me that this civic-minded radical has been in my corner since the '90s when my first record came out. Later, when Beto grew more famous, a lot of people would claim they were "early Foss fans" in El Paso. But that's like if everyone who claimed to be at the Sex Pistols gig at Randy's Rodeo in San Antonio were actually there; Madison Square Garden wouldn't have been big enough. It's OK, I'm sure Beto knows Foss were no Sex Pistols, but you get the point.

Fast-forward to 2017 and my wife Emily's longtime close friend Caroline Frye-Burruss calls us to say she's doing a fundraiser for Beto O'Rourke in her backyard in Austin and that Beto is running against Ted Cruz. Every time Beto's name came up, I would say, "Yeah, that dude used to play in a punk-rock band" and everyone would look at me like a dog hearing a high-pitched whistle. Just for the record, I couldn't stand Ted Cruz and still can't to this day. He's your classic square, un–rock 'n' roll, uncool, Frank Burns from *M*A*S*H*, hall monitor, tattletale, fearmongering, fake-religious, dirty-multinational-corporation-hooker Republican politician who is not even from Texas and was born in Canada. Was that too mean? Trust me, that was gracious; it could've been a lot worse. Anyway, I walk into the fundraiser in Caroline's backyard with my friend Jack McFadden and his wife, Cortney, and I see a big, tall, lean, dynamic guy who looks like he just jumped out of the balls of Robert and Jack Kennedy. I hear this time and time again from people, about how much Beto looks like a Kennedy and how close his oratory skills are to Robert and Jack Kennedy's. The guy could fire a crowd up, big-time. He could talk without pandering or dumbing down with stupid nationalist macho language and still excite folks with informed, scientific, fact-based ideas. We ended up about three inches away from each other, and he turns and says hello to me and looks at my wrist and sees my X tattoo. Beto says to me, "Is that an X tattoo?" I said, "Yeah, it's the band from Los Angeles X." Beto's face lights up and he says, "I love X!" Sometimes folks think it's a Malcolm X tattoo. (I read *The Autobiography of Malcolm X* in eighth grade.) So I tell him, "Well, I just filled in for their guitar player, Billy Zoom, who was diagnosed with cancer and did a whole North American tour with them." So Beto says to me, "Wow, can we take a picture together? I'm a huge X fan." I had every intention of asking *him* to take a photo, but he beat me to it. There were people all over him so we talked a few more minutes and he told me a little bit about his punk-band days in El Paso and it was, all in all, a great night.

Later in 2018 we would hang again at a Beto fundraiser I played in Dallas, Texas, with Ryan Bingham, Stephen Stills, Margo Price, Nathaniel Rateliff, Hayes Carll, Joe Ely, Jimmie Dale Gilmore, Cake, and others. Ryan Bingham's team helped put it on, and it was an amazing show. All the musicians were lined up backstage to take a picture with Beto, who at that moment was at rock-star level himself in terms of fans. I stood out of the way and Beto looked over at me and said, "Hey, Jesse Dayton, of course you're here!" I went over to take a picture with him, and though he was completely surrounded by people with cameras going off everywhere, he leaned over into my ear and said, "Did you ever used to read *Maximumrocknroll* magazine?" I said, "Hell, yeah, I bought my first copy at Sunrise Surf Shop in Beaumont, Texas!" He laughed and said that he ordered the record *Los Angeles* by X out of the back of that same magazine because you couldn't find it in the record stores in El Paso. This was all blowing my mind, that a punk rocker turned politician who had exploded onto the national television debate stage was talking to me about an underground punk-rock magazine. And just for the record, none of the Republican politicians I had ever met would say something like that, and none of them I've met, and I've met a few, have had any connections whatsoever to counterculture, be it hippie, activist, punk rock, or anything else.

This wouldn't be the last time I saw Beto, and as fate would have it, a few months later we were onstage together at the Willie Nelson Fourth of July Picnic in Austin singing "On the Road Again" with Willie. (Also onstage were Margo Price, Ryan Bingham, Willie's daughters Amy and Paula, and a few others.) Beto and I hung out backstage and had another similar short discussion about music, but once again he got mobbed. Also, Willie told us a story about how his bus, the *Honeysuckle Rose*, was pulled over by the highway patrol in Louisiana on the way back to Texas to make it in time for the funeral of Willie's friend, Texas governor Ann Richards. Willie's legendary roadie, Ben Dorcy, who has since passed on but was as old as dirt when this happened, was lying down, sleeping, when the cops came onto Willie's bus. A cop looked at Ben and said to Willie, "Is he OK?" Willie said, "Oh, that's Ben, he's dead. We're bringing him back to Texas to bury him next to Ann Richards." By the way, Ben Dorcy was the first roadie ever. He started out as John Wayne's personal valet when he was a kid, then went to work for Elvis Presley, Johnny Cash, Hank Thompson, and Ray Price in the 1950s, when roadies were called "band boys," and then stuck with Willie till the very end. Fascinating character to say the least. Sadly, Ben did transition on to the big hillbilly concert in the sky.

Word is Amy Nelson, Willie's daughter, is making an incredible documentary about Ben's life.

Just for the record, Ted Cruz did not win the Senate race by a landslide as he claimed. Cruz had 50.9 percent of the vote to Beto's 48.3 percent, and it was the closest Senate race in Texas since 1978. Beto O'Rourke earned over 4 million votes, which was the most ever for a Democratic incumbent in Texas, and he did it by taking a page out of Bernie Sanders's book and raising the money predominantly from individual contributions. Yes, I've heard he did take some money from some Big Oil folks, but if this is true, ya gotta remember: it's a Texas U.S. Senate race and the chances of him getting as many votes as he did were slim to none. The close race propelled him to the national stage, and he would eventually run for president but bow out after not getting enough traction with mainstream Democrats in California and New York.

I haven't seen Beto lately, but I hope he's at home enjoying his beautiful family and getting some well-deserved rest after having his life completely turned upside down during those years of heavy campaigning. He's a good man, and I know I'll see him again. I also know we haven't seen the last of him on the American political stage.

It's very important that we don't let cynicism win. I see cynicism on the far left and the hard right, and it's where bad ideas, prejudgment, ridiculous rumors, propaganda, and conspiracy theories are born. Cynicism is where bruised egos and disenfranchised, voiceless voters dwell. Cynicism is where people in bad relationships or exploitive jobs, people with unfulfilled potential or unacknowledged abusive childhoods settle. I actually have to work at not being cynical, and it requires a great deal of effort and discipline on my part, just like raising my hand to say no to the Shitty Committee when it tries to talk me out of going to the gym or going for a run or talk me into eating trashy fast food. When I catch myself rolling my eyes at someone younger, or when I catch myself tuning out and glazing over at someone's new music, motorcycle, clothes, or politics, I know that I've become more self-aware and that consciousness is the work I've put in. Catching myself is the fruits of my labor, the work I've put in so I don't dumb down and become some Archie Bunker cliché.

Without getting too New Age on ya, the true cynics I meet are people who have no spiritual foundation. Whether they're the grumpy old right-wing neighbor, the overreactive PC liberal, or the young idealistic anarchist in the streets setting everything on fire, they all seem to have the same issue, which is they don't believe in a power greater than themselves. This whole "believing in a power greater than yourself" philosophy is a universal theme that shows up in everything from self-help books to drug and alcohol recovery programs to religion, and has been proven to heal the hearts of human beings who are plagued by a lack of humility and a destructive self-image. Cynicism is still alive and well and thriving in America right now, and I hope we can overcome it. Until then, stay vigilant, mis amigos, and don't let up! It's OK to pick a side and it's OK to stand for something, which usually means not everyone's going to like you. And that's OK too. Money comes and goes, but we can never, ever get the time back. How much time do you have left? Fifty, forty, thirty, twenty years? What are you going to do with it?

I've chided myself countless times in my head, *You're not supposed to be here. What the fuck are you doing here?* In fact, here's how the dialogue from the Shitty Committee plays out whenever I'm surrounded by rock stars, politicians, actors, artists, whoever. It usually starts out with the whole belittling *JD, you're a Beaumonster and you're a long way from home, son.* Then it gets progressively worse: *They're going to find out you're completely full of shit* or *You're definitely not as talented as these people, so keep your mouth shut.* By the way, I never listen to that last one, but I probably should. I'm better at being quiet now than I was back when this story took place, that's for sure. Sometimes all this head stuff has some grain of truth to it, and sometimes it's just me and my lack of self-confidence and wanting to make everything OK.

But all in all, since I had my awakening about six years back and actually started working on the old, fucked-up Jesse (meditation, working out, partying less, eating clean, praying, all that humility stuff I used to think was fluffy hippie Eastern bullshit but now completely live by), I rarely get screamed at by the old Shitty Committee anymore. Sure, my inner voice still taunts me when I know I need to go to the gym, or when I'm intentionally trying to not react to the latest lie that some politician or corporation is telling in front of God and everybody. But I'm a work in progress and self-love is probably the toughest concept that I've ever had to embrace. But just being conscious of it is everything. I was way more of a fuck-up back when I had no clue about these lofty ideas about loving yourself, healing yourself, not blaming yourself, and discovering them started to influence everything I do, from how I treat my wife and son to the way I eat to the way I treat other people and especially how I engage with politics. It's as weird out there right now as it's ever been in my lifetime, so try to send love and strength to others, even if you think it's bullshit, because I'm here to tell you that it works.

OUTRO

Well, this is it so far, folks. I'm making memories, new stories if you will, right now as I write this, that are just as exciting, just as pathetic, and just as terrifying as anything I've ever done, so who knows what'll happen next! While I was writing this, Sirius Outlaw Country radio program director Jeremy Tepper left me a text (by the way, I should have an altar made with this guy's picture on it for all the cool shit he's done for me) saying, "Hey, you and your band are going to back up Lee Scratch Perry while the Outlaw Country Cruise is in Jamaica!" I've worked with a lot of folks from different scenes, from Waylon to the punk band X, but this will be the first time working with an OG Jamaican icon. See? It's still happening! There were a lot of stories I left out of the book that happened with other folks. But the ones here are the stories I felt needed to be told now.

One more thing: Dream bigger than they told you to. If you feel trapped in your situation (whatever it may be), just remember that every morning you wake up is a new opportunity to get your shit together. Six and a half years ago I woke up one morning and changed my entire life. After a doctor's visit that told me my blood pressure and cholesterol were dangerously high, I said fuck it and started to exercise, change my eating habits, and cut way back (almost to nothing) on my partying. If you're finishing this book right now, maybe it's late at night and your partner's already sleeping, or maybe it's right after another massive dinner and drinks with friends and you're just tired of it all. Well, tomorrow morning you have the universe's undivided approval and attention to change your behavior, go for a hike, a walk, or a run, stop eating foods that are gonna clog your arteries and kill you in a few years, stop drinking and smoking like you're twenty-one years old, and most important, embrace happiness. I've had to say goodbye to a few friends who were on another journey, had to reaffirm who and what is most important to me, but yeah, that's what I did and I'm a hell of a lot happier because of it.

I can tell you this firsthand, though, if you're waiting on "success" or that "one last big deal" to make you happy, it ain't comin'! The house, the hot rods and motorcycles, the money in the savings account . . . if anything, it just makes it all worse. But every time I do something good for myself like eat that clean lunch instead of a bunch of fried BS, or run up to the gym for an hour workout, or sit alone in a room and meditate in total quiet and darkness for thirty minutes, or most important, refuse to listen to the Shitty Committee in my head, well, the chemicals in my brain immediately start producing whatever it is that they produce in there to make me happy. I feel better, or at the very least, I wear myself out enough to turn my brain off and get a good night's rest! Anyway, hope y'all enjoyed the book. Sending love and strength to you and your families.

Onward,

JD

★ ACKNOWLEDGMENTS ★

Thanks to Emily and Sam for your undying moral support and love and laughter. Big love to Niels and Kirk and Eddie and all of the folks at Blue Élan for their patience and help. Thanks Aggie for being there after all the gigs, shows, and concerts went away. Massive thanks to the one and only Ben Schafer and the entire Hachette team for our conversations and their counsel that developed and nurtured the book. Thanks to all the people I've worked with in the book for figuring out a way to include this Beaumonster somehow along the way . . . what an honor. And lastly, this book would not have happened without the guidance and follow-through of Rynda Laurel. Thank you!

★ ABOUT THE AUTHOR ★

Jesse Dayton is a creative tour de force. He is a multi-genre guitarist, singer and songwriter, film writer and director, radio personality, and author. Along with a thriving solo career, Dayton has worked with the biggest legends in country, punk, Americana, and alternative genres. This is his first book. Born and raised in Beaumont, Texas, Dayton is now a longtime resident of Austin.